CHINA'S INDUSTRIAL DEVELOPMENT IN THE 21ST CENTURY

Series on Contemporary China   (ISSN: 1793-0847)

Series Editors: Joseph Fewsmith *(Boston University)*
Zheng Yongnian *(East Asian Institute, National University of Singapore)*

*To view the complete list of the published volumes in the series, please visit:
http://www.worldscibooks.com/series/scc_series.shtml

Series on Contemporary China – Vol. 27

CHINA'S INDUSTRIAL DEVELOPMENT IN THE 21ST CENTURY

editors

Mu YANG
East Asian Institute, National University of Singapore, Singapore

Hong YU
East Asian Institute, National University of Singapore, Singapore

World Scientific

NEW JERSEY · LONDON · SINGAPORE · BEIJING · SHANGHAI · HONG KONG · TAIPEI · CHENNAI

Published by

World Scientific Publishing Co. Pte. Ltd.

5 Toh Tuck Link, Singapore 596224

USA office: 27 Warren Street, Suite 401-402, Hackensack, NJ 07601

UK office: 57 Shelton Street, Covent Garden, London WC2H 9HE

British Library Cataloguing-in-Publication Data
A catalogue record for this book is available from the British Library.

ISBN-13 978-981-4324-74-8
ISBN-10 981-4324-74-4

Typeset by Stallion Press
Email: enquiries@stallionpress.com

Printed in Singapore.

Contents

Acknowledgements

This book on China's industries and the post-economic crisis era started as a series of policy-oriented research documents in 2009. The early drafts of chapters were previously submitted as Background Briefs, a policy-oriented report, for the Singapore government's reference. We wish to extend our sincere gratitude to many people. First, we express deep thanks to Prof. Zheng Yongnian for his support of the publication of the book and his encouragement during the writing process. He is a brilliant, humorous but also humble scholar. Second, we are deeply indebted to Prof. John Wong. He has not only spent much time in giving us valuable comments and revision suggestions, but also provided encouragement throughout our research. The dedicated research spirit that John has shown will be a lifelong inspiration to us.

Third, we would also like to express thanks to Dr. Sarah Tong for her professional comments. The book is a collaborative project and shows the strong teamwork of many scholars at the Economic Research Group of the East Asian Institute (EAI), National University of Singapore. Without them, this book could not have been completed, let alone published in such a short time. Indeed, the EAI has offered us a premium research environment.

In addition, we want to acknowledge our appreciation to Prof. Phua Kok Khoo from World Scientific Publishing for welcoming this book. Our thanks also go to Ms. Dong Lixi and Mr. James Tan. Without their kind assistance, publication of this book would not be possible at this time. And Ms. Jessica Loon provided valuable proof-reading assistance.

Mu YANG and Hong YU
Singapore
May 2010

List of Contributors

Mu YANG is a Visiting Senior Research Fellow and Co-ordinator of the China Cooperation Programme at the East Asian Institute, National University of Singapore. He was previously a CEO and Executive President of several companies in Hong Kong and Mainland China. In the 1980s, he was Deputy Director and Senior Research Fellow of the Institute of Industrial Economics, Chinese Academy of Social Science and had participated in China's central government policy formulation in industrial development, the reform of state-owned enterprises (SOEs) and others. He is the author of China's first academic book on "产业政策研究" (Industrial Policy Research). In 1988, he was awarded the Sun Ye Fang Economics Prize for his article in the *People's Daily*. Now, his research focuses on the world financial crisis, China's macroeconomic policy, China's industrial development, and Chinese companies' M&A abroad.

Hong YU is a Research Fellow at the East Asian Institute, National University of Singapore. He obtained his PhD in Economic Geography from the University of Sheffield in 2008. His research interests lie in the field of regional economy. He also has a parallel interest in the areas of industrial development and political economy of China. He is the author of the chapter "Impact of the Global Economic Crisis on the Pearl River Delta and Yangtze River Delta Regions" in the book *China and The Global Economic Crisis* (World Scientific, Singapore, 2010). He is also the author of the book *Economic Development and Inequality in China: The Case of Guangdong* (Routledge, London and New York, 2010). His research articles have appeared in journals such as Asian Politics & Policy, East Asian Policy.

Xiuyun YANG is an Associate Professor at the School of Economics and Finance, Xi'an Jiaotong University, China. She obtained her PhD in Industrial Economics from Xi'an Jiaotong University in 2003. Her main research interest lies in industrial economics. She has been involved in several national and provincial-level research projects in China, covering topics such as China's airport ownership structure, management strategy and market performance and price mechanism and practice for passenger traffic of China's civil aviation. She has published around 30 articles in journals such as *Journal of Air Transport Management*, <<经济学家>> (*jingji xuejia*) and <<经济科学>> (*jingji kexue*).

Rongfang PAN is currently a Research Assistant at the East Asian Institute of the National University of Singapore, having received her Masters of Science Degree (International Political Economy) from the S. Rajaratnam School of International Studies at the Nanyang Technological University in 2009. She was awarded the Lion Group Gold Medal for being the most outstanding student in the IPE programme during the academic year 2008–2009. Her publications have appeared as book chapters and in journals such as *World Economics* and *China & World Economy*. Her research interest covers economic nationalism under globalizing China, the political economy of China's strategic industries, and the internationalization of Chinese currency. She has an ongoing interest to examine the impact of China's economic reform and domestic transformation on its changing role in international politics.

Cuifen WENG obtained her BA double degree in the science of diplomacy and in economics from Beijing University, and her MA in political science from the National University of Singapore. Her primary research interests cover the history and transformation of China's public administration and the making and implementation of public policy in China. Her ongoing interests are central-local relations, administrative reforms and urban-rural integration in contemporary China.

Jinjing ZHU obtained her Bachelor of Computing in Information Systems at the National University of Singapore, and Master of Arts in Chinese Studies at the same university. Her previous research covers the application and influence of information systems in the organizational and social context, and Chinese intellectual history from classical China to modern-contemporary period. Her current research is mainly on China's science & technology policy, including the structure and changes of China's government research institutions, China's R&D investment, and the role of Chinese overseas returnees in China's efforts for technological advancement.

Chapter

1

Introduction

Mu YANG and Hong YU

CHINA'S INDUSTRIAL DEVELOPMENT IN THE GLOBAL ERA

During the pre-reform period before 1980, in showing preference for the development of heavy and defence industries, the Chinese central government put tight control on almost every aspect of industrial production: from goods price, raw materials and energy distribution to workers' welfare and salaries. For the individual industrial firms, no operational or managerial autonomy was allowed. Their investment and production decision had to strictly follow state industrial plans. They were not responsible for either production costs, or their financial losses and profits. As a consequence, not surprisingly, in general China's industrial sector suffered from high production costs, poor financial performance, slow technological progress and overall low efficiency. Nevertheless, with the introduction and implementation of reforms by the central government, the operation, management and performance of industrial firms have been fundamentally changed since the 1980s. They have been granted more autonomy in areas

1

ranging from investment and production to marketing and sales.[1] Performance and productivity have improved dramatically over the last three decades. Both the fast expansion of production capacity and the opening up of foreign markets to an increasing range of industrial goods in many industrial sectors have been impressive over the past few years.

China has recently been undergoing rapid industrialization, achieving one of the world's highest rates of industrial growth. Total industrial output was up to 50,744.8 billion *yuan* in 2008 from 423.7 billion *yuan* in 1978, with annual growth of around 17.3%. China is a fast developing nation with a population of 1.3 billion and this, combined with the rapid urbanization which is taking place, will inevitably lead to a further increase in the demand for industrial goods. With its vast land size and increasing population of middle and rich classes, China is now also one of the largest consumer markets for industrial products.

The global economic crisis, triggered by the American sub-prime mortgage crisis in 2007, has badly hit the world economy and led to a worldwide economic slowdown. Many countries witnessed a sharp decline in economic growth, foreign trade and industrial output, a shutdown of industrial firms and rising unemployment. Indeed, this crisis has been the worst for more than 60 years and China has not been immune to it. For example, China's shipbuilding industry has suffered from production slowdown and cancellation of existing foreign orders due to weak external demand. Worse, compared to the corresponding figure in 2008, a sharp decline of 55% in new shipbuilding orders to 26 million deadweight tons (dwt) was recorded in 2009.

In particular, the export-oriented Pearl River Delta and Yangtze River Delta regions have been hard hit by this crisis, as indicated by the sharp fall in their total exports. As orders from overseas markets plunged, many exported-oriented and labour-intensive manufacturing

---

[1] Lin Yifu Justin, Cai Fang and Li Zhou, *The China Miracle: Development Strategy and Economic Reform* (Hong Kong: Chinese University Press, 1996).

factories have been shut down since 2008. The domestic industrial problems caused by the global economic downturn required drastic measures from the Chinese government. The government has been quick to take action to boost industrial growth and support domestic manufacturing sectors, mainly through a 4-trillion-*yuan* government stimulus package released in November 2008 and efforts to add value to domestic industries through upgrading. The increasing share of new and high-tech exports in China's total export value indicates the progress made by China's industries and a gradual transformation from manufacturing low-end to high-end and value-added industrial products. According to official data, value added to China's high-tech industries was up to 1,162.1 billion *yuan* in 2007 from 108.1 billion *yuan* in 1995, with annual growth of 21.9%. Export of high-tech products had jumped to US$415.6 billion in 2008 from only US$10.1 billion in 1995, with annual growth of 33.1% (Figure 1). The ratio of high-tech exports to total exports of industrial products in China had increased to 30.8% in 2008 from 7.9% in 1995 (Figure 2).

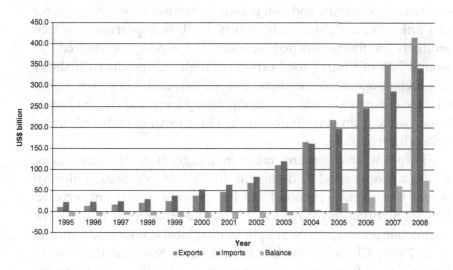

Fig. 1. Trade of high-tech products from China.

Source: The Ministry of Science and Technology of the People's Republic of China, 2009.

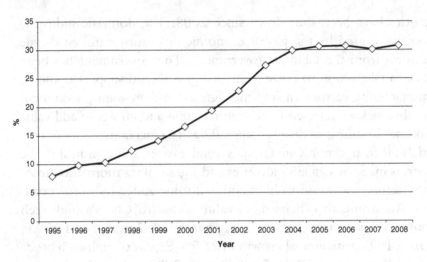

Fig. 2.   High-tech exports as a percentage of China's industrial products.
Source: The Ministry of Science and Technology of the People's Republic of China, 2009.

However, foreign-owned enterprises have played a crucial role in China's high-tech exports and contributed the majority share. In contrast, the domestic and indigenous enterprises have accounted for very little of China's high-tech exports. In 2008, exports of high-tech products by foreign-owned industrial enterprises accounted for around 70% of China's total exports of high-tech products. It shows that technological advancement and self-oriented innovation within Chinese companies is still at a disappointing level, and cheap Chinese labour is the main contributor to the fast growth of high-tech trade, rather than technology.

Thanks to the measures taken by the government, after experiencing a short period of decline in 2008/2009, domestic industrial output was quick to rebound and has shown a subsequent increase. Perhaps no other sector reflects this rapid ascendancy as much as the automobile industry. Even in light of the global economic downturn, since 2009, China has replaced the United States as the world's largest automobile market. This growth is especially apparent in the production of small-engine cars. Taking many people by surprise, the Chinese automobile industry has continued to develop and has been less affected by the economic crisis. Total auto sales in China reached over 13 million in 2009. More significantly, with the collaboration with research institutes and private companies, the Chinese government is making efforts to drive the development of green-energy technology to become the world's leading producer of green vehicles. The development of vehicles using renewable energy will be a key driving force in reducing greenhouse gas emissions and transforming China's economic development into an environment-friendly one in the future.

More importantly, China is currently the world's third largest economy, and it has become the world's largest manufacturing and production base for a wide range of industrial goods: from low-end toys and textiles to relatively high-end automobiles, high-speed rail and electronic goods. It has become a major global industrial power. Taking into account the significance of the Chinese economy to the world, its industrial development will generate both domestic and international implications.

Particularly, China's high-speed railway sector has also been prominent over the last ten years. China leads the world in the development of high-speed railway. The length of operational high-speed railways in China increased to nearly 3,800 kilometres (km) in 2009 from only 147 km in 1998, forging the world's largest high-speed rail network. The expansion of high-speed rail has ridden on the technological progress achieved by China. Backed by the central government, Chinese railway firms have adopted the "going out" strategy to enhance its global competitiveness. China is eager to actively join and play an important role in high-speed railway construction all over the world, and it has already signed a number of memorandums of understanding and cooperation agreements with other nations, including Russia, the United States, Saudi Arabia and Brazil.

THE WORLD'S MANUFACTURING BASE

China has now replaced Germany as the world's largest exporter, and is set to replace Japan as the world's second largest economy in 2010.

It is the largest manufacturing base in the world. In 2009, the value created by China's manufacturing sector accounted for around 15.6% of total value of the world's manufacturing sector, very close to the corresponding ratio of 17% for the United States. The competitiveness of Chinese manufacturing goods in the world is based on five aspects.

The first aspect of China's competitiveness is its abundance of cheap labour. In contrast to Japan and the Four Dragons (South Korea, Singapore, Taiwan and Hong Kong), where labour-intensive industries were competitive only over a ten-year period, China, with its 1.3 billion people, has continuously maintained its competitiveness in the world market for more than 30 years. The second aspect lies in the scale economy of its manufacturing enterprises. Its status as the world's largest domestic market makes it possible for the manufacturing enterprises and factories located in China to operate on the world's largest production scale. Scale economy also creates large profit margins, drawing inward foreign direct investment (FDI) and advanced technologies from all over the world.

The third aspect of competitiveness is the externalities. During the 30 years of high growth since 1978, industrial clusters in the Pearl River Delta (PRD), Yangtze River Delta (YRD), and Bohai Gulf Area (BGA) regions have gradually emerged. In these three regions, many industrial enterprises produce similar products. They compete with each other, learn from each other and also cooperate with each other. It is difficult to find any place in today's world with the same know-how, spillover effect, cheap transaction costs and strong capacity to learn new technology and complete the entire manufacturing process locally.

The fourth source of competitiveness is a world supply chain and sales network. In today's China, exports by multinational companies (MNCs) and other foreign investors account for 50–60% of its total export value. Supported by the developed transportation network with highways, container ports, airlines and high-speed railways, these MNCs, foreign investors and all kinds of domestic companies form a global logistic network based on China's manufacturing capacities. The raw materials and resources from Australia, Africa, Latin America, the Middle East, and components made in the East

Asian economies are imported into China, where they are processed and assembled, and finally, the finished manufactured products, with the label of "Made in China", are re-exported to Europe, the United States and other large consumer markets.

The fifth aspect is the capacity of China's research and development (R&D). There are many R&D centres in the major industrial regions, particularly in the PRD, YRD and BGA regions. Famous MNCs such as Microsoft, Intel, Motorola, Philips and Samsung have all set up large R&D centres in these areas, in proximity to China's best universities and research institutes. Moreover, many cash-rich Chinese enterprises have introduced high-quality design and research from Western countries. According to the 2010 Brandz Top 100 Most Valuable Global Brands survey, 7 of the world's leading 100 brands come from China. Huawei, ZTC, Lenovo and BYD are known by more and more people around the world.

A new phenomenon in recent years is that more and more Chinese companies are venturing abroad to compete with foreign counterparts. China's outward FDI was up to US$43.3 billion in 2009 from only US$0.9 billon in 1990. China's outward FDI in the United States was around US$5 billion in 2009, well below the Japanese foreign investment in the United States, with a peaking level of US$148 billion in 1991. Nevertheless, this represented a large increase in terms of China's previous outward investments, the average of which was merely US$500 million a year.

NEW DIRECTION OF STATE INDUSTRIAL POLICY

During the global economic crisis between 2008 and 2009, along with a 4-trillion-*yuan* stimulus package, the Chinese central government successively announced revitalization plans for ten key industries, including steel, automobile, shipbuilding, petrochemical, non-ferrous metals and equipment manufacturing, as well as textile, light industry, information technology and logistics. This policy with 165 detailed plans (e.g. tax incentives, government subsidies and bank loans to support these industries) successfully arrested the decline in China's industrial output experienced at the beginning of

2009, and made China the first "V-turn" recovery country in the world.

However, China's industries have faced serious long-standing problems of low efficiency, production overcapacity, high energy consumption and pollution, which are the inevitable by-products of the GDP growth-first state development strategies over the past three decades. The new goals for the central government are very clear now: they include reducing energy consumption per unit of GDP by 20% in 2010 compared to the year 2005 and 40–45% reduction in carbon emissions per unit of GDP from 2005 to 2020, whilst at the same time maintaining the pace of economic development.

A new industrial policy package is expected to be introduced by the State Council of China in August 2010. It is expected to consist of three main targets. First, promotion of new industrial priorities, ranging from the electronic and information industry, high-tech equipment manufacturing, new energy industries (namely wind power, nuclear energy, solar energy, geothermal heat, biomass and ocean energy), biopharmaceutical industry and software service industry to the logistics industry.

Second, the new policy is expected to focus on industrial restructuring in industries such as the mechanical industries, shipbuilding, metallurgical industry, automobile industry, non-ferrous industry, electronic and information industry through mergers and acquisitions (M&A) and eliminating outdated capacities via selection and competition. For example, the central government aims to strengthen the global competitiveness of the domestic shipbuilding industry by exerting control over capacity and encouraging M&A of small shipbuilding factories by large state-owned shipbuilding giants. Moreover, it plans to develop high-tech and high value-added shipbuilding R&D capabilities. In 2010, the Chinese government is planning to eliminate outdated capacity in steel (16 million tons), iron (21 million tons), cement (74 million tons), electrolytic aluminum (310 thousand tons) and coke (18 million tons).

Third, the state will offer preferential policies to support the small and medium-sized enterprises (SMEs), for example, helping the SMEs to get bank loans for development and setting up funds from the central government budget to support SME development (9.6 billion *yuan*) and technology upgrading (3 billion *yuan*).

Bearing in mind all its achievements, enormous problems and challenges still remain for China's industrial sector, the most prominent issue being significant overcapacity in production. Repeated warnings from the central government have proved to be very ineffective in curbing this. Overcapacity applies particularly to the domestic steel sector. In addition, production fragmentation is an unresolved issue for China's steel industry as most of the steel companies are small and suffer from low production output.

NEW ENERGY INDUSTRY: HELPING CHINA MOVING TOWARD A GREEN FUTURE

Due to the boom in the economy, China's energy consumption has shown a trend of fast growth during the reform period. Increasing amounts of energy are needed principally to fuel China's rapid industrial and economic growth, particularly for energy-intensive goods like automobiles and steel. China is hungry for energy resources and seeks them all over the world, from Central Asia, Russia, Africa and the Middle East to Latin America. However, although average per capita greenhouse gas (GHG) emissions are still low, in 2007, China replaced the United States as the world's largest GHG producer. Environmental pollution has become a prominent issue and directly threatens the health and daily life of the general public in China. In the interests of sustainable economic development and the future of the planet, instead of relying on heavily polluting oil and coal, the development priority of China's energy industry should be to use clean and renewable energy resources, particularly wind, solar and nuclear power.

Clean and renewable energy sources are destined to be predominant in China in the future. The share of the conventional energy sources of coal and oil in China's total production and consumption is expected to fall, accompanied by a steady increase in abundant and environmentally friendly energies such as nuclear and solar power.

With its rapid ascendancy as an economic giant, China's status in the world's new energy sector has become increasingly influential over the past few years. China now produces more than 50% of the world's solar cells. China has developed its core and independent technology and taken a lead in the world in the manufacture of solar collectors and solar water heaters. Chinese-made solar water heaters have been exported to many other countries, with a twentyfold increase in total export value between 2001 and 2009. It also replaced Spain as the world's second largest wind power producer in 2009. The development of China's new energy sector and government policies on energy will not only have major consequences for China itself, but also significant implications for the global environment and climate change.

The Chinese central government plays a crucial role in the formulation and implementation of new energy policy by providing financial incentives and acting as an advocate and regulator of energy sustainability.[2] The Chinese policymakers have realized the urgent need to accelerate development of clean energy technology and shift to renewable energy production. A ten-year development program issued by the government aims to increase the proportion of non-fossil, renewable energies in China's total primary energy consumption from 9.9% in 2009 to 15% by 2020. The government has also offered large-scale investment funding for the R&D of new energies.

Despite their current relatively low share in national energy production and consumption, the fast expansion of wind, solar and nuclear energy sectors reflects the government's will and commitment toward economic development driven by clean, renewable and reliable energy. Nevertheless, the Chinese government should not only provide more preferential policies and funds to encourage development of renewable energy technology and application, but also eliminate various barriers of grid connection and transmission for clean energy. For example, issues over access to power grid and feed-in have now become a major roadblock to the future development of China's wind power.

---

[2] J.E. Sinton *et al.*, "Evaluation of China's Energy Strategy Options", paper prepared for and with the support of the China Sustainable Energy Program, 2005, pp. 1–26.

Moreover, if it is to meet China's huge energy demands, the main issue which needs to be dealt with by the new energy sector is the high average production price. For example, according to the data given by the International Energy Agency, a megawatt-hour of electric power generated by solar cells costs up to US$600.[3] Therefore, the key for China is to reduce the production costs of these new energy resources as much as possible, and enable them to directly compete with the conventional energies without state subsidies.

THE AIM OF THIS BOOK

The book intends to provide a focused analysis of selected major Chinese industrial sectors through case studies, data analysis and review of state-initiated policies. This book on China's industrial development will offer extensive and quality research and original insights. The authors have conducted detailed studies in this field in order to bridge the research gap and it is hoped that this policy-oriented research will give rise to useful and illuminating discussion.

In response to the global economic crisis in the short run and to cope with the existing structural problems of production in the long run, the Chinese central government has successively released new development outlines for ten key industries since 2008. In this book, the authors will use key sectors including automobile, steel, high-speed railway and new energy to analyse the latest development of China's industries, along with their problems and future prospects. The effectiveness of state-oriented policies in rejuvenating these industries will be evaluated. After discussing the motivations for the new government-initiated policies, through detailed analysis of these policies, the authors will assess the contribution they have made to industrial development. The authors will also identify and analyse existing and potential challenges to the sustainable development of China's industries.

How did the industries respond to climate change and the development of a low-carbon economy in China? What measures have

---

[3] "The Rise of Big Solar: Growing Pains", *The Economist*, 17–23 April 2010.

been taken by these industries to reduce GHG emissions and overall energy consumption? What are the latest developments in China's conventional industries in terms of technological progress and upgrading? What are the developments in China's new energy industries? What is productivity performance like in the industrial sectors? What are the potential challenges facing the industrial sector in the post-economic crisis era? This study intends to address these issues.

The authors anticipate that this book will enhance understanding of the developments in China's key industries and the factors underlying their rapid growth, and will thus become an essential resource and reference for scholars, policymakers and business people concerned with China's industrial and economic sectors. It will also offer valuable reference material for both undergraduate and postgraduate students of Chinese economic studies.

BOOK STRUCTURE OVERVIEW

There are three main parts to this book, presented in nine chapters on various industries. The first part will discuss the development of conventional industries in China, with the steel, shipbuilding and automobile sectors selected for detailed analysis. The second part analyses China's new industries, including solar and wind power as well as water. The third part focuses on industries related to infrastructure. The high-speed railway and airport sectors will be discussed here. The detailed structure is as follows:

Discussion of China's automobile sector in Chapter 2 by Hong Yu and Mu Yang aims to analyse the factors underlying the rapid development of this sector in light of the global economic crisis. Key measures regarding green-energy technology and new forms of engine-driven vehicle adopted by the government to strengthen the global competitiveness of domestic automobile enterprises will be put under the microscope. This chapter also identifies potential challenges facing the domestic auto sector and offers some policy recommendations. The development of auto giants with large production capacity is expected to be the key strategy for reducing production costs and strengthening the competitiveness of domestic automobile enterprises.

Chapter 3 by Mu Yang and Jinjing Zhu attempts to provide an update on China's shipbuilding industry. It is a typical export-driven industry and traditionally dominated by large state-owned enterprises. Development of the domestic shipbuilding industry is still relatively promising in light of the global economic downturn. This chapter will focus on the analysis of a new development plan issued by the Chinese central government to rejuvenate the domestic shipbuilding industry which currently suffers from being low-technology-intensive, and strengthen its global competitiveness via technology upgrading and innovation. In addition, this chapter will discuss the recent development of the rig industry as a potential alternative to the conventional shipbuilding industry in China.

As will be discussed in Chapter 4, production in China's steel sector reached 500 million metric tons in 2008 and growth has been encouraged by rapid national economic development and strong domestic demand. Hong Yu and Mu Yang will identify and analyse the two main challenges faced by the steel sector: overcapacity and production fragmentation. For long-term sustainable development, domestic steel enterprises will have to put a cap on their production output. The chapter will also offer policy recommendations for achieving sustainable development of the steel sector.

Chapter 5 by Mu Yang and Rongfang Pan analyses China's wind power industry. Ahead of the 2009 Copenhagen summit, the Chinese government made a promise to reduce by 40–45% the carbon emissions per unit of GDP by the year 2020. Wind power is one of the key new industries in meeting the target of transforming China into a low-carbon economy. China is rich in both onshore and offshore wind energy resources, and wind farms are distributed in line with the wind belts. By 2009, China's total installed wind power capacity had doubled in comparison with the corresponding figure in 2006 and reached 25,805 megawatts. However, the authors argue that in terms of technological progress and innovation, a large gap still remains between China and the world's leading players in wind turbine manufacture. Local Chinese wind turbine components suppliers are still weak in proprietary technology. In addition, China's wind power industry has been subject to rampant overinvestment and blind expansion which has led to serious overcapacity.

Chapter 6 by Mu Yang and Cuifen Weng analyses China's water industry. China has suffered from a chronic water shortage for years. The per capita water resource is only 2104 cubic metres, which is 25% of the corresponding figure in the world averages. Worse, the authors have found that the regional water distribution is unequal; the eastern YRD and PRD account for a large portion of national water resources. This chapter will discuss the main measures taken by the government to deal with this water shortage issue through ground-water exploitation and "south-north water transfer" projects, emphasizing the limitation and problems of such schemes. Moreover, it will analyse the development of China's new water industry and wastewater treatment industry. Although the national wastewater treatment rate increased to 62.9% in 2007 from 14.9% in 1991, this was still much lower than the corresponding figure in the developed nations. It indicates huge market potential for expansion of the waste-water treatment capacity in China; this applies particularly to the rural areas. China's new water industry is still in its infancy and mainly focuses on wastewater treatment to meet quality standards of discharge, rather than wastewater reuse. The authors will also analyse the new state policies (e.g. preferential tax treatment) to support the new water industry and the institutional obstacles affecting the devel-opment of the new water industry.

Chapter 7 provides an update on the development of and chal-lenges to China's solar energy sector, particularly with regard to solar thermal energy (STE) for the utilization of solar heat. Mu Yang and Rongfang Pan argue that China has become the world's largest mar-ket for solar thermal applications and the largest producer of solar heat collectors, sharing nearly two-thirds of the global total capacity excluding unglazed collectors. Given their cost efficiency and conser-vation of energy, it is expected that the household penetration rate nationwide of solar water heating applications will rise to 20–30% by 2015 from below 10% currently. Nevertheless, despite the rapid growth, the authors stress that China's unique production structure poses major challenges to future development. In addition, the lack of effective communication and coordination between solar thermal producers and the building industry, poor regulation of small businesses and low quality of products, as well as safety risks resulting from unprofessional installation, are issues which urgently need to be addressed by both the industry and the government.

Chapter 8 by Mu Yang and Rongfang Pan provides a detailed analysis of China's solar photovoltaic industry (solar PV). Although China has been making impressive achievements in the utilization of solar energy in terms of solar thermal applications, the solar PV is an infant industry in China. In comparison with conventional power generation, the high cost has impeded development of the solar PV industry, although growth has accelerated since the enforcement of the Renewable Energy Law. This chapter discusses the development potential and challenges faced by this industry, and the state-initiated policies to boost it. In particular, two programs, namely the Township Electrification Program and China Village Electrification Program, have been effective in boosting solar PV development and local economic growth. Moreover, this chapter discusses the main structural challenges faced by the industry. From a long-term perspective, this chapter argues that the sustainable development of domestic solar PV industry largely depends on the expansion of domestic demand, the reduction extent of high PV power prices and state decisions on feed-in tariffs. The government may also need to spend more on R&D to advance the technological level of silicon material production and make solar PV competitive with conventional types of electricity generation.

Chapter 9 attempts to provide an illuminating and detailed analysis of the development, challenges and prospects of China's high-speed railway industry. Hong Yu and Mu Yang first offer a historical overview of China's railway development, and focus on a discussion of the key factors underlying the fast expansion of high-speed railways. The fast pace of industrialization and economic development has greatly spurred on domestic high-speed railway construction over the last decade. China's vast geographical area and its population of 1.3 billion have naturally created a high demand for freight and passenger travel. Also, the government's 4-trillion-*yuan* stimulus package announced in 2009 has stimulated the construction of domestic high-speed railways. The Medium and Long-Term Railway Network Plan, which is the principal government policy document on the design and implementation of railway development, is addressed in this section. The appeal of high-speed railway lies in its environmental friendliness. A substantial reduction of GHG output can be achieved through the development of high-speed railways. Whilst high-speed rail development has benefited from China's dramatic technological progress, this chapter also critically analyses the major challenges and obstacles facing the domestic railway sector.

Chapter 10 by Xiuyun Yang and Hong Yu offers a study of China's airport industry. The first section will discuss the development of the airport sector. The capacity of China's airports has been expanded over the last two decades. Not only has China's air transport sector been the fastest developing among its various transportation modes, China has also recorded the highest growth of air passenger traffic in the world. Section 2 will focus on the deregulatory reform of China's airports which has been largely responsible for the impressive improvements in China's airport industry since the early 1990s. The authors argue that the decentralization process of the reform period has led to local airport authorities enjoying more autonomy and power in providing airport services and running operations. Section 3 will analyse the problems and challenges facing the full modernization of the domestic airport sector, namely, unequal airport development and uneven regional distribution, overall poor performance and fierce competition within the transport industry. The rapid development of high-speed railways is expected to provide a serious challenge to domestic airport and airline development.

2

China as the World's Largest Automobile Market

Hong YU and Mu YANG

China made history in the first quarter of 2009 to become the largest auto market in the world for the first time. Thanks to China's sound economic fundamentals and government stimulus package, China's automobile industry is now the only automobile market to exhibit robust growth. The formation of auto giants with large production capacities is expected to be the key strategy to strengthening the global competitiveness of domestic automobile enterprises. However, the implementation of the mergers and acquisitions (M&A) strategy is a difficult task. Also, China is seeking to drive the development of green-energy technology to become the world's largest producer of alternative fuel vehicles; while the development of new forms of engine-driven vehicle will be a long-drawn-out business.

RAPID DEVELOPMENT OF THE CHINESE AUTOMOBILE INDUSTRY

The fast developing auto sector has been one of the mainstays of the Chinese economy. It achieved an annual growth rate of 15% between 1978 and 2008. Overall vehicle production increased to 9.34 million in 2008 (Figure 1), representing 13.2% of world auto production in 2008, an increase from just 4.1% in 2001 (Figure 2). The auto sector has strong linkages with more than 100 upstream and downstream industries, including steel, plastic, aluminum, glass and rubber. Their combined industrial output could amount to around 4 trillion *yuan*.[1]

Thanks to China's sound economic fundamentals and state-oriented preferential policies (e.g. tax cuts for vehicle purchases

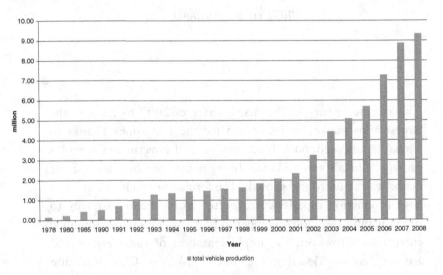

Fig. 1.   Total vehicle production in China, 1978–2008.

Sources:
1. *China Yearbook 2008.*
2. China Association of Automobile Manufacturers (CAAM), 2009.

---

[1] "2008 Chinese Auto Market: The Slowest Growth Year for Almost 10 Years", *Economic Reference Newspaper*, 12 January 2009.

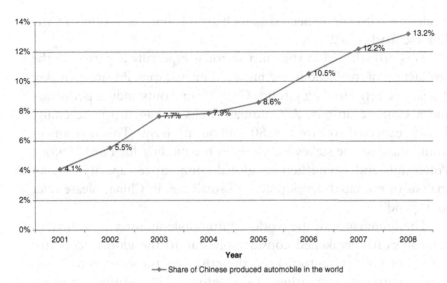

Fig. 2. Share of Chinese-produced automobile in the World.

Sources:
1. CAAM, 2008.
2. *The Industrial Map of China 2006–2007.*
3. Organisation Internationale des Constructeurs d'Automobiles (OICA), 2009.

and direct government subsidies), the development of the Chinese automobile industry is good and has the potential for further strong development. Many foreign automobile manufacturers like General Motors, Ford and Toyota have pinned their hopes on China to offset their huge losses in the home market.[2] The 13th Shanghai International Automobile Industry Exhibition attracted more than 1,500 international and domestic automakers and parts manufacturers, making it the biggest auto show ever held in China in terms of the number of participants and size and number of booths and pavilions.[3] However, competition in the automobile market is also

---

[2] "China may be the Bailout Global Car Industry Seeks", *The Straits Times*, 16 April 2009.

[3] "China Drives Sales for Global Majors", *China Daily*, online edition, http://www.chinadaily.com.cn/bizchina/2009-04/21/content_7697905.htm, 21 April 2009.

escalating with the expected launch of 80 new car models in the Chinese market in 2009.[4]

This growth within the auto sector is especially apparent in the production of small and low-emission domestic cars. Private carmaker Zhejiang Geely Holding Group (Geely) is one outstanding performer and a Chinese upstart. A Goldman Sachs-managed private equity fund is expected to invest $250 million in Geely.[5] This investment would increase the stakes for Geely in the bidding for Ford Motor's Volvo unit and strengthen its global competitive capacity. For an analysis of the rapid development of small cars in China, please refer to Appendix 1.

The dominance of the world's automobile industry by American companies has weakened considerably due to the global economic crisis. For Chinese automakers, the crisis has turned out to be an opportunity to strengthen their global competitive capacity. Zhejiang-based Geely is a shining example of this phenomenon. Its rapid growth and ambitious development plans does demonstrate the rise of privately owned Chinese auto firms, and more importantly, the potential for a power shift in the world's auto industry towards China in the future. Frank Zhao, president of Geely's research and development department, comments that "GM is big but moving down. We are small but moving up". Annual sales of Geely vehicles reached 221,900 in 2008, a tenfold increase from around 21,000 in 2001. Considering that Geely only began to sell vehicles in 2001, this is an impressive achievement. Over the last few years, Geely has developed a long-term strategy to strengthen global competitiveness and become a powerful international competitor. It has been investing heavily in research and development (R&D) (expenditure on product development accounts for 8% or so of its total revenue) and working hard to build advanced manufacturing capabilities. Geely is also

---

[4] "China Car Sales", *Financial Times*, http://www.ftchinese.com/story.php?storyid=001027498&lang=en, 12 May 2010.

[5] "Goldman Invests $250 Million in Geely Auto's Expansion", *The Wall Street Journal*, http://online.wsj.com/article/SB125336135937225281.html, 12 May 2010.

recruiting highly talented personnel with modern management, engineering and technological research skills.[6]

In contrast to many Chinese firms which are manufacturing and selling vehicles via joint ventures with foreign companies, Geely is one of the few domestic automakers relying on its own efforts to produce independently owned car brands. Also, it is planning to diversify into the production of more luxurious models, such as sport-utility vehicles, which are currently dominated by global leading automakers in the West. Geely is expected to export its own models to the highly competitive European and American markets over the next three years.

THE FACTORS UNDERLYING ITS RAPID GROWTH

Worldwide, the Chinese automobile industry is now the only automobile market to exhibit robust growth due to a number of factors. First, Chinese economic fundamentals remain sound. China has been achieving a remarkable annual GDP growth of 10% over the last two decades. The potential demand is still huge. The new rich and middle classes are willing to purchase vehicles as vehicles are largely reflective of high social and economic status. The American experience suggests that with the rapid increase of average household income, China is moving toward a period of car consumption boom in the coming years. China's average family income is approaching the income levels of America in the 1950s which represented the golden period of vehicle consumption.[7] By 2008, the average urban family income in China had risen to around 24,302 *yuan* ($3,522) from 16,159 *yuan* ($1,973) in 2005.[8]

---

[6] "Chinese Upstart Geely Expands to Take On Detroit", *The Wall Street Journal*, 18–19, 16 July 2009.

[7] The US experienced a dramatic boom of vehicle sales during the 1950s and 1960s. Compared to the corresponding figure of 4.8 million in the 1940s, the total number of domestic car sales jumped to 7.2 million and 11.1 million respectively in the 1950s and 1960s. The US average household income was about $4237 in 1950. (*Sources*: US Bureau of Labour Statistics; Consumer Expenditure Survey; and US Census Bureau, Statistical Abstract of the United States.)

[8] National Bureau of Statistics, People's Republic of China, 2009.

Second, the government has effectively stimulated domestic vehicle demand by implementing various policies to expand vehicle production, boost domestic consumption and speed up the development of alternative fuel vehicles. Government stimulus packages, such as lower purchase tax on small-engine cars and direct subsidies for peasants to purchase minivans and light trucks, have boosted consumer spending on new vehicles. Backed by the central government, the Chinese automobile sector is expected to play a more important role in the world auto industry in the future.

Government incentives have effectively stimulated domestic vehicle consumption. Auto sales in China decreased to 2.04 million in the third quarter of 2008 from 2.57 million in the first quarter of 2008. Due to the government's stimulus package and strong domestic demand, the downward trend of automobile sales has been reversed since the first quarter of 2009. Total auto sales rose by 73.5% to 3.54 million in the third quarter of 2009 from the corresponding figure in the previous year (Figure 3).

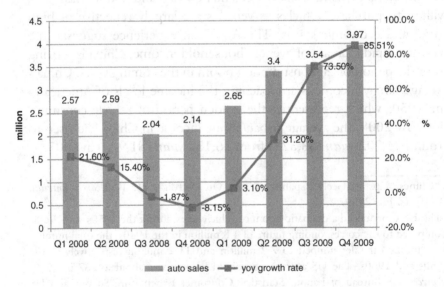

Fig. 3.   Quarterly auto sales in China.

Source: Ministry of Industry and Information Technology, the People's Republic of China, 2009.

Third, the fast expansion of the highway system in China has also helped to boost domestic vehicle consumption. The Chinese government has acknowledged that the transportation infrastructure is an important pre-condition for the development of its automobile industry and has been working hard on highway construction over the last two decades. In 2008, the total length of operational highways reached 60,300 kilometres, and a domestic highway network linking the whole nation was preliminarily established (see Appendix 2).[9]

IMPACTS OF THE GLOBAL ECONOMIC CRISIS

The auto industry worldwide has been badly hit by the global economic crisis. Due to a dip in demand for new vehicles, auto enterprises in North America have, since 2008, been experiencing a considerable decline in sales from the previous double-digit rates. In contrast, the Chinese automobile industry has continued to develop and has been less affected by the crisis. The severe effects of the credit crisis and economic recession have led to a sharp drop in total auto sales in the US to 2.2 million in the first quarter of 2009, compared to 2.65 million in China (Figure 4). For the first time, China has surpassed the US in auto sales to become the world's largest auto market. The total auto sales in China reached 3.97 million in the last quarter of 2009. Total auto sales in China reached over 13 million in 2009.

However, the year 2008 was also a difficult year for the Chinese auto industry after it was hit by the global economic crisis. In 2008, total sales of domestically manufactured vehicles were 9.38 million. Overall sales growth was down to 6.7% from 21.8% in 2007. The overall domestic vehicle production was 9.34 million in 2008 while the annual growth rate of domestic vehicle production fell to only 5.2% from 22% in 2007 (Figure 5).[10] Both vehicle sales and production

---

[9] "From a Backward Position, China Becomes the World's Leading Automobile Market in Terms of Production and Sales", *Yazhou Zhoukan*, 27, 12 July 2009.

[10] "China to Consider Steel, Vehicle Support Programs", http://English.people.com.cn/90001/90776/90884/6573360.html, 7 May 2010.

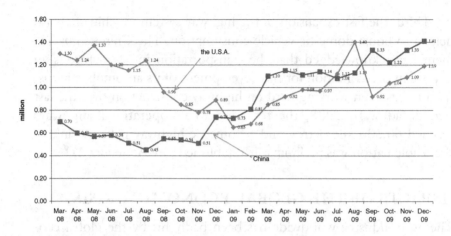

Fig. 4.   Total automobile sales in the US and China.

Note: The forecast data for December 2009.

Source: CAAM and Autodata Corp.

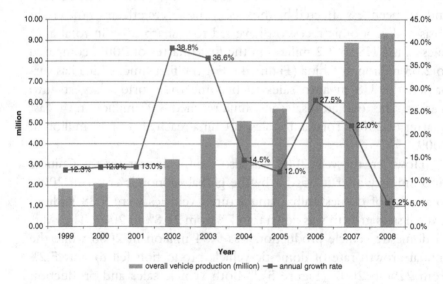

Fig. 5.   Vehicle production in China, 1999–2008.

Sources:
1. *China Statistical Yearbook 2008*.
2. CAAM, 2009.
3. http://auto.sohu.com/20090316/n262813521_1.shtml.

growth figures were down to single digits, registering the poorest growth rates since 1999.

The weakening consumer confidence triggered by the crisis has caused a rapid decrease in global vehicle consumption. Consequently, official statistics have been recording a substantial slump in Chinese auto exports since 2008. During the first two quarters of the year, growth rates were up to 79.3% and 44.9%. However, the corresponding figures were sharply down to 2.6% and −38.8% in the last two quarters of 2008.

GOVERNMENT-BACKED SUPPORT

A Newly Initiated Development Outline

Against the backdrop of the global crisis, the government issued a new development outline for the automobile industry which forms an important part of the support plans for ten key industries. Through the Outline, the central government has been using various stimuli to boost domestic consumption and speed up the development of alternative fuel vehicles to cope with the sudden plunge in external consumption and foreign investment.

In March 2009, the State Council of China released a new development outline for the automobile industry 2009–2011 (referred to as the Outline). This Outline maps out comprehensive development schemes, such as industrial upgrading, technological enhancement and promotion of new engines, and at the same time addresses other issues such as the lack of economic scale and production fragmentation. The Outline also intends to make significant progress in mergers and acquisitions (M&A) of auto enterprises. Regional clustering of vehicle production is believed to be the major development goal (Table 1).

In response to the economic crisis in the short run and to cope with the existing problems of production structure in the long run, there are two main objectives unveiled by the Outline. First, production should be diverted from low-end vehicle assembly to high-end manufacturing and product design. This will hopefully enable the

Table 1.   Highlights of the new development outline for the automobile industry

Summary

Production Expansion

1   Targets have been set at 10% annual growth in vehicle production and sales for the next 3 years, and in the manufacturing and sale of 10 million cars in 2009.
2   By 2011, passenger vehicles with engine capacity of below 1.5 litres are expected to account for 40% of market share, with those below 1.0 litres taking 15% of the market.

Mergers and Acquisitions

3   Two to three large auto giants with production and sales capacities reaching 2 million, and four to five smaller auto giants with capacities reaching 1 million are expected to be developed by 2011.

Domestic Consumption

4   The purchase tax for vehicles with engine capacities below 1.6 litres would be reduced to 5% from 10% between 20 January and 31 December 2009.
5   The government is expected to allocate 5 billion *yuan* in one-off allowances to farmers who replace their three-wheeled vehicles and low-speed trucks with minivans or buy new minivans with engine capacities below 1.3 litres.
6   A discount of 10% will be given to farmers who buy a minivan or light truck between 1 March and 31 December 2009, with a ceiling subsidy of 5,000 *yuan*.
7   Farmers who scrap their old three-wheeled vehicles or low-speed trucks will be able to enjoy 2,000 and 3,000 *yuan* subsidies respectively during the same period.

Technological Upgrading

8   The state aims to spend 10 billion *yuan* on special investments to support auto enterprises in technological upgrading, such as developing new car engines using alternative energies and recycling battery sets.
9   It is envisaged that vehicles manufactured by domestic independent companies will account for more than 40% of the total auto market; these vehicles will make up 10% of overall export production and sales.

Development of Alternative Energy Vehicles

10   The production and sales of electronic vehicles are expected to achieve scale economy status by 2011. The combination of hybrid and pure electricity-driven vehicles is to achieve a production capacity of half a million by 2011 and the sales of passenger cars with new engines have been set at 5% of total passenger vehicles sales.

Source: National Development and Reform Commission, the People's Republic of China, 2009.

auto enterprises to compete more effectively on a global scale. The reliance on low-end and labour-intensive manufacturing using imported technology is no longer sustainable, and development of the auto industry requires production restructuring and technological upgrading. According to the Outline, passenger vehicles manufactured by domestic independent companies will account for more than 40% of the total auto market, making up 10% (around one million) of overall export production and sales in 2011.

Second, boosting domestic vehicle demand is seen as a key means to stimulating economic growth. The government is expected to evaluate tax and financial stimulation policies in an effort to give consumers the confidence to spend more on the purchase of new vehicles. The regulations on car purchase restrictions are expected to be abolished. As unveiled in the Outline, the government is expected to implement the "selling automobiles to peasants" policy. By providing one-off allowances on the replacement of three-wheeled vehicles and low-speed trucks, the authorities hope to encourage farmers to purchase new light minivans. However, the possibility of farmers rescuing the auto industry is highly uncertain. In contrast to the people living in the cities, the financial means available to the farmers are very limited as banks and other financial institutions are more reluctant to offer car purchasing loans to farmers.

State Plans on Green-Energy Vehicles

The industry is expected to place much more emphasis on research in energy-saving and environmentally friendly vehicles. The development of renewable energy vehicles is a key factor in reducing emissions, protecting the environment and achieving environmentally friendly development for China in the future. China is seeking to drive the development of green-energy technology and become the largest producer of alternative fuel vehicles in the world.

The Chinese central government has realized that long-term competitiveness and sustainable development for the automobile industry lie in the promotion of green-energy technology. Wan Gang, Minister for Science and Technology, a former technical manager in the Production and Planning Department of the German Audi corporation, has been influential in promoting green-energy technology and development of alternative fuel vehicles in China. On various occasions, he has reiterated in speeches that the central government will speed up the development of alternative energy vehicles to cope with the global financial crisis and enhance long-term industrial competitiveness.

As an important part of the central government's ambition to develop green-energy technology and expand the production of alternative energy vehicles, 60,000 alternative fuel cars will be on the road and energy-saving and alternative energy vehicles will reach 1 million and account for 10% of total annual auto output by 2012.[11] Various means of financial support, from tax benefits to direct subsidies, are expected to be offered to carmakers engaging in the production of alternative fuel vehicles, and to domestic consumers purchasing green-energy cars.

In new efforts to support the development of green-energy vehicles, the Ministry of Finance and Ministry of Science and Technology have jointly launched a trial program and given subsidies to 13 Chinese municipalities[12] to purchase hybrid and electric vehicles for public transportation services (e.g. buses, taxis and postal service cars). The local governments have also been employing various strategies to promote the development of new energy vehicles (e.g. direct subsidies for green-energy vehicles purchases). For example, between 2010 and 2011, Shanghai's authority is expected to provide up to 20% of subsidies for purchases of new vehicles which have energy savings of 15% and above.[13]

---

[11] "60,000 Alternative-Energy Vehicles to Hit Roads by 2012", *Xinhua News*, http://www.chinadaily.com.cn/china/2009-03/19/content_7597301.htm, 19 March 2009.

[12] These 13 trial municipalities include Beijing, Shanghai, Chongqing, Changchun, Dalian, Hangzhou, Jinan, Wuhan, Shenzhen, Hefei, Changsha, Kunming, and Nanchang.

[13] "Greener Cars Get Cash Infusion", *China Daily*, online edition, http://www.chinadaily.com.cn/bizchina/2009-05/20/content_7794342.htm, 20 May 2009.

Indeed, state plans on green-energy vehicles are ambitious. However, the promotion of new energy-fuelled vehicles is costly while average retail prices are still too high.[14] Only when environmentally friendly vehicles and their associated alternative energies become affordable for the ordinary people will domestic consumption shift from gas-guzzling to energy-saving and environmentally friendly cars. Moreover, for the purely electricity-driven and hybrid vehicles, there is a lack of working proposals to address the issue of supporting infrastructure (e.g. electricity recharging network). For many municipalities, building electricity-charging ports for recharging electric and hybrid vehicles will create financial difficulties; as a result, meeting operational needs will take many years.

The development of green-energy technology and alternative energy vehicles are difficult tasks for the Chinese automobile industry. The promotion of environmentally friendly vehicles has lagged behind that of the other advanced nations while the development of new forms of engine-driven vehicles will be a long-drawn-out business. The Chinese leaders are overwhelmingly optimistic regarding the future development of alternative energy vehicles. Although the state has been encouraging domestic consumption of small-engine, low-emission vehicles and new energies, concrete results towards this end have yet to become apparent. There is a lack of policy details for achieving this objective.

M&A: A KEY DEVELOPMENT STRATEGY

One of the important characteristics of the Chinese automobile industry is regional production fragmentation. There are more than 120 vehicle makers, which is almost equal to the combined figure of all auto enterprises in Europe, Japan and the US.[15] Most of these firms suffer from weak competitiveness and low production capacity.

---

[14] "Hopes for Chinese Rescue Reined In", *Financial Times*, 18, 21 April 2009.
[15] Yang Mu and Teng Siow Song, "China's Automobile Industry Post-WTO: Surging Growth", EAI Background Brief No. 293, National University of Singapore, Singapore, 2006.

The Shanghai Automotive Industry Corporation (SAIC), First Automobile Works (FAW) and Dongfeng Motor Corporation (DFM) are the top three vehicle producers in China. However, they shared less than 50% of overall auto sales in 2008. In contrast, the market share of the five largest US automobile firms (General Motors, Ford, Chrysler, Toyota Motor Sales USA Inc. and American Honda Motor Co.) accounted for more than 76% of total automobile sales in 2008.[16] FAW, China's largest automaker, manufactured only 0.63 million vehicles and ranked only No. 20 in the world in 2008. In contrast, total vehicle production of Toyota, the top vehicle manufacturer, was more than 14 times that of the figure for FAW, at 9.23 million vehicles in 2008 (Figure 6).

The auto sector is an industry that enjoys economies of scale; the strong effects of economic externalities generated from scale

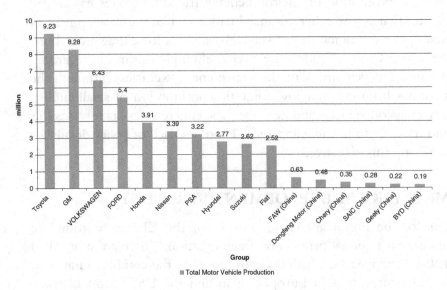

Fig. 6.   World ranking of motor vehicle manufacturers, 2008.

Source: OICA, 2009.

---

[16] "Sales and Share of Total Market by Manufacturer", *The Wall Street Journal*, online edition, http://online.wsj.com/mdc/public/page/2_3022-autosales.html #autosalesD, 12 May 2010.

economies and industrial agglomeration can substantially reduce the production cost per vehicle. Moreover, regional production agglomeration could benefit automakers through the spillover of knowledge.[17]

Therefore, rationalization of the highly fragmented Chinese automobile industry in the form of production clustering is badly needed. As M&A are believed to be the key to achieving the beneficial effects of scale economies, over the next three years, the formation of auto giants with large production capacities is expected to strengthen the global competitiveness of domestic auto enterprises against their Western counterparts.

Li Shufu, Geely's Chairman, believes that Geely can develop faster via mergers and acquisitions of established foreign vehicle-producing companies. Since January 2008, the firm has established itself as the front-runner in the bidding for Ford Motor's Volvo unit. If the anticipated US$2 billion acquisition deal is successfully completed, it is expected to shape the future of the world's auto industry. Moreover, SAIC and GM formed a US$100 million joint venture in December 2009. This new venture would manufacture and sell vehicles in India which were developed by Shanghai GM and SAIC-GM Wuling Automobile Co.[18] This joint venture is expected to achieve annual sales of 225,000 vehicles in India by 2012.[19] These two events represent the latest effort by the Chinese automobile industry to adopt an outward M&A strategy to expand production capacity and strengthen global competitiveness. The automakers may also intend to strengthen their domestic position via overseas M&A activities. Under the current global economic crisis, the Chinese carmakers are seeking opportunities to enter other emerging markets beyond China.

However, problems such as a lack of international management skills and the difficulties in restructuring internal management teams and blending different cultures into a united whole could be the

---

[17] M.E. Porter, *The Competitive Advantage of Nations* (London: Macmillan, 1998).
[18] "GM Teams Up With SAIC for $100m Joint Venture", *China Daily*, http://www.chinadaily.com.cn/china/2009-12/05/content_9123704.htm, 12 May 2010.
[19] "SAIC and GM Reshape Partnership", *The Wall Street Journal*, 25, 7 December 2009.

roadblocks impeding further development of Geely and other emerging privately owned automakers in China. Nevertheless, that the interior of a Buick car selling in the American market was designed by Geely's technical centre in Shanghai shows that China is making progress in obtaining high-tech product development and high-level design capabilities. The plentiful and consistent supply of high-quality engineering graduates from top universities in China has further enhanced the potential of R&D capability for Geely. Backed by the Chinese government's supportive policies and direct subsidies for high-tech vehicle research, China is soon expected to become the most influential low-cost engineering base within the world's automobile sector.

STATE-DOMINATED M&A: CHALLENGES FACED BY THE AUTOMOBILE INDUSTRY

The state has played a key role in M&A activities, as evidenced by the FAW acquisition of Tianjin Auto Corporation in 2003 and the merger of Nanjing Automobile (Group) Corp (NAC) with the SAIC in 2007.[20] This state-dominated style of M&A has been hampered by high acquisition costs, difficulties in restructuring internal management teams and overall low competitiveness.

Although it is believed that M&A will strengthen the automobile firms' competitiveness on a global scale, implementation of this strategy is a difficult task for the Chinese automobile firms. For example, the total transaction amount of China's cross-border M&A dropped by 30% in 2008, compared to the figure in 2007.[21] They faced at least three serious challenges.

---

[20] "The Merger of Changfeng Auto Group by Guangzhou Automobile Industry Group Co., Ltd.: The New Charter of Free Merger for the Chinese Automobile Industry", *Sina News*, http://auto.sina.com.cn/news/2009-05-22/0911493777.shtml, 22 May 2009.

[21] "China's Cross-border M&A Dropped by 30% in 2008", *China Daily*, online edition, http://www.chinadaily.com.cn/bizchina/2009-01/19/content_7410335.htm, 19 January 2009.

First, the Chinese auto enterprises generally lack international M&A experience. They should apply caution in the consolidation and acquisition of auto enterprises in the light of past failures. The acquisition case of Ssangyong Motor has taught the Chinese auto companies a hard lesson: without understanding different business environments and labour cultures, hasty M&A are doomed to fail.[22] The SAIC has suffered huge losses brought on by expansion. More than half of the acquisition investment made by the SAIC was lost with the shrinking market value of Ssangyong Motor. The total sales profit for the SAIC decreased by 50% in 2008 in comparison to the corresponding figure in 2007.[23]

Second, in attempting M&A, Chinese automakers have encountered resistance from local authorities; a big proportion of local tax revenue is contributed by auto firms which employ a large number of workers.[24] Due to self-interest, local governments are more eager to safeguard local jobs and tax revenue than to support auto sector mergers.

The third issue is inadequate external financing sources. The underdevelopment of the Chinese financial market has undermined the ability of many small and medium-sized automobile companies in raising funds to effect such M&A activities (e.g. leverage buyout). At the same time, government policy is biased towards large state-owned companies, which can obtain preferential funds from the policy banks.[25] Due to these government policies and regulations, commercial banks have been placing numerous restrictions (e.g. registered capital requirement) on the provision of acquisition loans to domestic companies for onshore and outbound M&A activities.

---

[22] "Expansion Spells Difficulties for SAIC Group", *China Business Feature*, http://www.cbfeature.com/chinese_company/news/expansion_spells_difficulties_for_saic_group, 3 January 2010.

[23] "Will SAIC Walk Out of Ssangyong's Shadow?" *Gasgoo*, http://autonews.gasgoo.com/auto-news/1009323/Will-SAIC-walk-out-of-Ssangyong-shadow.html, 12 May 2010.

[24] "Automakers May Restructure Soon", *China Daily*, online edition, http://www.chinadaily.com.cn/bw/2009-03/16/content_7580742.htm, 16 March 2009.

[25] "Experts: Overseas M&A Deals May Slow", *China Daily*, online edition, http://www.chinadaily.com.cn/bizchina/2009-04/28/content_7722693.htm, 28 April 2009.

APPENDIX 1

The Development of Small-Engine Cars in China

The rapid growth of auto sales in China has been largely driven by small-engine and low-emission domestic cars. Chinese consumers have been taking advantage of government programmes designed to increase spending on small-engine vehicles, which include measures such as lower purchase tax on small-engine cars below 1.6 litres and a 5-billion-*yuan* direct subsidy for peasants purchasing minivans and light trucks. This has had the effect of dramatically stimulating the production and sales of domestic small-engine car producers.

Private carmakers Chery Automobile, Brilliance Auto and Zhejiang Geely Holding Group have performed particularly well. In January and February 2009, Chery, known for its popular QQ model, reported sales growth of 25%. It has become the fourth largest vehicle manufacturer in China. In January 2009, Geely recorded sales of 28,502 vehicles, up by 14.5% on the corresponding figure in the previous January. Brilliance Auto, which has been achieving rapid growth since the company's establishment 13 years ago, aims to become the No.1 vehicle maker in China by 2015.

However, the fierce industrial competition among domestic small-engine carmakers raises concerns over the future development of the automobile industry. In order to increase market share, these car producers have been in price competitions. Even though sales have jumped substantially, the negative price competition has caused many small-engine carmakers to experience a decrease in net profits or even face financial troubles. For example, although the auto sales growth of Chongqing Changan Automobile Co. was 22%, its profits dropped by 89% in the first quarter of 2009 compared to that in the previous year.

Second, under the negative impacts of the ongoing global economic downturn, future economic growth and employment in China is hard to forecast. Facing uncertain economic situations, the Chinese consumers would prefer to save more money and exercise caution over automobile purchases in the future. According to a report by the People's Bank of China, the central bank of China, 47% of urban residents would like to increase their savings in the second quarter, registering an increase of 9.5% on the first quarter of 2009. Only 15.1% of urban residents intend to increase spending during the same period, a fall of 14.6%. Also, the rising vehicle consumption is mainly driven by the government stimulus policies. It would not be sustainable in the long term. These factors will inevitably have an effect on the recent strong growth in domestic consumption of the small-engine automobile sector and the future continuation of such rapid development should not be taken for granted.

Sources:

1. "Autos: Small Car Sales Boom in Jan on Tax Cut", *China Daily*, online edition, http://www.chinadaily.com.cn/bizchina/2009-02/06/content_7452135.htm, 14 April 2009.
2. "Reviving China's Auto Industry", *BBC News*, online edition, http://news.bbc.co.uk/2/hi/programmes/from_our_own_correspondent/7779261.stm, 14 April 2009.
3. "A Lean, Green Detroit", *Newsweek*, 22–25, 4 May 2009.
4. "Auto Firms Headed for Tougher Times", *China Daily*, 15, 6 May 2009.
5. "Carmakers Vie for China Sales", *China Daily*, 9, 20–26 April 2009.
6. "Consumer Resilience", *China Daily*, 4, 15 June 2009.

APPENDIX 2

China's Current Highway Network

Nine Vertical Lines

1. Hegang–Dalian, 2. Shenyang–Haikou, 3. Changchun–Shenzhen, 4. Jinan–Guangzhou, 5. Daqing–Guangzhou, 6. Erlianhaote–Guangzhou, 7. Baotou–Maoming, 8. Lanzhou–Haikou, 9. Chongqing–Kunming

Eighteen Horizontal Lines

1. Suifenhe–Manzhouli, 2. Hunchun–Wulanhaote, 3. Dandong–Xilinhaote, 4. Rongcheng–Wuhai, 5. Qingdao–Yinchuan, 6. Qingdao–Lanzhou, 7. Lianyungang–Huoerguosi, 8. Nanjing–Luoyang, 9. Shanghai–Xi'an, 10. Shanghai–Chengdu, 11. Shanghai–Chongqing, 12. Hangzhou–Ruili, 13. Shanghai–Kunming, 14. Fuzhou–Yinchuan, 15. Quanzhou–Nanning, 16. Xiamen–Chengdu, 17. Shantou–Kunming, 18. Guangzhou–Kunming

Seven Radial Lines

1. Beijing–Shanghai, 2. Beijing–Fuzhou, 3. Beijing–Hong Kong and Macau, 4. Beijing–Kunming, 5. Beijing–Lhasa, 6. Beijing–Urumqi, 7. Beijing–Haerbin

Source:

1. "From a Backward Position, China Becomes the World's Leading Automobile Market in Terms of Production and Sales", *Yazhou Zhoukan*, 27, 12 July 2009.

China's Shipbuilding Industry Facing Crisis and Challenge

Mu YANG and Jinjing ZHU

INTRODUCTION

In facing the difficulties of the Chinese industries caused by the financial crisis of 2008, the executive meeting of the State Council approved the adjustment and stimulus plans for ten key industries from January to February 2009. These industries include automobile, iron and steel, textiles, equipment manufacturing, shipbuilding, electronics and information technology, petrochemicals, light industries, non-ferrous metals and logistics.[1] As one of the ten key industries, China's shipbuilding industry has been developing rapidly in recent years. Its gross industrial output increased from 39.7 billion *yuan* in

---

[1] "10 Major Industries to Become China's Economic Engines", *People's Daily Online*, February 27, 2009, http://english.peopledaily.com.cn/90001/90778/90857/90862/6602754.html.

2000 to 419.7 billion *yuan* in 2008. The growth was particularly fast from 2006 to 2008, with 49.3% and 63.2% growth rates in 2006–2007 and 2007–2008, respectively.

However, as export occupies more than 60% of the total production, China's shipbuilding industry was severely influenced by the crisis since end 2008. It experienced significant slowdown in the production completion, cancellation of existing orders, and a tremendous drop in new orders. The state council passed the Plan on the Adjustment and Revitalization of the Shipbuilding Industry on 11 February 2009. The plan states that the shipbuilding industry is a comprehensive and strategic industry for national defence and maritime development, instrumental in increasing exports, and closely related to other strategic industries such as steel and petroleum.[2] It is emphasized in the plan that from 2009 to 2011 it is necessary to adjust and revitalize the industry mainly towards three targets: 1) sustaining the declining demand: taking active supporting policies to sustain the existing orders and stabilize new orders, and reduce the risk of companies; 2) promoting mergers and acquisitions (M&A) and restructuring: promoting the conglomeration of CSSC (China State Shipbuilding Corporation) and CSIC (China Shipbuilding Industry Corporation), China's two largest state group corporation, strengthening large enterprises through value chain integration, and restructuring the business scopes of SMEs through M&A; 3) encouraging indigenous innovation and R&D: expediting the technology assimilation and indigenous innovation process, and dedicating more R&D to infrastructural and high value-added shipbuilding and equipments.[3]

The following sections will examine each of the three policies. We will analyse the details of the policies, their concrete implementation

---

[2] "China Approves Stimulus Plan for Shipbuilding Industry", *Xinhua News Agency*, February 11, 2009, http://www.china.org.cn/business/news/2009-02/11/content_17262273.htm.

[3] "The Plan on the Adjustment and Revitalization of the Shipbuilding Industry", www.gov.cn, 9 June 2009, http://www.gov.cn/zwgk/2009-06/09/content_1335839.htm.

and the difficulties encountered. Meanwhile China's existing industry structure and its problems will be identified and linked to the policy initiatives. We will also have a discussion on the two latest developments in China's shipbuilding industry: offshore drilling rigs as a potential high-tech alternative to traditional ship models; and construction of the Changxing Shipbuilding Base, expected to be the world's largest shipyard, to increase China's future production capacity.

SUSTAINING THE DECLINING DEMAND

Among the three main areas of the adjustment plan, the most urgent is sustaining the declining demand. According to the report of the first quarter of 2009, the major problem that China's shipbuilding industry faced was that the demand for new ships had become almost stagnant, with the completion of the production of new ships exceeding new orders.

China's shipbuilding industry has been developing rapidly in recent years. As seen in Figure 1, the industry increased its gross

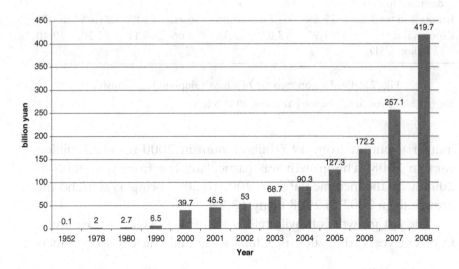

Fig. 1. Gross industrial output of China's shipbuilding industry.

Source: China Shipbuilding Industry Yearbook 2009, 5.

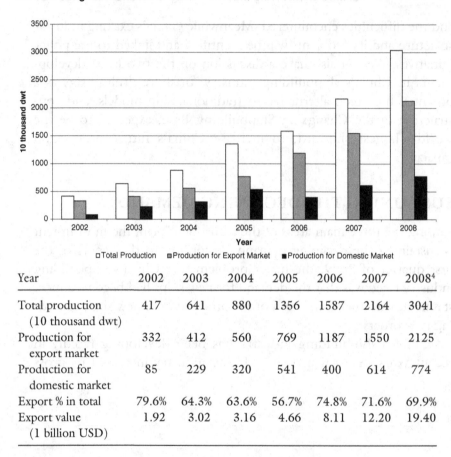

Year	2002	2003	2004	2005	2006	2007	2008[4]
Total production (10 thousand dwt)	417	641	880	1356	1587	2164	3041
Production for export market	332	412	560	769	1187	1550	2125
Production for domestic market	85	229	320	541	400	614	774
Export % in total	79.6%	64.3%	63.6%	56.7%	74.8%	71.6%	69.9%
Export value (1 billion USD)	1.92	3.02	3.16	4.66	8.11	12.20	19.40

Fig. 2.   Production capacity of China's shipbuilding industry.

Source: China Shipbuilding Industry Yearbook 2009, 5 & 8.

industrial output from 39.7 billion *yuan* in 2000 to 419.7 billion *yuan* in 2008. The growth was particularly fast from year 2006 to 2008, with the incremental from 2006 to 2007 being 49.3%, and the growth from 2007 to 2008 being 63.2%.

The fast growth is heavily reliant on export. As seen in Figure 2, in recent years, the value of China's shipbuilding export products

---

[4] There is some inconsistency in data in the 2008 figure in the yearbook: the addition of the export and domestic production does not equal the total production capacity.

increased from US$1.92 billion in 2002 to US$19.40 billion in 2008. Production for the export market in total production capacity is higher than 60%; while production for the domestic market is lower than 40% for most of the years. Take 2008 for example, when the export percentage in total almost reached 70%.

As a result, China's shipbuilding industry is severely influenced by the global financial crisis. Since August 2008 there was a sharp decline in new orders in the global shipbuilding market, and in the global market of 2009, new ship transactions declined by more than 80% from 2008, and prices for the major ship types dropped by more than 30%. Consequently, China's shipbuilding industry experienced significant slowdown in production completion, cancellation of existing orders, and a drop in new orders. In December 2008 alone, China received only 20,000 dwt new orders, a decrease of 99.8% from the same period of last year.[5] In 2009, the national total production completion was 42.43 million dwt, still an increase of 47% from 2008. Existing orders and new orders, however, both decreased. Existing orders totalled 188.17 million dwt, a decrease of 8% from the beginning of 2009; the decrease in new orders was even more serious, with only 26 million dwt, a decrease of 55% from 2008. While China's shipbuilding industry (enterprises above designated size) reached an industrial output value of 548.4 billion *yuan* in 2009, an increase of 28.7% from 2008, the incremental rate dropped 31.1% compared to 2008.[6]

Realizing the tremendous demand drop, the government has been implementing two concrete policies to help the enterprises in the revitalization plan. First, in viewing that the inadequacy of funding is the main reason for the demand drop, the government tries to provide financial support for enterprises, both domestic and foreign, to encourage banks to provide sufficient credit loans to enterprises.

---

[5] "Tremendous Demand Drop of China's Shipbuilding Industry", China Machinery Web, 20 January 2009, http://news.machine365.com/content/2009/0120/206857.html.

[6] The figures in the following paragraphs are from: "China Shipbuilding Industry Overcomes Economic Difficulties", *Xinhuanet*, 20 January 2010, http://news.xinhuanet.com/mil/2010-01/20/content_12844024.htm.

Particularly, those with deferred orders should get relatively long-term credit loans. Banks should also offer loans to ship-buying and ship-producing enterprises with good credit. One important aspect of this policy is that the government also encourages the banks to provide credit loans to foreign ship buyers, so as to sustain the existing orders of enterprises, especially those of large domestic enterprises.[7]

The second policy is to stimulate the domestic shipbuilding market. Currently, the domestic demand of China's shipbuilding industry is yet to be fully developed. In 2008, for example, only around 30% of the total national production completion is for domestic demand. Thus the government is trying to promote domestic ship demand by various means. One traditional approach is that the state invests and orders more ships for infrastructure and government usage. Another approach is to encourage the domestic petroleum and gas companies to invest in maritime engineering products such as rigs. As an alternative to the traditional ship model, maritime engineering adds high technology value to the shipbuilding industry and could promote the domestic petroleum industry as well, and thus serves as a good candidate as the domestic shipbuilding demand stimulator.

Though the effect of these policies is not evidently identifiable and China is expected to continue to face a shortage of demand in the coming two years, China's shipbuilding industry seems to excel other countries in sustaining demand. The comparative position of China's shipbuilding industry in the global market was strengthened in 2009. Though new orders of China's shipbuilding industry were only 26 million dwt in 2009, 45% of that in 2008 and 26% of that in 2007, China's share in the global shipbuilding market in terms of new orders increased significantly from 37.7% to 61.6%. And China's production completion was 34.8%, existing orders 38.5%, and new orders 61.5% of the global total in 2009, an increase of 5.3%, 3% and 23.9% respectively compared to 2008. According to the statistics from January to October 2009, China's existing orders and new

---

[7] "Analyzing the Plan on the Adjustment and Revitalization of the Shipbuilding Industry", *China Waterway Transportation*, 30 March 2009, http://www.zgsyzz.com/Article/ShowInfo.asp?ID=851.

Table 1. Three indicators of the global shipbuilding industry market 2009

Indicator/Country		Global	China	Korea	Japan
Production completion	10 thousand dwt	12203	4243	4378	2899
	%	100%	34.8%	35.9%	23.8%
New orders	10 thousand dwt	4219	2600	1487	90
	%	100%	61.6%	35.2%	2.1%
Existing orders	10 thousand dwt	48884	18817	17224	8831
	%	100%	38.5%	35.2%	18.1%

Source: Ministry of Industry and Information Technology. The global source is from Clarkson PLC, with modification from China's statistics.

orders exceeded Korea, becoming No. 1 in the world (see Table 1 for more details).[8]

PROMOTING MERGERS AND ACQUISITIONS AND RESTRUCTURING

To resolve the industry's problems of low value-added and over-capacity, the plan also emphasizes promoting mergers and acquisitions (M&A) and restructuring. There are three targets to be achieved. First, the plan promotes conglomeration, as China encourages its two largest state group corporations, i.e. CSSC and CSIC, and its major subsidiaries to enter into M&A and restructuring, so as to make them globally competitive. Second, it aims to strengthen large enterprises: it encourages large enterprises to form strategic alliances with upper-stream and lower-stream enterprises, such as ship equipment manufacturing enterprises and R&D institutes, so as to increase their value-added and technology component in the value chain. Third, it encourages small and medium-sized enterprises (SMEs) to restructure their business scope. Instead of continuing to build more lower value-added ships, SMEs should be restructured to specialize in niche areas, such as ship repairing, ship equipment manufacturing, etc, so as to gain

---

[8] "Development and Situation Analysis for China's Shipbuilding Industry", www.chinaequip.gov.cn, 4 March 2010, http://www.chinaequip.gov.cn/2010-03/04/c_13196719.htm.

a competitive edge. The main reason to promote M&A and restructuring is to target the structural problem of China's shipbuilding industry, mainly to avoid over-capacity and increase the value added to the industry. In the long run, this policy is conducive to upgrading the shipbuilding industry and building stronger technological capacity.

Currently, China's shipbuilding industry is composed of three main players. The first major component is made up of large SOEs with mega-sized production and technology capacity, many of which belong to CSSC or CSIC, the two monopoly conglomerates owned by the state. CSSC occupies the east and the south coastal area, including the Yangtze River Delta and Pearl River Delta Region, covering provinces such as Jiangsu, Shanghai, Zhejiang, Guangdong, etc; and CSIC occupies the north and the west, including the Circum-Bohai-Sea region, covering Liaoning, Shaanxi and Shanxi, etc. Both corporations originated from the previously larger China State Shipbuilding Corporation which was divided into two in 1999. They have state authorization for investment and capital management, and are directly under the supervision of the central government, specifically, the Commission for Science, Technology and Industry for National Defense. In 2009, CSSC as a conglomerate completed the production of 170 ships, with 10.76 million dwt, 3 million dwt more than 2008. Its market share in the national total reaches 27%, No. 1 in China, and its global share is 9.1%, No. 2 in the world.[9] Many of the ten largest shipbuilding companies in China belong to either CSSC or CSIC (refer to Appendix 1 for more details).[10] For example, CSSC has Shanghai Waigaoqiao Shipbuilding Co., Ltd. (SWS), Hudong-Zhonghua Shipbuilding (Group) Co., Ltd., Jiangnan Shipyard (Group) Co., Ltd. (JN), the Changxing shipyard, etc. CSIC has Dalian Shipbuilding Industry Co., Ltd., Bohai Shipbuilding Heavy Industry Co., Ltd., Qingdao Beihai Shipbuilding Heavy Industry Co., Ltd., Wuchang Shipyard, etc.

The second major component of China's shipbuilding industry is private enterprises, which have become increasingly important in

---

[9] "China Shipbuilding Industry Overcomes Economic Difficulties", *Xinhuanet*, 20 January 2010, http://news.xinhuanet.com/mil/2010-01/20/content_12844024.htm.
[10] *China Shipbuilding Industry Yearbook*, 2008.

recent years. In 2008, for instance, private shipbuilding enterprises completed 55% of the national total production. Among them are some private enterprises that can be very large; famous examples include Rongsheng Heavy Industry Corporation, a purely private enterprise, and Jiangsu Yangzijiang Shipbuilding Co., Ltd., restructured to be a private enterprise from an SOE.[11] (For details on the two corporations, refer to Appendix 2.) There are also many private SMEs dispersed in coastal provinces such as Jiangsu and Zhejiang, mainly in the form of collective investment by small private shareholders. These SMEs usually produce low value-added ships, and thus could be the targets to be acquired and restructured.

The third component of China's shipbuilding industry is joint venture between foreign companies and Chinese companies. For example, Japan and Korea, China's two major competitors in the global shipbuilding market, in fact have invested quite intensively in China. Nantong COSCO KHI Ship Engineering Co., Ltd. (NACKS), for example, is a joint company by China Ocean Shipping (Group) Company (COSCO) and Japan's Kawasaki Heavy Industries, Ltd. (KHI), and is among the top ten producers in China. Korea has also invested heavily in the Circum-Bohai-Sea Region. One example is Qingdao Hyundai Shipbuilding Co., Ltd., a joint investment between Korea's Hyundai General Trading Company and Qingdao Lingshan Shipbuilding Co., Ltd. Moreover, Singapore has also invested in China's shipbuilding industry. One example is the Jiangsu New Century Shipbuilding (NCS). The motivation for foreign companies to invest in China is mainly the cheap labour cost. On the China side, how to assimilate advanced foreign technology into domestic companies and increase the value added is the main concern.

According to the plan, M&A and restructuring takes several forms. The first is to promote conglomeration. It is emphasized in the plan that the two mega conglomerates, CSSC and CSIC, should be supported to implement M&A and restructuring. It is targeted that the two mega group corporations will be more competitive in

---

[11] *China Shipbuilding Industry Yearbook*, 2009, 4.

the higher end of the global shipbuilding market in the near future, having advanced technology in maritime engineering and equipment manufacturing. In fact, conglomeration has long been China's strategy to form globally competitive large SOEs. It is believed by the government that through conglomeration, China can collectively concentrate its R&D and production capacity to restructure the industry and lead the nation's industry to be globally competitive.

The second is to strengthen large corporations. To increase the production capacity of China, the plan encourages large shipbuilding corporations to ally with each other to mutually reinforce their production capacity. Also, in order to optimize the value chain and improve production efficiency, large corporations should also acquire upper-stream and lower-stream corporations, such as ship equipment manufacturing companies. In fact, many of the subsidiaries of CSSC and CSIC are in alliance with ship equipment manufacturing and ship repairing subsidiaries.

Third, the plan encourages SMEs to be acquired and restructured through the help of large enterprises, to specialize in niche areas, such as ship repairing and ship equipment manufacturing, so as to stay competitive. According to the plan, such restructuring and specialization of SMEs are instrumental in reducing the existing over-capacity problem of SMEs, and conducive to forming a competitive shipbuilding value chain for the nation's entire industry.[12]

Compared to the grand M&A and restructuring blueprint, the plan has less concrete policies in implementing and facilitating it. There are only some vaguely mentioned details in the plan. First, similar to adding financial stimulus to sustain demand, the government will provide government capital funds, financing and credit loans for M&A cases, particularly for those large enterprises and group corporations' M&A projects. Second, the government also gives priority to technology improvement projects between large enterprises and their acquired enterprises. Moreover, the plan also mentions that the government

---

[12] "Detailed Policies on the Shipbuilding Industry Revitalization Plan Have Come Out", *China Securities*, 27 March 2009, http://finance.jrj.com.cn/2009/03/2704393951100.shtml.

should cooperate with enterprises to settle staffing and capital reloca-tion, debt and tax issues during the M&A and restructuring process.

Admittedly, the M&A and restructuring policy faces significant challenges. First, it is questionable whether large enterprises have enough motivation to acquire other enterprises, or to be acquired by others. It will be difficult for two compatible large enterprises to merge, as very often they are competitors wishing to retain their own brand names rather than become collaborators. Moreover, if there is not sufficient stimulus for large enterprises to feel the necessity to penetrate the entire value chain, it will also be difficult for a large enterprise with a high-end product range to acquire an SME with a low-end product range, facing an incompatibility of product ranges and possibly the SME's reluctance to be restructured.

Second, SMEs may not appreciate being restructured to specialize. If those SMEs view the acquisition by large enterprises as a threat to com-petition and survival, then it will be impossible for large enterprises to help SMEs to specialize and restructure their product range. Instead of considering the help of large enterprises as a means to overcome financial difficulty and upgrade their production, they may consider themselves to be facing fiercer competition with their larger counterparts.

Although both the government and industry leaders have been emphasizing the necessity of M&A and restructuring, there seems to be insufficient motivation for it to take place. According to *China Enterprises*, so far there has not been any significant case of M&A of enterprises since the financial crisis. Instead, there are some cases of cross-industry M&A, such as Grand China Logistics purchasing 50% of the stock of Golden Gulf Shipbuilding Corporation.[13]

ENCOURAGING INNOVATION AND R&D

One essential long-term problem in China's shipbuilding industry is its low technology and innovation capacity. China's shipbuilding capacity with high value added and high-tech is less than 10% share of

---

[13] "Shipbuilding Restructuring Faces Challenge", *Chinese Enterprises*, 26 May 2010, http://finance.eastmoney.com/news/1355,2010052676764498.html.

the global total, significantly lower than its 34.8% share of the global total production output. Technologies such as maritime engineering equipment design, assembling technology and core internal equipment of the ship are still heavily reliant on foreign technology.

The Chinese government is thus calling for indigenous innovation and R&D. There are four aspects that the government is aiming at. The first is to promote optimization and upgrading for the existing three mainstream ship models, including oil tankers, bulkers and containerships. The second is to develop high-tech and high value-added R&D capabilities for new ship models and technologies; particularly, those with environment-saving and energy-efficient ship-building technologies, and those with maritime project equipment and products, such as offshore drilling rig, get prioritized in the restructuring plan. Third, besides upgrading existing and new ship models, China also wants to have indigenous research on internal critical equipments and components within ships, such as automation of the navigation system, etc. Fourth, China aims to build common infrastructural R&D for shipbuilding and maritime devices and equipments.

The plan has four concrete policies to implement the target. First, China will increase the R&D expenditure on advanced high-tech ship models and equipments, and basic and infrastructural technological research on the shipbuilding industry generally. It is emphasized that technological improvement on them are essential in R&D activities. Second, given the lack of a common standard in China's shipbuilding industry, the plan also states that China needs to speed up the standardization of the industry. These two policies are more abstract policies to improve the R&D expenditure generally.

The third and fourth policies are more specific to enterprises. The plan states that the government will encourage and support large shipbuilding enterprises to merge and restructure each other, and to engage in informationalization, automation and production process restructuring. Fourth, it also encourages SMEs to restructure their business scope to be consistent with the industry policies. This could implicitly mean the government will support those SMEs which are willing to restructure and specialize in certain niche areas of the entire shipbuilding production cycle, but abandon those SMEs which continue wasting its capacity in building lower value-added ships.

Indeed, R&D and industrial upgrading is also one of the deeper causes for the Chinese government to promote M&A in the shipbuilding industry. By its nature, shipbuilding industry requires very intensive investment and technology support. It is only through large enterprises that the government can concentrate its resources in developing R&D and increase the technology capacity of the industry. It is usually difficult for SMEs to commit such technological investment on the overall ship other than by choosing a niche area to specialize in.

However, it remains vague how the government will proceed to implement these four policies and measure their effect. Moreover, as R&D takes a long time to have an effect on the industry, it will be difficult to see any immediate result. Whether China will be able to promote R&D and innovation in the shipbuilding industry remains a challenge.

OFFSHORE DRILLING RIG: MARITIME ENGINEERING

As one of the potential candidates of indigenous innovation and R&D, maritime engineering and technology is promoted throughout the revitalization plan. One of its promising areas is the offshore drilling rig, which requires advanced maritime engineering technologies. Unlike the traditional usage of ships, rigs are used for offshore oil exploration. It refers to offshore platforms and equipments that are used for the discovery and development of underwater oil and gas resources. Types of rigs range from shallow-water steel jackets and jackup barges, to floating semi-submersibles and drillships able to operate in very deep waters.[14]

Due to the onshore oil price surge and the huge potential of offshore oil exploration, the global drilling rig industry is flourishing. With the world's increasing need for new energy, rigs become a great

---

[14] Typology of offshore rigs from: http://en.wikipedia.org/wiki/Offshore_drilling.

potential area for maritime engineering. Many large enterprises in China are starting their business in rigs. Examples include China National Offshore Oil Corporation, Shanghai Waigaoqiao Ship building Corporation, Cosco Corp., Yangzijiang Shipbuilding, etc.

In October 2007, Shanghai Waigaoqiao Shipbuilding Co. signed a contract with China National Offshore Oil Corp. to build a semi-submersible drilling rig[15] with a working deepwater drilling capability of 3000 m and the capability of drilling oil wells as deep as 12,000 m. The project utilizes the latest technological development of the 6th generation global offshore rig equipment design. It is one of the major corresponding projects related to China's long-term national offshore oil exploration strategy. China's Marine Design & Research Institute (Research Institute No. 708) is responsible for its research and design, while Shanghai Waigaoqiao Shipbuilding Corp. is mainly responsible for its construction. The rig was completed in February 2010. The project is considered to be a great achievement of the state's move to indigenous R&D and construction in the rig industry.[16]

Recently in March 2010, Cosco Corp., a subsidiary of China Ocean Shipping Group, landed a US$500 million contract for a deepwater semi-submersible drilling rig with Norway's Sevan Drilling, a unit of Norway-based oilfield services group Sevan Marine. The rig is expected to be delivered in the first quarter of 2012. According to Cosco, it secured a full engineering, procurement, construction and installation contract to build a deepwater semi-submersible drilling rig. Previously, Cosco Nantong had already

---

[15] Semi-submersible drilling rig: The floating platform has a hull (columns and pontoons) that, when flooded with seawater, cause the pontoons to submerge to a predetermined depth. Semi-submersibles are generally used for offshore deepwater drilling operations with water depth ranging from 600 metres to 3,600 metres. Description from http://www.cimc.com/res/products_en/ocean/rig/semi_submersible/200912/t20091228_2493.shtml.

[16] See "Indigenous Innovation of China's Offshore Drilling Rig", http://china.cippe.net/, 26 March 2009, http://china.cippe.net/news_sec/12290.htm; and "World Most Advanced Semi-submersible Drilling Rig Produced in Shanghai", CNOOC website, 26 February 2010, http://www.cnooc.com.cn/data/html/news/2010-02-26/301109.html.

worked with Sevan Drilling on a rig delivered in November 2009. This project shows how a Chinese company gradually assimilates and transfers advanced foreign technology into a domestic company through international cooperation.[17]

Another example took place in April 2010, when China's Yangzijiang Shipbuilding teamed up with a Middle Eastern investor Baker Technology to buy a 15% stake in oil-rig maker Sembcorp Marine PPL Shipyard for US$155 million. Both companies are listed on the Singapore Exchange. With the purchase of this stake holding, Yangzijiang Shipbuilding seems to be making a move into the international rig industry.[18]

The current challenge for China's rig industry is that its technology is still far behind the most advanced in the world. For example, the semi-submersible drilling rig produced by Waigaoqiao Ship building Co. was based on the initial design of Friede & Goldman, Ltd., an US-based naval architecture and marine engineering company. The core technology for Cosco's new rig is also from Norway's Sevan Drilling. How to balance between promoting indigenous innovation and assimilating foreign core technology thus becomes the main challenge for China's future rig development.

CHANGXING SHIPBUILDING BASE

As China is striving to build its production capacity to be the world No. 1 shipbuilder, it is necessary to construct many mega-size shipbuilding bases. One latest and biggest move is the construction of the world's largest shipbuilding base on Changxing Island, off the deepwater coast of Shanghai. The project has an overall investment of 35 billion *yuan*, and is targeted to be completed from 2003 to 2015. Its main stakeholder is CSSC, especially its subsidiary Jiangnan Shipyard (Group) Co., Ltd., which has been relocated to Changxing Island from its previous location, the current Shanghai Expo site.

---

[17] "Cosco Corp Lands $698m Rig Contract", *The Straits Times*, 16 March 2010, B13.
[18] "China-based Shipbuilder to Buy Stake in PPL Shipyard", *The Straits Times*, 19 April 2010, B16.

It is expected that the Changxing Shipbuilding Base will become the world's largest shipbuilding base upon its completion. It is expected that the Jiangnan Shipyard Co., Ltd. will expand its shipbuilding capacity from the current 800,000 dwt a year to 4.5 million by 2010. CSSC is expected to have an annual capacity of 8 million dwt, half of China's current production capacity by 2015. Shanghai will also become the world's largest shipbuilding base, tripling its capacity to 12 million dwt by 2015.[19]

There are three main production lines for the Changxing Shipbuilding Base. The west line, the No. 1 line, is mainly under the construction of Shanghai Waigaoqiao Shipbuilding Co., Ltd. The middle line, the No. 2 line, is mainly under the construction of Hudong-Zhonghua Shipbuilding (Group) Co., Ltd. Both lines are for civil shipbuilding. The east line, the No. 3 line, is under the construction of Jiangnan Shipyard Co., Ltd., and is mainly for military shipbuilding. Some sources even say that given its capacity to build large naval vessels, it is constructing China's first aircraft carrier in this line.

The construction of the new Changxing Shipyard began in November 2003. In the first phase, four large dry docks, nine outfitting piers, and two cargo piers were built along a 3.8 km coastline. It became the new location for CSSC's Jiangnan Shipyard Corporation in 2008. In the second phase, CSSC's Hudong-Zhonghua Shipbuilding Corporation and Waigaoqiao Shipbuilding Corporation will construct more shipyards along the island's 8 km coastline.

The Changxing Shipbuilding Base offers the capability to build large naval vessels, including aircraft carriers. The largest dockyard in the facility is 580 m in length and 120 m in width. According to some sources, China is planning to build 1–2 medium-size aircraft carriers in Changxing's No. 3 production line. If this is true, China would have its own first indigenously built aircraft carrier by 2015.[20]

---

[19] "Changxing Island Shipbuilding Base Building China's Aircraft Carrier", *Sina Military*, 5 June 2009, http://www.chnqiang.com/article/2009/0605/article_86104.shtml.

[20] "New Facility Offers Carrier Building Capability", *SinoDefence.com*, accessed on 17 May 2010, http://www.sinodefence.com/research/new-facility-carrier-building/default.asp.

APPENDIX 1

Ten Largest Shipbuilding Corporations (Production Completion) in 2008

Ranking	Corporation	Chinese Name	Property	Production Completion (10 thousand dwt)
1	Shanghai Waigaoqiao Shipbuilding Co., Ltd. (SWS)	上海外高桥造船有限公司	Subsidiary of CSSC	356.1
2	Dalian Shipbuilding Industry Co., Ltd. (DSIC)	大连船舶重工集团有限公司	Subsidiary of CSIC	292.4
3	Jiangsu New Century Shipbuilding (NCS)	江苏新世纪造船股份有限公司	Joint investment by Singapore company and the original New Century Shipbuilding Co., Ltd.	200.5
4	Hudong-Zhonghua Shipbuilding (Group) Co., Ltd.	沪东中华造船（集团）有限公司	Subsidiary of CSSC	127.4
5	Shanghai Jiangnan-Changxing Shipbuilding Company Limited (SCS)	上海江南长兴工业造船有限责任公司	Subsidiary of CSSC	102.4

(Continued)

(*Continued*)

Ranking	Corporation	Chinese Name	Property	Production Completion (10 thousand dwt)
6	TSUNEISHI Shipbuilding Co., Ltd. (Zhoushan)	常石集团（舟山）造船有限公司	Foreign investment by TSUNEISHI Holdings Corporation (Japan)	93.2
7	Jiangsu Yangzijiang Shipbuilding Co., Ltd.	江苏扬子江船厂有限公司	Founded in 1956 as an SOE, restructured to be private in 1999, listed in Singapore in 2005.	83.9
8	Bohai Shipbuilding Heavy Industry Co., Ltd. (BSHIC)	渤海船舶重工有限责任公司	Subsidiary of CSIC	81.6
9	Guangzhou Shipyard International Company Limited (GSI)	广州广船国际股份有限公司	Subsidiary of CSSC	69.7
10	Nantong COSCO KHI Ship Engineering Co., Ltd. (NACKS)	南通中远川崎船舶工程有限公司	Joint investment by China Ocean Shipping (Group) Company (COSCO) & Japan Kawasaki Heavy Industries, Ltd. (KHI)	63.2

Source: China Shipbuilding Industry Yearbook, 2009.

APPENDIX 2

Two Cases of Large Private Shipbuilding Enterprises in China

Rongsheng Heavy Industries Corporation (江苏熔盛重工有限公司)[21] is one of China's largest private shipbuilding enterprises. The company was founded in June 2006, with a registration capital of USD 297 million. It is located in the southern end of Chang Qingsha Island, Rugao Port of Nantong, Jiangsu Province, and is in Shanghai's 1.5 hour economic circle. It has a coastline of 6.0 km. As of June 2009, the company has more than 16,000 employees. It is equipped with four large docks, three sets of 900-T gantry cranes, one set of 1600-T gantry crane, eight outfitting quays and two material quays. It applies a modern general assembly shipbuilding mode, advanced shipbuilding concept and process flow, and completely follows the modern general assembly shipbuilding mode to make scientific allocations in terms of productivity calculations, process design, production workshop layout, selection of equipment and facilities, etc, which obtains maximum performance from the productivity of core facilities and reduces the transportation cost of intermediate products.

Yangzijiang Shipbuilding (Holdings) Ltd. (江苏扬子江船业控股有限公司)[22] is a large shipbuilding enterprise with Jiangsu Yangzijiang Shipbuilding Ltd. and Jiangsu New Yangzi Shipbuilding Ltd. as the core. Founded in 1956 as an SOE, restructured to be private in 1999, the company is the first shipbuilding enterprise in China that entered the stock market in Singapore, becoming one of the Straits Times Index stocks in the Singapore Exchange. The company covers a area of 2.2 million m² and a wharf line of 3,000 m, and employs over 10,000 staff and workers. Equipped with one large dry dock and five large and medium-sized slipways, the company boasts a shipbuilding capacity of over 1 million dwt annually in terms of ship tonnage.

---

[21] Description from the Corporation website, accessed in June 2010, http://www.rshi.cn/about1.html.

[22] Description from the Corporation website, accessed in June 2010, http://www.yzjship.com/en_about.asp.

The mainstream products of the company range from large and medium-sized containerships, large bulk carriers to medium multi-purpose ships. The company has been building container ships, oceanographic engineering ships, chemical tankers, multi-purpose ships and bulk carriers for numerous domestic and overseas customers over the last 50 years. The company has been widely approved and commended by the international classification societies such as GL, LR, ABS, BV and CCS for its quality products.

Chapter

4

Challenges for China's Steel Industry: Overcapacity and Production Fragmentation

Hong YU and Mu YANG

China's steel production reached 500 million metric tons in 2008. The growth of the steel sector has benefited from the rapid economic development and strong domestic demand. However, it is facing two challenges: overcapacity and production fragmentation. First, for long-term sustainable development, domestic steel enterprises will have to put a cap on their production output. Second, China's steel industry is perhaps the most fragmented in the world. The lack of production consolidation results in duplicated development and cut-throat competition among domestic steel enterprises. Most of these steel firms suffer from weak competitiveness and low production output. The steel industry is big, but not strong. Mergers and acquisitions (M&A) are the key strategy for the development of China's steel industry.

RAPID DEVELOPMENT OF CHINA'S STEEL INDUSTRY

The steel sector has been the mainstay of the Chinese economy since the early 1950s. China has been one of the key steel producers in the world over the last decade, as evidenced by its leading world position, with production reaching 500 mmt in 2008. Its total production capacity surpassed the combined output of the next seven largest steel-producing countries (Table 1). The share of Chinese-produced steel in the world increased to 37.6% in 2008 from 5.1% in 1980, with a production of merely 37.1 mmt (Figure 1).

The growth of the steel sector has benefited from the strong domestic demand over the last decade. Likewise, the steel industry has also contributed to China's economic growth. The rapid industrialization of China has led to an increase in demand for steel products.[1] Indeed, China's steel sector has benefited from the rapid development of the Chinese economy over the last decade; especially after

Table 1.   World's top ten steel-producing countries, 2008

Country	Rank	Production 2008 (million metric tons)	World Share (%)
China	1	500	37.6
Japan	2	118	8.9
US	3	91	7.2
Russia	4	68	5.2
India	5	55	4.1
South Korea	6	53	4.0
Germany	7	45	3.4
Ukraine	8	37	2.8
Brazil	9	33	2.5
Italy	10	30	2.3

Source: The World Steel Association, 2009.

---

[1] Feng Lintong, "China's Steel Industry: Its Rapid Expansion and Influence on the International Steel Industry", *Resources Policy* 20 (1994), 219–34.

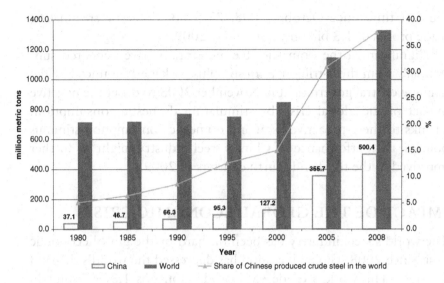

Fig. 1. China's global share of produced crude steel.

Source: The World Steel Association,[2] 2009.

China became a member of the World Trade Organization (WTO) in 2001. The rapid growth of China's key industries such as its automobile and shipbuilding sectors has boosted the demand for high-end steel products. Also, owing to the huge state investment in high steel-consumption sectors such as infrastructure and housing construction, low-end steel production has been reporting decent growth.

As the fundamentals of the Chinese economy remain sound and state-oriented capital investment, such as low-cost housing, infrastructure construction and Sichuan earthquake reconstruction, in key high steel-consumption areas is high, there is cause for optimism for the future development of China's steel industry. For example, for

---

[2] The World Steel Association (WSA) is one of the most powerful and largest industry associations in the world. It represents 18 of the world's 20 biggest steel enterprises and around 170 steelmakers, steel industry associations and steel research institutes across the world. In total, its members produce 85% or so of the world's annual steel output.

the first time since October 2008, 72 major domestic steelmakers made profits of 1.3 billion *yuan* in May 2009.[3]

Significantly, the domestic steel enterprises have benefited substantially from the 4-trillion-*yuan* stimulus package announced by the Chinese central government in November 2008 to offset the negative impact of the global crisis by stimulating domestic consumption. Thanks to these proactive fiscal and domestic consumption stimulus policies, the performance of China's steel industry might be further improved in the third and fourth quarters of 2009.

IMPACT OF THE GLOBAL ECONOMIC CRISIS

The world's steel industry has been hit hard by the global economic crisis since 2008. Global recession has depressed the world's demand for steel. The world's crude steel production was 1,329.7 mmt in 2008. If China's figures were excluded, annual growth of crude steel production would show a contraction of 3.3% in 2008 compared to an expansion of 3.4% in 2007 (Figure 2).

Many major steel-producing countries, such as the US, Japan and Russia, recorded a sharp fall in steel production in 2008.[4] For example, the total steel production in the US was down to 91.5 mmt in 2008 from 98.2 mmt in 2007, a decrease of 7%. More than 50% of its steel production capacity has become idle since January 2009, marking the lowest levels of production for several decades.

The year of 2008 was a difficult year for China's steel industry. It had been suffering from high export dependency, with semi-manufactured and finished steel products exports accounting for 23% of total steel production in 2008.[5] The sharp fall of external consumption had severely affected the export of steel products from China. The export of finished steel products decreased to 1.4 mmt in April 2009 from 7.5 mmt in August 2008. Compared to 11.4 mmt in

---

[3] "Major Steel Mills Back in Black", *China Daily*, 30 June 2009.
[4] *The World Steel Association*, 2009.
[5] China Iron & Steel Association, 2009.

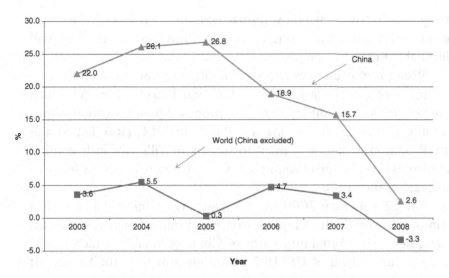

Fig. 2. Growth of crude steel production in the world.
Source: The World Steel Association, 2009.

the first quarter of 2008, the export of finished steel products was down by 51.8% to reach only 5.5 mmt in the first quarter of 2009.[6] Total export value of finished steel products hit only US$7.5 billion during the first four months of 2009, a decrease of 47.8%.

The global economic crisis has also exacerbated the existing problems of excessive capacity and production fragmentation in the steel sector. Due to the impact of this crisis and decreasing steel prices, up to 62% of 72 large and medium-sized steelmakers in China recorded losses of 29.1 billion *yuan* in 2008.[7] During the first quarter of 2009, these key domestic steel enterprises recorded further losses, totaling 3.3 billion *yuan*, according to the China Iron and Steel Association. Moreover, the road to global economic recovery is proving to be sluggish and problematic. Facing depressed external demands,

---

[6] General Administration of Customs of the People's Republic of China, 2009.
[7] "China's Steel Industry to Consolidate Amid Global Crisis", *Xinhua News*, http://news.xinhuanet.com/english/2009-03/12/content_10995040.htm, 12 March 2009.

triggered by the worsening global economic crisis and uncertain economic future, the foreign trade of China's steel industry will inevitably further decline.

Rising iron ore prices also significantly increase production costs for many of China's large and medium-sized steel companies which are now in financial difficulties.[8] The proposed joint venture between leading global mining companies, Rio Tinto PLC (Rio Tinto) and BHP Billiton, would lead them to surpass Brazil's Vale in becoming the largest iron ore producer in the world. Iron ore prices are likely to increase in the future.

On 12 February 2009, Anglo-Australian mining concern, Rio Tinto, the world's third biggest iron ore producer, signed a planned agreement with Aluminum Corp of China (Chinalco) which would make an investment of US$19.5 billion investment in the former.[9] If successful, the deal would mark the biggest overseas investment in a foreign company made by a Chinese firm. The deal would also help Rio Tinto reduce its overall debt and meet repayment obligations. However, Rio Tinto called off the deal with Chinalco on 5 June 2009, and announced that it would pay a US$195 million break fee to Chinalco. Instead, Rio Tinto and its rival, BHP Billiton, the world's second largest iron ore producer, would combine their iron ore assets and set up a joint production venture in Western Australia. In order to achieve 50:50 share ratio in this joint venture between these two companies, BHP Billiton is expected to pay US$5.8 billion to Rio Tinto.[10]

Both companies and the Australian government argue that the abandonment of the original deal with Chinalco and the decision to establish a new joint venture was purely based on market considerations and commercial interests. However, the termination of the

---

[8] "China's Steel Sector Just Keeps Growing", *Asia Times*, http://www.atimes.com/atimes/China_Business/HH03Cb03.html, 12 May 2010.

[9] "China Steel Association Opposes Rio–BHP iron ore JV", *Xinhua News*, http://www.chinadaily.com.cn/bizchina/rio_chinalco/2009-06/10/content_8328150.htm, 10 June 2009.

[10] "Rio Tinto-Chinalco $19.5B Deal Now Dead", *China Daily*, online edition, http://www.chinadaily.com.cn/china/2009-06/05/content_8252601.htm, 5 June 2009.

planned deal between Rio Tinto and Chinalco has caused wide concern and discontent in China. China claims that by arguing that one of the key strategic assets of Australia should never be controlled by China, the acquisition deal between Chinalco and Rio Tinto had been politicalized by Western politicians and media. China claimed that the consolidation deal between Rio Tinto and BHP Billiton had clear monopolistic characteristics and expressed strong opposition to their joint venture.[11]

As the world's largest iron ore importer, China's discontent is understandable. China has become the world's largest iron ore importer since 2003. More than 50% of its consumed iron ore needs to be imported. China's steel industry is very sensitive to any strategic cooperation and alliance between the major iron ore suppliers. China has expressed the concern that this kind of move would give suppliers a monopoly over iron ore assets and more power in setting their prices.[12] Currently, more than half of China's iron ore imports come from Rio Tinto and BHP Billiton. The joint venture between these two giants would strengthen their say on the world's iron ore pricing. It would inevitably put China in a vulnerable position in bargaining iron ore prices and force it to accept higher prices in the long term. The Chinese government and steelmakers have expressed strong opposition to the Rio Tinto–BHP Billiton consolidation deal on the grounds that it has clear monopolistic characteristics. The Chinese government makes it clear that it would carefully watch any move of this joint venture and use the anti-monopoly law to eliminate market manipulation if necessary.

There is a lesson to be learnt from this investment failure. It is not easy for high-profile state-owned Chinese enterprises to succeed in overseas investments especially when strategic resources or industries

---

[11] Chong Siew Keng and Desmond Chua, "The Rio Tinto Affair", EAI Background Brief No. 468, National University of Singapore, 2006; "Chinese Steel Group Opposes Rio-BHP Venture", *Yahoo News*, http://finance.yahoo.com/news/Chinese-steel-group-opposes-apf-2622493996.html?x=0&.v=1, 3 January 2010.
12 "Rio Tinto, BHP Deal 'Monopolistic', Industry Warns", *China Daily*, 13, 9 June 2009.

like the oil and iron ore sectors are involved. Such success depends on not only well-planned investment proposals that consider commercial interests and various market factors, but also, possibly, a good lobbying strategy to deal with the frequent criticisms of the Western media and politicians. Their influence on investment deals cannot be ignored.

GOVERNMENT'S STIMULUS PROGRAMMES

In January 2009, the State Council of China released a new development outline for the steel industry 2009–2011 (referred to as the Outline). This Outline maps out comprehensive development schemes, such as structural readjustment and technological upgrading, and at the same time addresses other issues such as the lack of economic scale and production fragmentation. The Outline also sets up important working tasks for conserving resources and protecting the environment for the steel industry.

In response to the global economic downturn in the short run, and to cope with the existing problems of excessive overcapacity and production fragmentation in the long run, apart from the specific development goals identified in Table 2, there are three main objectives unveiled by the Outline. First, in order to strengthen global

Table 2.   Highlights of the new development outline for the steel industry

Summary

General Development

1   The total production capacity of crude steel is expected to be maintained at around 500 mmt in 2011. The 4% ratio of value-added industrial output of the steel industry in GDP is achievable.

Mergers and Acquisitions

2   The central government is seeking to establish around five key steel giants with annual production capacity reaching 50 mmt and several large steel companies with annual production capacity of 10–30 mmt by 2011.

(*Continued*)

Table 2. (*Continued*)

Summary

3   These leading domestic steel enterprises should develop strong self-innovation capability and be competitive globally. The share of the top five steelmakers is expected to account for 45% of total steel production capacity in China in the next three years.

Outdated Production Capacity Elimination

4   The Chinese government would do well to consider shutting down blast furnaces with a capacity of 300 cubic metres or less and electric arc furnaces with a capacity of 20 tons or less by 2010. Blast furnaces with a capacity of 400 cubic metres or less and electric arc furnaces with a capacity of 30 tons or less could be next in line for elimination by 2011.

5   In total, up to 72 mmt in outdated iron-making and 25 mmt obsolete steel-making capacity are expected to be eliminated in the steel industry over the next three years.

Technological Upgrading

6   China's steel industry is expected to speed up in its technological upgrading. The quality of 60% of finished steel products manufactured by important large- and medium-sized steel enterprises is expected to achieve general world standards by 2011. Self-sufficiency in key finished products is expected to reach 90% by 2011.

7   The central government would provide around 15 billion *yuan* in subsidies and loans to support technological research and upgrading and enhance product quality in the steel sector.

Export Promotion

8   Export tariffs on key steel products will be scrapped to encourage exports and ease pressure on domestic steelmakers. The export tax rebates for high-tech and high value-added steel products will be increased. From 1 April 2009, the export tax rebate for 59 finished steel products has been increased to 13% from 5%.

Environment Protection

9   The Outline also sets up important working tasks for resources conservation and environmental protection for the steel industry. Specific targets have been set up for energy consumption reduction per unit of production output: by 2011, energy consumption per ton of steel products should not exceed 0.62 tons of standard coal equivalent. The rate of second-hand energies, which can be reused, will reach 100%.

Source: National Development and Reform Commission, the People's Republic of China, 2009.

competitiveness, the steel sector is expected to undergo major industrial restructuring. The central government is expected to provide subsidies and loans to support technological research and upgrading in the steel sector.

Second, the steel sector is expected to make significant progress in acquisitions. The central government hopes that China's steel industry can compete more effectively on a global scale and encourages foreign acquisitions by domestic steel enterprises. Third, addressing the prominent issue of production overcapacity is believed to be the top priority. Total production capacity of crude steel should be maintained at around 500 mmt by 2011.

Wen Jiabao, Premier of China, during his recent visits to large iron and steel firms, has reiterated in speeches that the domestic steel industry faces huge tasks in restructuring production and eliminating outdated capacity, and linking the steel industry with a green economy and new materials to cope with the global financial crisis and enhance long-term industrial competitiveness.[13] The Chinese steelmakers should take a proactive role in diversifying products and enhancing quality to meet the demands of the manufacturing, new energy vehicles and shipbuilding industries. The 4-trillion-*yuan* state stimulus package and rejuvenation plans for the ten key industries are expected to provide new opportunities for the development of the steel industry.

However, the problems of production overcapacity and fragmentation in the steel sector are nothing new, and have existed for a long time. To resolve these problems is a major challenge for the government. Although the central departments of China are attempting to deal with these problems, concrete results have yet to become apparent. There is a lack of policy details to achieve these objectives.

---

[13] "Premier Wen: Economy Making Steady Progress", *China Daily*, online edition, http://www.chinadaily.com.cn/bizchina/2009-06/23/content_8311301.htm, 23 June 2009.

SEVERE CHALLENGES AND PROBLEMS

Large-Scale Overcapacity

Although the Chinese government has outlined an ambitious plan to strengthen the domestic steel industry's competitiveness on a global scale and to become an influential steel player in the world, the implementation of this outline is a difficult task. It faces at least three serious challenges. First, large-scale overcapacity in production is the most prominent problem. According to the Ministry of Industry and Information Technology's (MIIT) forecast, in 2009, the apparent domestic consumption (including production, net imports and inventory adjustment) of crude steel will be merely 470 mmt while the steel production capacity is expected to be more than 600 mmt, a production overcapacity of around 25%.[14] The steel enterprises are simply making too much steel.

Despite facing a sharp fall in external demand and uncertain economic circumstances, domestic steel production, surprisingly, recorded growth during the first six months of 2009. The monthly production reached 47.2 mmt in November 2009 from 41.2 mmt in January 2009, with a monthly growth of 2.3% (Figure 3). The growth in steel production is also reflected in the sharp increase in imports of iron ore, a key raw ingredient for steel making. For example, the imports of iron ore increased to 53.4 million tons in May 2009, up by 63% from 32.6 million tons in January 2009.[15]

China is now the world's largest iron ore importer. In particular, a large proportion of imported iron ore comes from Rio Tinto. China is expressing strong opposition to the consolidation deal between Rio Tinto and BHP Billiton, arguing that it would give suppliers a monopoly on iron ore assets and more power in setting their prices.

In recent years, China has been working hard to engage in the negotiation of iron ore prices and to achieve influence consistent with its status as the world's largest steel producer and biggest iron ore importer. On 31 May 2009, China rejected the iron ore price cut of

---

[14] Ministry of Industry and Information Technology, People's Republic of China, 2009.
[15] General Administration of Customs of The People's Republic of China, 2009.

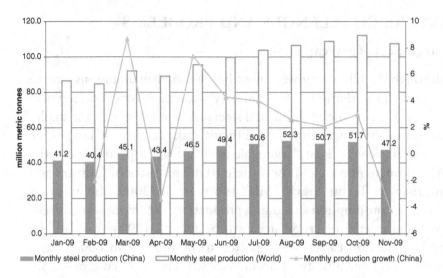

Fig. 3.   Monthly steel production of China and the world.

Source: The World Steel Association, 2009.

33% negotiated by Rio Tinto, Japanese and South Korean steelmakers, claiming that the price was still unacceptably high. The China Iron and Steel Association said that this price would hurt China's steel industry and cause overall losses for domestic steelmakers. It insisted that a minimum 40% price cut in the annual contract for iron ore purchase, which had already been resisted by the world's leading suppliers, must be achieved before China's steel firms could sign this year's iron ore supply contract. China is threatening to abandon the benchmark system of annual iron ore negotiations, which has been a key symbol of the world's steel industry for 40 years, and to turn to the spot market for supplies.[16]

On 9 July 2009, Shanghai's State Security Bureau arrested Stern Hu, General Manager of iron ore sales and marketing at Rio Tinto's

---

[16] "Last Attempt to Save Iron Ore Benchmark", *Financial Times*, http://www.ft.com/cms/s/0/04e61204-448f-11de-82d6-00144feabdc0.html; "Rio Case Shakes Foreign Groups into Reassessing China Methods", *Financial Times*, 3, 18/19 July 2009.

Shanghai office, and three other Rio Tinto staff. China accused Stern Hu of stealing state secrets with his bribes to staff of Chinese steel-making enterprises. It said that according to evidence obtained, Hu's behaviour had caused huge losses to China's economic interests and was a threat to the national economic security.[17] It is believed that some senior staff from the Chinese steel mills were also involved in this case and might be investigated by the Chinese security department.[18] However, the Western media widely speculated that the arrest of Hu and the other three Rio Tinto staff was connected to the Chinalco deal cancellation by Rio Tinto. The case is seen as payback for the broken deal.[19] The arrest of Hu has aroused the concern of the Australian government and negatively affected relations between China and Australia.

Stern Hu's detention is expected to worsen the hostile relations between Rio Tinto and China's steel industry caused by the failure of the Chinalco deal. It could also affect and delay the ongoing iron ore price talks between Chinese steelmakers and global major iron ore producers. By announcing these arrests, China intends not only to show the iron ore giants that it means to take a more proactive role in the bargaining of iron ore prices, but also more importantly, to clean up all irregularities within the iron ore trade in China (see Appendix 1 for detailed analysis).

In April 2009, the MIIT issued a strong warning to the steel industry to avoid excessive investment and prevent overcapacity by eliminating backward production methods and ceasing bank loans.[20] However, the warning from the central government, and even

---

[17] "Rio Employee Accused of Bribery", *Financial Times*, http://www.ft.com/cms/s/0/5cf0e9fc-6d15-11de-9032-00144feabdc0.html, 12 May 2010.

[18] "Australia Warns China on Spy Case", *BBC News*, http://news.bbc.co.uk/2/hi/business/8150985.stm, 12 May 2010.

[19] "Rio Worker 'Stole Secrets'", *BBC News*, http://news.bbc.co.uk/2/hi/business/8141766.stm, 12 May 2010.

[20] "MIIT Issued the Emergency Public Report to Restrain the Over Expansion of Production Capacity in the Steel Industry", *China Iron & Steel Association*, http://www.chinaisa.org.cn/show.php?newsid=2152377, 2 January 2010.

repeated remarks by Premier Wen Jiabao himself, proved to be ineffective in curbing production overcapacity. In fact, due to robust domestic demand, steel production growth is projected to have sped up in the third and fourth quarters of this year.

China's steel sector is dominated by a few large state-owned enterprises (SOEs) with numerous small and medium-sized enterprises (SMEs) accounting for only a small portion of steel output. Overcapacity has been mainly due to the rapid production expansion of the SMEs. This is in contrast to the reduction efforts made by the large steel firms. For example, average daily production of the SMEs jumped to 0.34 mmt from 0.29 mmt.[21] Overcapacity might add additional pressure to the downward trend of steel prices in the light of the plunge in external consumption. The fall in domestic steel prices would further hit the profit performance of China's steelmakers. For long-term sustainable development, domestic steel enterprises need to exercise self-restraint in expanding production capacity. The priority task for the steel sector is to curb over-production.

In examining unfair practices such as subsidies and dumping, the US Department of Commerce successively raised three anti-dumping and countervailing investigations into the imports of finished steel products from China during June 2009.[22] Taking into account the frequency of these investigations and specific target industry, this was a very unusual move. The Chinese steelmakers might need to turn to the export of cheap steel products to the US in light of domestic oversupply. However, it is very easy to trigger anti-import and protectionist sentiments in the US. This case shows that China's steel sector needs to speed up its structural readjustment process and eliminate outdated production methods.

---

[21] "China Steel Makers Report Losses as Output Rises", *China Daily*, online edition, http://www.chinadaily.com.cn/bizchina/2009-04/23/content_7708515.htm, 23 April 2009.

[22] "China Scraps Anti-Dumping Duty on Newsprint Imports", *Reuters*, http://www.guardian.co.uk/business/feedarticle/8583969, 30 June 2009.

Production Fragmentation

Second, production fragmentation is another challenge facing the steel industry. China has more than 7,000 iron and steel companies, far more than any other country. Most of these firms suffer from a lack of competitiveness and low production output. China's steel industry is big, but not strong. Among the 76 key large- and medium-sized enterprises in China, only ten firms have 10 mmt annual production capacities (Table 3).[23]

Compared to the world's leading steel companies, Chinese steel enterprises have employed far more workers. However, crude steel output per employee for domestic steel enterprises was much lower than that for leading firms in the world (Table 3). Jiangsu Shagang Group has the highest productivity in China, but its output per employee was barely one third that of the world's leading steel companies. This indicates that labour productivity in the Chinese steel firms is low and technical progress is still slow. Looking at the pre-reform period between 1957 and 1980, Jefferson's empirical study (1990) found that China's steel industry had achieved productivity growth at an annual rate of 2.5% during the reform era.[24]

The low technological capability of China's steel industry is also reflected in the measurement of energy efficiency. For example, in comparison to the world's leading nations, the average coke consumption per ton of crude steel in China was 2–3 times higher (Table 4). Technological advancement is not only important for enhancing energy efficiency and thus improving steel production, but also crucial to achieving sustainable steel development and environmental protection. Although China produced around 36% of the world's steel output in 2007, it accounted for more than 50% of carbon dioxide emissions generated from world steel

---

[23] The steel-making companies with annual production capacity reaching at least 10 mmt are internationally recognized as "internationally competitive" firms.

[24] Jefferson Gary H., "China's Iron and Steel Industry: Sources of Enterprises Efficiency and the Impact of Reform", *Journal of Development Economics*, 33 (1990), 329–55.

Table 3. Productivity of China's large steel-making enterprises and the world's leading firms, 2007

Enterprise	Crude Steel (mmt)	Total Employees (1,000)	Output per Employee (tons)
China			
Baosteel Group	28.5	40	712
Angang-Bengang Group	23.5	196	119
Jiangsu Shagang Group	22.8	26	876
Tangshan Iron & Steel Group	22.7	96	236
Wuhan Iron & Steel Group	20.1	87	231
Shougang Corporation	15.4	80	192
Magang Group	14.1	59	238
Jinan Iron & Steel Group	12.1	41	295
Laiwu Iron & Steel Group	11.6	39	297
Hunan Hualing Iron & Steel Group	11.1	46	241
Other 66 Iron & Steel Groups	Less than 10	n/a	n/a
Comparison with the World			
Nippon Steel (Japan)	35.7	14	2550
JFE (Japan)	34.0	14	2428
POSCO (South Korea)	31.1	17	1829
US Steel (US)	21.5	21	1023

Source: Compiled by the authors based on various information from China Iron and Steel Association (2008); *China Steel Yearbook (2008)* and the World Steel Association (2009).

Table 4. Coke consumption per ton of crude steel output of China and leading steel-producing countries (unit: kg)

Country	2004	2005	2006
China	740	720	710
Japan	380	380	420
South Korea	230	190	180
US	200	170	170

Source: *China Steel Yearbook 2008.*

production.[25] The steel sector still has a long way to go to achieve energy conservation and efficiently utilized input energy.

The lack of production agglomeration results in duplicated development and cut-throat competition among domestic steel enterprises. China's steel industry is perhaps the most fragmented in the world. On average, there are more than 230 iron and steel enterprises in each province (Figure 4). As the steel sector is an industry with economies of scale, it makes no sense to maintain so many steel-making firms.

The share of the top five domestic steelmakers in the total steel production of China was merely 27% in 2007. Baosteel Group, China's flagship steel enterprise, made only 35.4 mmt of steel products. In contrast, the world's leading steelmaker, Luxembourg-based ArcelorMittal, produced 103.3 mmt of steel products in 2008, nearly

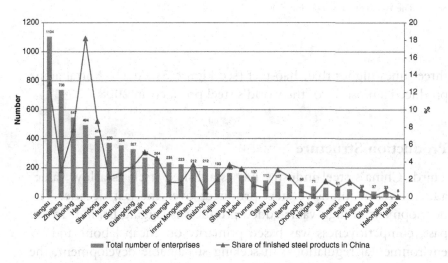

Fig. 4. Regional distribution of domestic iron and steel enterprises and their shared output in China, 2007.

Source: China Steel Yearbook 2008.

---

[25] "Meeting the Challenge of Climate Change", International Iron and Steel Institute (IISI) (2008).

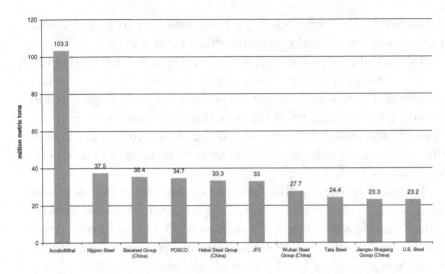

Fig. 5.   Top ten steel makers in the world, 2008.

Source: The World Steel Association, 2009.

three times higher than Baosteel (see Figure 5). ArcelorMittal alone produced almost 8% of the world's steel products in 2008.

Production Structure

Third, China's steel industry has established itself as a low value-added, labour-intensive steel producer over the last decade. The development of high value-added products is lagging behind. In the past, competitiveness was based primarily on cheap labour and lax environmental regulations. In seeking sustainable development, the Chinese government needs to take prompt measures to readjust the production structure of the steel sector and move it up the value chain. As a top priority, the government has to adopt certain key measures to promote technological upgrading including tax incentives and state capital subsidies.

The rapid growth of energy-intensive steel production has paid the price of serious environmental degradation in areas near to the iron and steel firms.[26] To protect the environment and build an energy-conserving economy in China, elimination of production methods which use outdated technology and technological upgrading are essential.

In particular, the lax environmental standards and regulations for the steelmaking sector need to be further strengthened. The highly polluting and energy-guzzling small steel enterprises should be shut down. The rapid expansion of high energy-consuming steel production is unaffordable, both economically and environmentally, in the long run.

M&A: A KEY DEVELOPMENT STRATEGY FOR CHINA'S STEEL INDUSTRY

M&A are the key strategy for the development of China's steel industry. They not only help the industry cope with the impact of global crisis via production cost reduction, but also strengthen the global competitiveness of the steel enterprises via market share expansion. M&A are also effective means to reduce outdated capacity and increase productivity in the steel sector. Acquisition is also important to enhance the negotiation position of domestic steelmakers in importing steel-making raw materials. Fragmentation has weakened the bargaining power of China's steel industry over iron ore prices as firms negotiate individually with the global suppliers. M&A would allow large domestic steel enterprises to act as a negotiation bloc to obtain a bigger say in iron ore price talks.

To be fair, China's steel industry has been making some progress in terms of consolidation and 17 mergers and acquisitions were successfully completed in 2008.[27] There is the shining

---

[26] Ma Jinlong, D.G. Evans, R.J. Fuller, and D.F. Stewart, "Technical Efficiency and Productivity Change of China's Iron and Steel Industry", *International Journal of Production Economics*, 76 (2002) 293–312.

[27] "Steel Sector Consolidation to Continue", *China Daily*, online edition, http://www.chinadaily.com.cn/bizchina/2009-03/09/content_7553574.htm, 9 March 2009.

acquisition example of Handan Iron and Steel and Chengde Xinxin Vanadium and Titanium Co. by Tangshan Iron and Steel (Tangsteel), the sole listed subsidiary of Hebei Steel Group. Since the merger, Hebei Steel Group has become the second largest steelmaker in China and challenged the dominant status of Baosteel Group.[28] Leading enterprises may need to play an influential role in the consolidation and acquisition of many small domestic steelmakers.

But consolidation and integration were never going to be easy for the domestic steel sector. For example, the Tonggang incident is a tragic symbol of the government-backed acquisition strategy. On 22 July 2009, the proposed deal for acquiring Jilin-based Tonghua Iron & Steel (Tonggang) by the large, privately owned Jianlong Steel Holding Group (Jianlong) was approved by the Provincial State-owned Assets Supervision and Administration Commission (SASAC), in Jinlin. Tonggang is the largest state asset in Jilin Province, with an annual steel production capacity of 7 mmt.[29] The planned acquisition by Jianlong was widely expected to increase the productivity of Tonggang and strengthen its overall competitiveness.

However, the proposed acquisition of Tonggang by Jianlong was permanently scrapped after a serious riot leading to Chen Guojun, the interim general manager and representative appointed by Jianlong, being killed by the company's angry workers on 24 July 2009.[30] The steel workers were concerned that they might lose their jobs after the company's takeover by Jianlong. In an attempt to stop the police, government officials and ambulances from rescuing Chen Guojun, who was beaten up, the workers blocked roads and threw

---

[28] "Hebei Iron Arms Merger to Challenge Baosteel", *China Daily*, online edition, http://www.chinadaily.com.cn/bizchina/2009-06/25/content_8320496.htm, 25 June 2009.

[29] "Size of Deadly Steel Factory Protest Exaggerated: Official", *China Daily*, online edition, http://www.chinadaily.com.cn/cndy/2009-07/29/content_8484267.htm, 29 July 2009.

[30] "Killing of China Steel Plant Boss Halts Sale", *Financial Times*, 1, 27 July 2009.

bricks at them.[31] The riot also led to the shutdown of production in Tonggang's seven blast furnaces, and Tonggang workers stopped supplies of raw materials by blocking railway tracks.[32] The deadly Tonggang incident and consequent acquisition deal cancellation has proven to be a serious setback for the restructuring of the steel industry and the reduction of overcapacity attempted by the central government.

During the pre-reform period, state workers enjoyed enormous welfare benefits in areas such as lifelong employment, education and health care. In their eyes, the state-owned enterprises were "iron rice bowls" and insurance of their lifelong employment and salary. The reform of state-owned enterprises (SOEs) and acquisition strategies within the steel industry have taken away many forms of welfare, which were taken for granted by the workers for many years. It is a painful process for the state workers. In the northeast provinces of China where there are high concentrations of state-owned industries and enterprises, state workers have expressed strong resentment towards privatization of state-owned firms and any plan by private enterprises to acquire SOEs.[33] It is believed that the SOE reforms and state-oriented consolidation strategy have paid too much attention to the commercial interest of local regions and development of their steel mills without addressing the interest of state workers.[34]

The death of Chen might be an isolated case. However, the Tonggang incident highlights the importance of establishing mechanisms for social dialogue and negotiation in China. This serious

---

[31] "Manager Killed in Plant Riot", *China Daily*, 27 July 2009, online edition, http://www.chinadaily.com.cn/life/2009-07/27/content_8475878.htm, 27 July 2009.

[32] "Jianlong Told to Drop Tonghua Buyout After Clashes (Update2)", *Bloomberg News*, http://www.bloomberg.com/apps/news?pid=20601087&sid=a0G6pTJV 10mM, 12 May 2010.

[33] "Chinese Steelworkers Fight Privatization Effort", *The Wall Street Journal*, http://online.wsj.com/article/SB124863589915981859.html#printMode, 12 May 2010.

[34] "Murder Bares Worker Anger Over China Industrial Reform", *The Wall Street Journal*, http://online.wsj.com/article/SB124899768509595465.html#printMode, 12 May 2010.

incident reflects the lack of communication between government, management and workers. Restricted access to information leads to the spread of rumours and false news among workers. In contemporary China, the lack of effective legal channels and other social forums for workers to voice their grievances and complaints has led them to adopt brutal and extreme means.

China's steel industry has been facing serious roadblocks in its M&A strategy. First, due to administrative divisions and self-interest considerations, local governments are extremely reluctant to support steel sector mergers. Although great acquisition efforts were made by large steelmakers, a growing number of newly established SMEs are also emerging in China, such as Dalian-based Dongbei Special Steel Group.[35] These firms have local government-dominated characteristics and are the result of local protectionism. In attempting M&A, domestic steelmakers have encountered resistance from local authorities, as steel firms are the backbone industry of many local regions with their huge contribution to local tax revenue.[36] The local governments are also concerned that the steel sector mergers might result in a big rise in unemployment rates and are likely to use various means to protect their steel sectors.

Second, many merging enterprises would face difficulties in restructuring internal management teams and building an integrated corporate culture. M&A success largely depends on coordinating and incorporating different internal management teams and blending different cultures into a united whole. This would involve substantial time and effort on the part of these enterprises.

---

[35] "The Agglomeration Dilemma for the Steel Industry: The Re-emergence of Small Iron and Steel Enterprises in China", China Iron & Steel Association, http://www.chinaisa.org.cn/show.php?newsid=2153382, 3 January 2010; Wu Yanrui, "The Chinese Steel Industry: Recent Developments and Prospects", *Resources Policy*, 26 (2000), 171–178.

[36] Li Zhongmin, "Three Strategies to Enhance the Global Competitiveness of China's Steel Industry", Policy Brief No. 09017, International Trade and Investment Series, Chinese Academy of Social Science, 2009.

APPENDIX 1

Analysis of the Arrest of Rio Tinto's Staff by China

On 12 August 2009, Stern Hu and three other Rio Tinto staff were formally arrested by the Chinese authorities on the allegation of giving bribes and stealing commercial trade secrets. However, in contrast to earlier reports made by the state media, the suspicion of their involvement in stealing state secrets from China was not mentioned.

The arrest of Rio Tinto's staff reflects serious problems facing China. First, China's entire legal system is still problematic, as reflected in the lack of transparency and independence, and in the ambiguity of national security and state secrets law. Lawyers do not have access to the detainees without investigators' permission. Second, the iron ore trade in China suffers from administrative irregularities and the monopolistic control by a few large steel enterprises and middlemen. Currently, there are only 112 steel firms and agencies in China trading in iron ore. Smaller steel firms need to negotiate with large domestic firms to obtain iron ore supplies for production. This creates huge price differences between imports of iron ore by these large monopolies and actual domestic re-selling of iron ore to other small steel firms in China. This allows a few monopolistic companies to maximize their profits and reflects the power of internal staff of the few large steel enterprises in deciding the quantity of iron ore imports, giving them the opportunity to take bribes from foreign companies. Besides, internal problems have actually weakened the power of domestic steel enterprises in their negotiations with global mining concerns.

To rectify this problem, China should designate a national stockpiling policy to help domestic steel mills. By establishing a national iron ore stock China's steel industry can not only avoid market fluctuation risks and stabilize import prices of iron ore, but also achieve other objectives including production cost saving, iron ore supply security and influencing world trade prices of iron ore. However, national storage is costly, and the optimal level of stockpiling is hard to be determined. It would not be possible to establish a national stockpile if serious irregularities within the iron ore trade sector in China persist.

Sources:

1. For the research on the role and impact of commodity price stabilization and national stockpiling, and the potential means to achieve price stabilization, please refer to D.M.G. Newbery and J.E. Stiglitz, "Optimal Commodity Stock-piling Rules" *Oxford Economic Papers*, 34 (1982), 403–27.
2. Chong Siew Keng and Desmond Chua, "The Rio Tinto Affair", EAI Background Brief No. 468, National University of Singapore, 2009.
3. "Rio Case Shakes Foreign Groups into Reassessing China Methods", *Financial Times*, 3, 18/19 July 2009.
4. "Beijing's Peculiar Definition of State Secrets", *Financial Times*, 7, 24 July 2009.
5. "The Disorderly Phenomenon of the Iron Ore Trade", *Xinhua News*, http://news.xinhuanet.com/fortune/2009-07/14/content_11705743_2.htm, 14 July 2009.
6. "China Arrests Rio Tinto Workers", *BBC News*, http://news.bbc.co.uk/2/hi/business/8196529.stm, 12 May 2010.

Chapter

5

China's Wind Power Industry: From Infant Stage to Growth Stage

Mu YANG and Rongfang PAN

Against the backdrop of China's determination to develop a low-carbon economy, wind power as a renewable energy with zero emission is now becoming a major driving force in the green campaign. Compared to other new energy industries, wind power is relatively mature in technology and is developing the fastest. Over the past 25 years, favourable policies, concession programmes and technology transfers have greatly boosted the wind power industry in China. By 2009, China had already become the third largest wind power generator and the largest wind turbine manufacturer in the world. However, challenges, such as weakness in technological innovation and a structural problem between limited access to the power grid and overheating production, have to be addressed to ensure sustainable development of the industry in China.

WIND POWER INDUSTRY LEADS CHINA'S "GREEN" LEAP FORWARD

China's National Development and Reform Commission (NDRC) emphasized that the country is now taking concrete steps to push forward with its low-carbon economy by boosting emerging industries of strategic importance.[1] The move is meant to achieve the goal of reducing energy consumption per unit of GDP by 20% by the end of the Eleventh Five-Year Plan in 2010 and to meet China's official target of 40–45% reduction in carbon intensity per unit of GDP from 2005 to 2020.

The wind power industry is rapidly emerging as one of the strategic energy industries utilized by China to meet the aforementioned targets. Among the new energy industries, namely nuclear energy, solar energy, geothermal heat, biomass and ocean (tidal and wave) energy, wind power is relatively mature in technology and developing the fastest in China.

As a renewable energy with zero emission, wind power will act as a major contributor to the reduction of carbon dioxide (CO_2) emissions, a primary cause of climate change. Against the backdrop of climate negotiations in Copenhagen, a study released on 14 December 2009 by the Global Wind Energy Council (GWEC) reveals that wind energy alone could contribute up to 65% of emission reduction targets for industrialized countries.[2]

As for China, wind energy is expected to produce up to 493 terawatt hours (TWh)[3] of electricity and cut 296 million tons of CO_2 emissions in 2020, which would account for 18.6% of the world's total reduction. The annual emission reduction resulting from the

---

[1] "Green Plans on Track, NDRC Says", *China Daily*, 31 December 2009, online edition, http://www.chinadaily.com.cn/bizchina/2009-12/31/content_9249945.htm.
[2] "Wind Energy Can Meet 65% of Tabled 2020 Emissions Reductions by Industrialised Countries", Global Wind Energy Council, 14 December 2009, http://www.gwec.net/index.php?id=30&no_cache=1&tx_ttnews%5Btt_news%5D=238&tx_ttnews%5BbackPid%5D=97&cHash=c4d07d5ebf.
[3] The terawatt hour, or TWh, is a unit of energy equal to one trillion watt hours. Energy in watt hours is the multiplication of power in watts and time in hours.

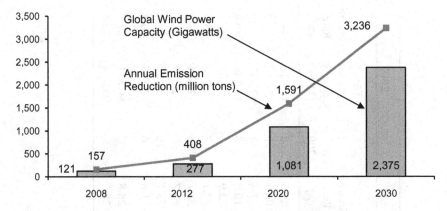

Fig. 1. Forecast: Global wind power capacity and emission reductions.

Notes: The gigawatt (GW) is equal to one billion watts.
Source: Global Wind Energy Council (GWEC).

increase in world wind power capacity will be 1,591 million tons in 2020 and 3,236 million tons in 2030 (Figure 1).

With such great potential, wind power is now becoming the driving force behind the green economy and sustainable development both in China and the world. Since the Renewable Energy Law was put into effect on 1 January 2006, China's wind power industry has witnessed dynamic growth. In particular, the boom continues despite global economic woes. In 2008, China's accumulative installed wind power capacity increased by 106.5% to reach 12,210 megawatts (MW),[4] overtaking India as the largest producer of wind power in Asia and the fourth largest in the world.[5] The figure doubled again in the year 2009: China's total installed capacity grew by 111.3% to 25,805 MW and surpassed Spain and Germany to become the second largest in the world (Table 1).[6]

The development over the past two years far outperforms the 2010 target of 10,000 MW previously planned in the Eleventh Five-Year

---

[4] Megawatt (MW): 10^6 watts; kilowatt (kW): 10^3 watts.
[5] "World Wind Energy Report 2008", World Wind Energy Association, http://www.wwindea. org/home/images/stories/worldwindenergyreport2008_s.pdf.
[6] "Global Wind 2009 Report," Global Wind Energy Council.

Table 1.   World top ten wind power producers

Rank 2009	Country	2009			2008			2007		
		Share of World Total (%)	Total Installed Capacity (MW)	Growth Rate (%)	Rank in 2008	Total Installed Capacity (MW)	Growth Rate (%)	Rank in 2007	Total Installed Capacity (MW)	Growth Rate (%)
1	USA	22.1	35,064	39.3	1	25,170	49.7	2	16,818	44.9
2	China	16.3	25,805	111.3	4	12,210	106.5	5	5,912	127.0
3	Germany	16.3	25,777	7.8	2	23,903	7.4	1	22,247	7.9
4	Spain	12.1	19,149	14.3	3	16,754	10.6	3	15,145	30.4
5	India	6.9	10,926	13.3	5	9,645	22.9	4	7,845	25.1
6	Italy	3.1	4,850	29.8	6	3,736	37.1	7	2,726	28.4
7	France	2.8	4,492	32.0	7	3,404	38.7	8	2,454	56.6
8	UK	2.6	4,051	25.0	8	3,241	35.7	9	2,389	21.7
9	Portugal	2.2	3,535	23.5	10	2,862	33.1	10	2,150	25.3
10	Denmark	2.2	3,465	9.0	9	3,180	1.8	6	3,125	-0.4
	Top Ten Total	86.5	137,114	31.7		104,104	28.8		80,811	27.8
	World Total	100.0	158,505	31.2		120,798	28.7		93,864	26.5

Source: Global Wind Energy Council (GWEC).

Renewable Energy Development Plan by the NDRC.[7] According to Shi Lishan, deputy director of the New Energy and Renewable Energy Bureau of the National Energy Administration (NEA), China's installed wind power capacity is expected to exceed 30,000 MW by the year 2010, more than tripling the same target.[8]

Moreover, the dramatic growth of wind power promotes a moderate greener trend in the electric power industry characterized by a slightly improving energy structure, where the proportion of non-fossil energy input rises while that of fossil energy declines. Though thermal electricity still took up almost three quarters of the total electricity supply in 2009, it experienced a drop of 1.45 percentage points compared to 2008. In the meantime, wind power capacity has nearly doubled and surpassed nuclear power as China's third largest source of electricity, after thermal and hydropower (Figure 2).[9]

China will complete construction of seven wind power bases, each with a capacity of 10,000 MW and have a wind power capacity of 100,000 MW by the year 2020, accounting for around 10% of the country's total power generation capacity, a great leap forward from the current 1.8%.[10] Furthermore, research by Harvard and Tsinghua Universities shows that wind energy alone has the potential to meet China's electricity demands projected for 2030.[11]

PAST AND FUTURE OF THE SUNRISE INDUSTRY

Since the first wind turbine generator system, Vestas 55 kW, was established in Hainan Dongfang Wind Farm in 1985, China's on-grid wind

---

[7] For details, see the "Eleventh Five-Year Renewable Energy Development Plan", available at http://www.sdpc.gov.cn/nyjt/nyzywx/W020080318390887398136.pdf.

[8] "Wind power gets set for huge thrust", *China Daily*, 3 June 2009, online edition, http://www. chinadaily.com.cn/cndy/2009-06/03/content_7965844.htm.

[9] "China's Power Generation Goes Greener with Total Capacity up 10%", *Xinhua*, 7 January 2010, online edition, http://news.xinhuanet.com/english/2010-01/07/content_12771880.htm.

[10] "Wind Power Gets Set for Huge Thrust", *China Daily*, 3 June 2009, online edition.

[11] "China Could Meet its Energy Needs by Wind Alone", *Harvard Gazette*, 10 September 2009, http://news.harvard.edu/gazette/story/2009/09/china-energy-needs-wind/.

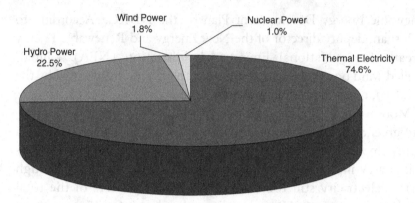

Fig. 2.   Energy structure of electric power industry.

power generation has experienced three stages of development.[12] The first stage (1986–1993) was dominated by small demonstrative wind farms that were fully financed by the government.

It was in the second stage from 1994 to 2003 that on-grid wind power was first developed as a new energy source for electrical power generation in China. Since then China has initiated the Ride the Wind Program (*chengfeng jihua*) and implemented import substitution policies for the production of turbines and parts, and its wind power gradually entered the stage of sector development. However, the process is fairly difficult because of technical constraints and uncertainties in on-grid pricing policies.

The third stage was characterized by expansion and localization of manufacturing (2004–2009). In 2003, the NDRC launched the Wind Power Concession Program[13] to build large-capacity wind farms and achieve scale economies. Through a competitive bidding process, investors and developers of wind farms are selected for the projects under the program. This stage saw a large expansion in the industry.

---

[12] "China Wind Power and Pricing Policy Research Report", Chinese Renewable Energy Industries Association (CREIA), http://www.crein.org.cn/uploads/News/2009-11-27/P020091126386872388651.pdf.

[13] *China Wind Power Report 2007*, China Environmental Science Press.

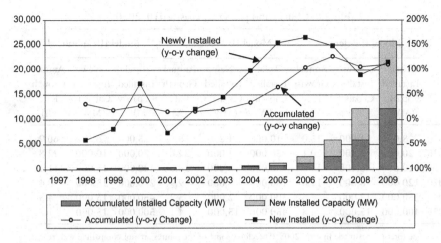

Fig. 3. China's installed wind power capacity, 1997–2009.

Sources: For 1997–2006, *China Wind Power Report 2007*, China Environmental Science Press.
For 2007–2008, *World Wind Energy Report 2008*, World Wind Energy Association.
For 2009, Global Wind 2009 Report, Global Wind Energy Council.

Figure 3 shows a relatively low level of growth rate at the second stage, from 16.3% to 28.4%, and at an accelerating pace in the third stage, from 34.7% to 127.5%. However, if the first stage is "conception", the second "birth", then in view of the forecast of the next 40 years described in the following sections, the third would be the "infant stage" at best. In this sense, China's wind power industry is now stepping out of its infant stage and moving towards the stage of growth.

The *China Wind Power Report 2008*, prepared by Li Junfeng, Secretary General of the Chinese Renewable Energy Industries Association (CREIA), provided three estimates for China's future development in wind power: a reference estimate, a moderate one, and an advanced one (Table 2). Now, even the advanced one seems somewhat underestimated: a total capacity of 25,000 MW had already been achieved by end 2009, instead of the projected 2010.

In comparison, the global wind power industry during the same period shows a different picture. Before 2003, the world's total installed capacity increased at a higher rate from 26% to 41.7% and at

Table 2. China wind power forecast 2010–2050

	Model I: Reference			Model II: Moderate			Model III: Advanced		
Year	Total Installed Capacity (MW)	New Installed Capacity (MW)	Annual Growth Rate (%)	Total Installed Capacity (MW)	New Installed Capacity (MW)	Annual Growth Rate (%)	Total Installed Capacity (MW)	New Installed Capacity (MW)	Annual Growth Rate (%)
2010	8,000	1,000	15.0	10,000	1,330	18.5	25,000	6,330	60.9
2015	20,000	2,400	20.1	30,000	4,000	24.6	70,000	10,000	22.8
2020	40,000	6,400	14.9	70,000	8,000	18.5	120,000	15,000	11.4
2030	120,000	8,000	11.6	180,000	11,000	9.9	270,000	15,000	8.4
2040	250,000	13,000	7.6	300,000	12,000	5.2	450,000	13,000	4.5
2050	400,000	15,000	4.8	450,000	15,000	4.1	500,000	15,000	1.7

Notes: The forecast was made in early 2008. Therefore, some of the figures are not compatible with recent development, especially those in Models I and II.

Source: China Wind Power Report 2008, China Environmental Science Press.

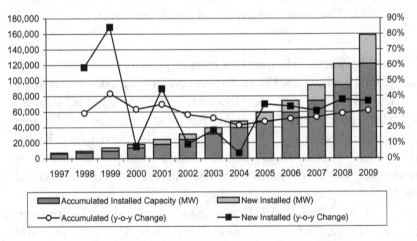

Fig. 4. World installed wind capacity, 1997–2009.

Sources: World Wind Energy Report 2008, World Wind Energy Association.
　　For 2009, Global Wind 2009 Report, Global Wind Energy Council.

a much lower rate from 21.4% to 30.8% after 2003 (Figure 4). This shows that China's wind power industry had a late start but gained its momentum after 2003. In the short term till 2015, China's wind power development is expected to have better prospects than the

Table 3.   World wind power forecast 2010–2050

	Model I: Reference			Model II: Moderate			Model III: Advanced		
Year	Total Installed Capacity (MW)	New Installed Capacity (MW)	Annual Growth Rate (%)	Total Installed Capacity (MW)	New Installed Capacity (MW)	Annual Growth Rate (%)	Total Installed Capacity (MW)	New Installed Capacity (MW)	Annual Growth Rate (%)
2010	129,000	19,998	10.0	172,000	28,904	19.0	186,000	36,468	22.0
2015	233,000	20,887	9.0	379,000	54,023	15.0	486,000	84,160	19.0
2020	352,000	24,180	9.0	709,000	81,546	11.0	1,081,000	142,674	12.0
2030	497,000	30,013	4.0	1,420,000	80,536	3.0	2,375,000	165,000	5.0
2040	599,000	36,196	1.0	1,696,000	97,548	1.0	3,163,000	165,000	1.0
2050	679,000	36,560	1.0	1,834,000	100,302	1.0	3,498,000	165,000	1.0

Notes: The forecast was made in early 2008. Therefore, some of the figures are not compatible with recent development, especially those for Models I and II.
Source: *Global Wind Energy Outlook 2008*, GWEC and Greenpeace.

world average. After that, China is likely to follow the overall global trend in wind power development (Table 3).

CHINA'S WIND ENERGY RESOURCES AND WIND FARM DISTRIBUTIONS

China is rich in wind energy resources and has great potential for the development of wind power generation. The most recent data published by the China Meteorological Administration (CMA) on 4 January 2010 shows that China's potential wind energy resources on land, measured at 50 metres above ground level, are about 2,380 gigawatts (GW).[14] The figure is about eight times the 297 GW measured at 10 metres from the ground between 2004 and 2006.

According to China Wind Power Centre, the wind-rich areas in China can be grouped into three "wind belts". The first belt covers coastlines and near-coast islands, including Shandong, Jiangsu,

---

[14] Gigawatt (GW): 10^9 watts. "我国风能资源详查和评价取得新进展", *China Meteorological Administration*, 4 January 2010, http://www.cma.gov.cn/mtjj/201001/t20100104_55673.html.

Shanghai, Zhejiang, Fujian, Guangdong, Guangxi and Hainan Provinces. The second is the northern China wind belt along the "Three Norths": northwest China (Gansu, Ningxia and Xinjiang), north China (Hebei and Inner Mongolia) and northeast China (Liaoning, Jilin and Heilongjiang). The third belt covers some inland areas with special geological and topographic characters.[15]

Accordingly, wind farms are distributed in line with the wind belts. Inner Mongolia, Liaoning, Hebei, Jilin, Heilongjiang, Jiangsu, Gansu and Xinjiang account for 30.7%, 10.3%, 9.1%, 8.8%, 6.9%, 5.3%, 5.2% and 4.7% of the total installed wind power capacity, respectively (Table 4).

In addition, China has a long coastline. Preliminary estimates show that in offshore areas with a 5–25 metre water depth line, the offshore installed wind power capacity at 50 metres above sea level could reach 200 GW. Despite the higher construction costs of offshore wind farms than those on land, the great potential and improved technologies may make offshore wind power an important source of green energy in future China. The first offshore wind power project in China, and also in Asia, is for the World Expo 2010 in Shanghai. Construction of the offshore wind farm started in April 2009 and was completed at the end of the same year. With an installed capacity of over 100 MW, it is connected to the power grid to provide electricity supply to the World Expo in May 2010.

STRONG IN PRODUCTION BUT WEAK IN R&D

While China is rich in wind power resources, its research and development of grid-connected wind turbine units is still lagging. Since the 1980s, China has conducted research on wind turbines with power capacities of 18 kW, 30 kW, 55 kW and 200 kW; however, before they were commercialized, larger wind turbines became dominant

---

[15] "China Renewable Energy Development Overview 2008", NDRC, http://www.cresp.org.cn/uploadfiles/7/977/2008en.pdf.

Table 4. Regional distribution of total installed wind power capacity, 2008

Provinces, Municipalities and Autonomous Regions	Total Installed Capacity (MW) as of 2008	Percentage (%)
Inner Mongolia	3,735.4	30.7
Liaoning	1,249.8	10.3
Hebei	1,110.7	9.1
Jilin	1,069.5	8.8
Heilongjiang	836.3	6.9
Jiangsu	648.3	5.3
Gansu	637.0	5.2
Xinjiang	576.8	4.7
Shandong	572.3	4.7
Ningxia	393.2	3.2
Guangdong	366.9	3.0
Fujian	283.8	2.3
Zhejiang	194.6	1.6
Shanxi	127.5	1.0
Yunnan	78.8	0.6
Beijing	64.5	0.5
Hainan	58.2	0.5
Henan	50.3	0.4
Jiangxi	42.0	0.3
Shanghai	39.4	0.3
Hubei	13.6	0.1
Chongqing	1.7	0.01
Hunan	1.7	0.01
Hong Kong	0.8	0.01
Total	12,152.8	100.00

Source: China New and Renewable Energy Statistical Yearbook (2009).

internationally.[16] Till 2005, China could only produce wind turbines no larger than 600 kW on its own while the international market has already been dominated by turbines in the 750 kW and 1.0 MW range. At that time, key components of 600 kW turbines and all turbines larger than 750 kW had to be imported.

---

[16] "China Renewable Energy Development Review (2008)", NDRC, http://www.cresp.org.cn/uploadfiles/7/977/2008en.pdf.

Because wind turbines account for 70% of total investment involved in a wind power generation project, cost reduction by import substitution strategies became a major solution to boost the development of the industry.[17] The major approach is to pay a technology transfer fee for licensing the production or to establish a joint venture with foreign companies. Such partnerships or acquisitions between the Chinese players and their foreign counterparts started in 2003.

Goldwind Science and Technology Co., Ltd. (Goldwind) is a pioneer in this effort. In 2002, Goldwind first signed an agreement with REpower Systems AG on licenced production and supply of components for 48 kW to 750 kW turbines.[18] It then acquired a production licence in 2003 from VENSYS Energiesysteme GmbH (Saarbrücken, Germany) for its VENSYS 62 turbine of 1.2 MW, and from then on, for turbines of increased output to 1.5 MW, 2.0 MW and 2.5 MW. Now Goldwind turbines are 90% locally produced (for more details, see Appendix 1).[19]

This approach prevailed among other local manufacturers and greatly enhanced China's manufacturing capability. As a result, China's wind power production technology has developed at a speed never seen before, especially for the 600 kW wind turbines in 2005, 750 kW in 2006, 1.5 MW in 2007, 2 MW in 2008 and 3 MW in 2009. In addition to the 3 MW wind power generators now operating in the Shanghai Dongdaqiao offshore wind farm, Sinovel started its 5 MW wind turbine project in Jiangsu Yandu in early 2010.[20] In the meantime, Dongfang Electric (DEC) also signed a contract with AMSC Windtec, a wholly-owned subsidiary of American Super-conductor

---

[17] *China Wind Power Report 2008*, China Environmental Science Press.

[18] European Wind Energy Association (EWEA), *Wind Energy — The Facts: A Guide to the Technology, Economics and Future of Wind Power* (London; Sterling, VA: Earthscan, 2009), 77.

[19] Ibid.

[20] "Sinovel Starts Construction of 5 MW Turbine Project", *Bloomberg New Energy Finance*, 12 January 2010, www.newenergymatters.com/?p=list&t=newsitems& id=36062.

Corporation, to jointly develop 5 MW wind turbines for the offshore wind power market.[21]

On the other hand, the Wind Power Concession Program, launched by the NDRC in 2003, and the subsequent six batches of concession bidding projects helped enlarge the market share of domestic manufacturers and extensively promoted the localization of wind turbine production. In addition, the Chinese government stipulated that "the localization rate of wind power equipment should be no less than 70% and wind farms failing to meet the requirement are not allowed to be constructed".[22]

Because of the supportive policies and protective regulations, the market share of domestic manufacturers and joint ventures increased rapidly while that of foreign manufacturers decreased over the past few years. Wind turbines made by domestic manufacturers and joint ventures accounted for only 25% of the total in 2004, but the share increased to 75.6% by end 2008 (Figure 5).

After six years of "learning" and government protection as an infant industry, domestic manufacturers have grown rapidly in size and number. In 2008, the three largest wind turbine manufacturers, Sinovel, Goldwind and Dongfang, took up 57.5% of the market share. In comparison, the largest foreign-funded manufacturer, Vestas, only accounted for 9.6% of the total (Table 5). Under such circumstances, the NDRC issued a circular on 25 December 2009 to lift the restrictions on foreign-made wind turbines and abolish the requirement of 70% local products for wind power projects,[23] thus establishing a level playing field for all manufacturers, domestic or foreign.

Furthermore, China overtook major competitors such as Denmark, Germany, Spain and the United States to become the

---

[21] "AMSC & Dongfang To Develop 5 MW Offshore Wind Turbines", 6 January 2010, http://www.renewableenergyworld.com/rea/news/article/2010/01/amsc-to-develop-5-mw-wind-turbines-with-dongfang.

[22] NDRC Energy Circular [2005] No. 1204, "*Guan yu feng dian jian she guan li you guan yao qiu de tong zhi*".

[23] NDRC Energy Circular [2009] No. 2991, "*Guan yu qu xiao feng dian gong cheng xiang mu cai gou she bei guo chan hua lu yao qiu de tong zhi*".

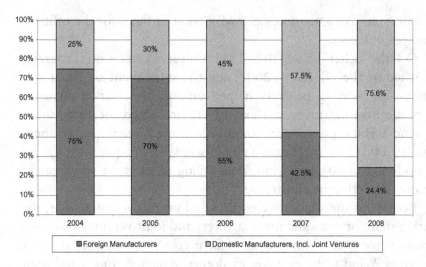

Fig. 5.   Market share of domestic and foreign manufacturers and joint ventures by newly installed capacity, 2004–2008.

Sources: For 2004–2006, *China Wind Power Report 2007*.
      For 2007–2008, *Global and China Wind Power Industry Report* 2008–2009.

Table 5.   Market share of manufacturers by newly installed capacity, 2008

Domestic Manufacturers			Foreign Manufacturers		
Manufacturers	Newly Installed Capacity 2008 (MW)	Percentage (%)	Manufacturers	Newly Installed Capacity 2008 (MW)	Percentage (%)
Sinovel (华锐)	1,402.5	22.5	Vestas	599.7	9.6
Goldwind (金风)	1,131.8	18.1	Gamesa	508.3	8.1
Dongfang Electric (东汽)	1,053.0	16.9	GE	145.5	2.3
Windey (运达)	233.3	3.7	Nordex	144.0	2.3
Sewind (上海电气)	178.8	2.9	Suzlon	128.5	2.1
Mingyang (明阳)	174.0	2.8			
CASC-Acciona (航天-安迅能)	150.0	2.4			
XEMC (湘电)	120.0	1.9			
New Unite (新誉)	73.5	1.2			
Beizhong (北重)	60.0	1.0			
Others	143.7	2.3			
Domestic Subtotal	4,720.4	75.6	Foreign Subtotal	1,526.0	24.4

Source: China Wind Energy Association (CWEA).

world's largest producer of wind turbines in 2009, and is poised to expand even further in 2010.[24] In actuality, some Chinese manufacturers have already expanded their business abroad by export, overseas mergers and acquisitions, outward direct investment or research group outsourcing.

However, in terms of independent innovation, a large gap still remains between China and the world leaders of wind turbine manufacture. Compared to the world's largest turbine in operation, the Enercon E126, which has a power capacity of 6 MW to 7 MW, China's 3 MW in operation and 5 MW in R&D still have quite a long way to go in terms of size.[25] At the same time, the capacity of the world's most powerful turbine in R&D is 10 MW.[26]

At the same time, local Chinese wind turbine component suppliers are still weak in indigenous technology over which they have intellectual property rights. Currently, core components for turbine units larger than 3 MW are mostly acquired through outsourcing. Despite the competitive advantage of China's domestic manufacturers in terms of cost reduction through large-scale production, it is the capability to independently carry out research and development, rather than expansion, that serves further development in the long run. Therefore, looking forward, it is imperative for China's manufacturers to cultivate in-house research groups and encourage local innovation.

CHALLENGES FACED BY THE INDUSTRY IN TRANSITION

While the rapid growth in China's wind power capacity looks impressive, it is less so when it comes to power transmission. Connection to the national transmission power grid is now the greatest challenge

---

[24] "China Powering Ahead in Clean Energy", *The Straits Times*, 1 February 2010.

[25] Enercon, 25 November 2009, available at: http://www.enercon.de/www/en/pressemitteilungen.nsf/6a7745841ee132cac1256eef0034a002/ab7f60a44e386594c125767a003c5d8e?OpenDocument.

[26] "AMSC and US DOE to collaborate on 10MW wind turbines", Windtech, 10 February 2009, available at http://www.windtech-international.com/content/view/2223/2/.

faced by wind farm operators. Because not all wind power can be transmitted, efficiency loss and blind expansion become prominent.

First, the construction of the power grid cannot keep pace with the development of wind power generation. Currently, wind turbines are erected in remote areas too far away from the transmission network and thus have limited access to the power transmission system for urban areas. Furthermore, the extension of current power grid networks is by no means a small project. According to research by Morgan Stanley, about 3.5 GW, or 29% of installed wind capacity in China, is lying idle and a lot of wind turbines have been "sunbathing". Citigroup also estimated that about 30% of wind power capacity in 2008 was not connected to the power grid.[27]

Second, even when connection to grid is settled, wind power feed-in is another big problem. Wind energy is an intermittent and erratic source of electric power, and thus the unstable electric flow is "polluting" or even damaging to the power grid. Therefore, the traditional power grid must be improved or upgraded to a modernized electricity network, namely, smart grids, which would require massive investment and a long construction period (see Appendix 2).

Another challenge is "overinvestment" and "overcapacity" owing to the government's subsidy policy or local governments' relentless pursuit of GDP growth. The problems are expected to become more prominent with more wind power farms being put into operation, a recent survey by the State Electricity Regulatory Commission showed.[28] Many wind farms are now being built even though necessary transmission is not available.

Blind expansion is also prevalent in wind turbine manufacturing. Holding a "panning for gold" attitude, some manufacturers even enter the sunrise industry without necessary technology and capital. The number of turbine makers has increased from 6 before 2005 to around 80 today. The only motivation is that the wind power

---

[27] "Weaknesses In Chinese Wind Power", *Forbes*, 20 July 2009, online edition, http://www.forbes.com/2009/07/20/china-wind-power-business-energy-china.html.

[28] "China Warns Against Blind Wind Power Expansion — Xinhua", *Reuters*, 28 July 2009, online edition, http://uk.reuters.com/article/idUKPEK19929320090728.

industry is one with supportive policies and a bright future. Duplication of low level development is not rare nowadays. Among the 80 local manufacturers, only 10 are capable of an annual batch production of over 100 units. The remaining 70 manufacturers accounted for only 2.3% of the total market share in terms of newly installed capacity in 2008 (see Table 5).

In brief, the three major challenges mentioned earlier reflect a structural problem in China's wind power industry: the mismatch between infrastructure (power grid and power feed-in) and production (wind farm construction and turbine manufacturing). The construction of infrastructure involves cross-regional coordination while production is more of a local issue. Therefore, the key is to promote wind power based on proportionate and coordinated development together with other facilities in the same industrial chain. An overall wind energy development plan, an incentive scheme for innovations and reasonable policies are indispensible to the sustainable development of the wind power industry.

APPENDIX 1

Goldwind Science and Technology Co., Ltd.

Goldwind Science and Technology Co., Ltd., or Goldwind, established in 1998, is a wind turbine manufacturer based in Urumqi, Xinjiang. The company is the largest turbine manufacturer in China in terms of accumulated installed capacity. As a 55% state-owned company, Goldwind is a primary beneficiary of government policies that protected the niche market and preferentially supported utilization of domestically manufactured wind turbines.

Goldwind specializes in R&D, product development and the manufacturing of large-sized wind turbines. It is principally engaged in researching, developing, manufacturing and marketing large-sized wind turbine generator sets. The company's major products include 600 kilowatt (kW), 750 kW, 1.2 megawatt (MW) and 1.5 MW series wind turbine sets. Its R&D models include the 2.5 MW direct-drive wind turbine, 3.0 MW first transmission permanent magnet wind turbine, and 5 MW series wind turbine. The company also provides wind power technology services, development and sale of wind power projects and technology transfer services.

Goldwind has enjoyed an annual 100% market share growth for eight consecutive years. By the end of 2008, the company implemented orders with a total capacity of 1,541.25 MW, including 750 kW units for 170.25 MW, and 1.5 MW units for 1,371 MW. In terms of newly installed capacity, Goldwind reached 1,131.75 MW for the year 2008 alone, representing 18.1% of the national total, after Sinovel with 22.5%.

At the beginning of 2010, Goldwind is planning to invest in an Australian wind farm as part of its efforts to expand its turbine technology business overseas. According to Wu Gang, the company chairman, Goldwind is also looking at markets in the United States, Central Europe and Africa, either by investing in local wind farms or by directly selling its products. Goldwind expects the overseas markets to account for 20 to 30% of its business over the next three to five years. Goldwind's current clients are mainly domestic wind power operators. It is also selling products to Pakistan, Turkey and several Central Asian countries.

Goldwind recently expanded its global footprint by acquiring a 70% stake in an American wind farm in Minnesota this year. In 2008, Goldwind acquired VENSYS, a Germany-based wind-turbine designer, to enhance its technology in wind turbine manufacturing. After the acquisition of VENSYS, Goldwind also bought the subsidiary companies that produced converters and variable propeller systems for VENSYS, through VENSYS in Germany. In general, it is now expanding into upstream and downstream businesses, from turbine blade manufacture to wind farm operation.

Sources:

1. http://en.goldwind.cn/
2. http://en.wikipedia.org/wiki/Goldwind
3. "Goldwind to Spread Wings Overseas for Growth", *China Daily*, 15 December 2009, online edition, http://www.chinadaily.com.cn/bizchina/2009-12/15/content_9178876.htm.

APPENDIX 2

China to Speed up Construction of Smart Grids

Smart Grids

A smart grid delivers electricity from suppliers to consumers using two-way digital technology to control appliances at consumers' homes to save energy, reduce cost and increase reliability and transparency. It includes a computerized monitoring system that keeps track of all electricity flowing in the system. It also incorporates the use of superconductive transmission lines for less power loss, as well as the capability of integrating alternative sources of electricity such as solar and wind.

Such a modernized electricity network is being promoted by many governments as a way of addressing energy independence, global warming and emergency resilience issues. The governments and utilities funding development of grid modernization have defined the functions required for smart grids:

1. Be able to heal itself
2. Motivate consumers to actively participate in operation of the grid
3. Resist attack
4. Provide higher quality power that will save money wasted from outages
5. Accommodate all generation and storage options
6. Enable electricity markets to flourish
7. Run more efficiently
8. Enable higher penetration of intermittent power generation sources

Asian Nations Spending Heavily This Year to Improve Efficiency of Energy Networks

Spending on smart grids by Asian governments, including China, Japan and South Korea, is expected to outpace that in the United

States, with China alone expected to invest $7.3 billion in the sector this year, according to Zpryme, a market research firm based in Austin, Texas. China could spend about $100 billion improving its power distribution over the next 10 years, said Min Li, an analyst at Yuanta Securities.

"China is pursuing smart grid as aggressively as or more aggressively than any other country in the world right now", said Brad Gammons, vice president of IBM's Global Energy & Utilities Industry. "They're very focused and have a very strong commitment to move in that direction", he said. IBM, along with other technology companies like Cisco and Microsoft, is also investing in the smart-grid market in China.

Sources:

1. http://en.wikipedia.org/wiki/Smart_grid
2. Cho Mee-Young and Leonora Walet, "Smart Grids in Asia Open Opportunities", 9 March 2010, *International Herald Tribune*.

China's Recycled Water/Water Treatment Industry in the Age of Water Crisis

Mu YANG and Cuifen WENG

China is facing a looming water crisis due to factors from supply and demand sides. Existing measures to increase water supply, including groundwater exploitation and large-scale water transfer projects, failed to solve the problem of water shortage. The Chinese government thus turned to recycled water at the beginning of 21st century. The wastewater treatment industry grew significantly in the past decade, while the recycled water industry is still in its infancy. As the government pays more attention to recycled water, there is much room for development in both industries. Though the government has continuously made efforts to reform the water price structure, low water price is still a major institutional obstacle to these industries at present.

CHINA'S WATER CRISIS

Although China has the fourth largest amount of water resources (2.8 trillion m³) in the world, it is facing a looming water crisis.[1] With a population of 1.3 billion, per capita water resources in China were only 2104 m³ in 2008 (Figure 1), one quarter of the world's average and one of the 13 lowest in the world.[2] Among China's 655 cities, over 400 cities face the problem of water shortage, 110 out of which are seriously water-scarce.[3]

Water shortage in current China is becoming more and more serious due to factors from the supply and demand sides. From the

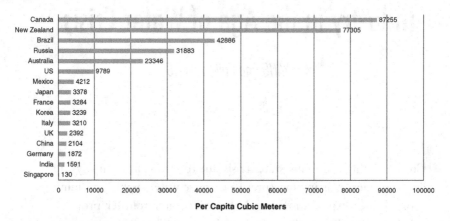

Fig. 1.   Per capita water resources in selected countries.

Source: AQUASTAT online database, accessed via http://www.fao.org/nr/water/aquastat/data/query/results.html on 10 May 2010.

---

[1] For detailed discussion on the situation of water crisis in China, refer to Yang Mu and Teng Siow Song, "China's Looming Water Crises", EAI Background Brief No. 386, 12 June 2008.

[2] http://www.unesco.org/water.

[3] Zhou Wangjun, "Report on the Current Situation of China's Water Resource and Water Prices", August 2009, http://jgs.ndrc.gov.cn/jgqk/t20091221_320454.htm, accessed on 10 May 2010. According to international standards, per capita water availability less than 200 cubic metres means water scarcity; less than 1000 cubic metres per capita, serious water scarcity; less than 500 cubic metres, extreme water scarcity.

supply side, the distribution of water resources in China is uneven in space and time. The south of the Yangtze River, which constitutes 36.5% of the country's total area, has 81% of total water resources, while the remaining 63.5% of the total area in the north has only 19% of total water resources. Time distribution of rainfall is also uneven. On average, over 70% of total rainfall occurs during late spring and summer every year. In the rest of the year, northern China always suffers from droughts. Therefore, the water shortage problem in northern China is more serious than in the south. As Figure 2 shows, the level of water scarcity between China's northern and southern provinces and municipalities varies dramatically.

To make things worse, China's scarce water resources are seriously polluted. The 7 major river systems, 28 major lakes and offshore waters in China are all polluted (see Figures 3, 4 and 5).[4] Moreover, water supply in China is inefficient. The leakage

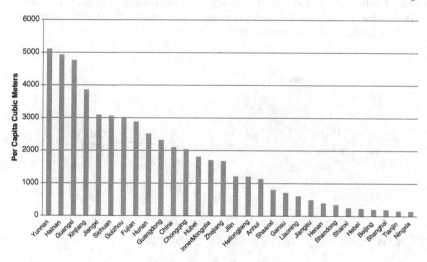

Fig. 2. China's per capita water resources in provinces (municipalities) in 2008.

Note: Per capita water resources in Tibet (159726.8) and Qinghai (11900.5) are excluded from this figure because they are outliers, dramatically larger than other provinces.
Source: China Statistical Yearbook 2009.

---

[4] For a discussion on the problem of water pollution in China, see Chen Gang, *Politics of China's Environmental Protection: Problems and Progress* (Singapore: World Scientific, 2009).

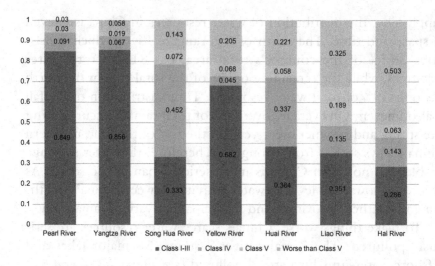

Fig. 3. Level of pollution in China's seven major river systems.

Note: Class I — best to consume, Class II — good to consume, Class III — alright to consume, Class IV — Industrial use, Class V — agricultural use, worse than Class V — totally unusable.
Source: China Environment Communiqué 2008.

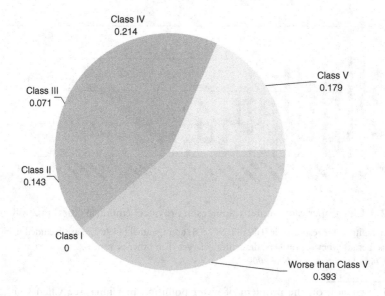

Fig. 4. Pollution in China's top 28 lakes/reservoirs in 2008.
Source: China Environment Communiqué 2008.

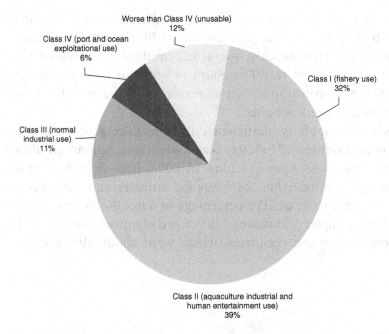

Fig. 5. Seawater pollution in China in 2008.

Source: China Environment Communiqué 2008.

problem of potable water supply during transmission is serious. In 2008, the leakage rate was about 20%, which is much higher than the 5–6% in developed countries. Due to the leakage problem, around 10 billion m³ of potable water is lost every year, which is even larger than the volume transferred by the Central Line of the South-North Water Transfer Project (*nanshui beidiao gongcheng*).[5]

From the demand side, with the increasing pace of urbanization in China, more and more water is needed for household consumption and industry use. Between 1992 and 2002, the industrial water use in China increased more than three times.[6]

---

[5] "Ministry of Construction Said that Water Prices in China are Low and There Is Room for Price Increase", 20 June 2008, http://www.qingquanshiye.com/newEbiz1/EbizPortalFG/portal/html/InfoContent.html?InfoPublish_InfoID=c373e919b4248bd88f7f1af24c169d33, accessed on 7 June 2010.

[6] *Statistical Yearbook for Asia and the Pacific 2009*, 206.

In 2008, the total amount of water used in industry was about 139.7 billion m³.[7] In the past decades, China's urban population has increased significantly, from 322 million (27.46% of total population) in 1992 to 607 million (45.68% of total population) in 2008.[8] As urban population increases, more water will be consumed by urban households.

As water supply is inefficient due to leakage problems, water usage in agriculture and industry is also inefficient. Agriculture always consumes the most water in China. In 2008, 62% of total water use was for agriculture, while 24% was for industry and 12% was for domestic use (Figure 6). The percentage of water use in agriculture is quite large compared to those of developed countries such as the US and some European countries, which were about 49% and 38%,

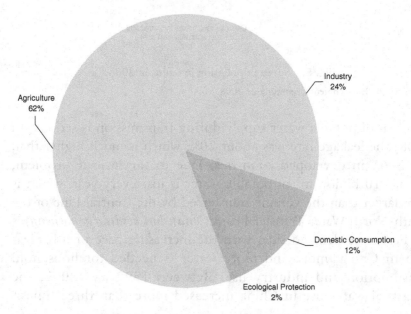

Fig. 6. Water use in different sectors in China in 2008.

Source: China Statistical Yearbook 2009.

---

[7] *China Statistical Yearbook 2009*, 349.
[8] Ibid.

respectively.[9] The efficiency of the largest portion of water use in irrigation is very low in China. In 2007, China's agricultural water usage rate[10] was only 0.47, much lower than that of developed countries (0.7–0.8).[11] In industry, the average volume of water used per 10,000 *yuan* GDP, which is one important indicator of water usage efficiency, was 297 m³ in 2007, twice the world's average.[12]

Water price is another factor that worsens the water shortage problem. Under the planned economy, the water fee was incorporated into the social welfare system and was thus kept at a very low level. Since 1998, with the start of the water industry reform, the Chinese government has been trying to establish a new water price system based on the market mechanism.[13] However, water prices in China today are still much lower than in many other countries. Low water prices have discouraged people to develop a conception of water conservation and water saving.

CURRENT MEASURES TO INCREASE WATER SUPPLY AND THE DILEMMAS

To cope with water shortage, the Chinese government has adopted a number of policies and measures. On the supply side, the government has tried to find new sources of water supply, improve water use efficiency, and restructure the water market in a more competitive manner. On the demand side, there are ongoing efforts to reform the water price structure to encourage water conservation.[14]

---

[9] "Status of Water-Saving Irrigation in China", 19 March 2010, http://info.chyxx.com/nlmy/201003/72098083533C9460.html, accessed on 7 June 2010.

[10] This is one of the most important indicators of agricultural water usage efficiency.

[11] "Status of Water-Saving Irrigation in China".

[12] *China Urban Construction Statistical Yearbook 2007.*

[13] Fu Tao, "On China's Water Price III", 10 August 2009, http://blog.h2o-china.com/html/62/251662-10211.html, accessed on 18 May 2010.

[14] For detailed discussion of these measures and policies, refer to Yang Mu and Teng Siow Song, "China Struggling to Cope with its Water Crises", EAI Background Brief No. 387, 12 June 2008.

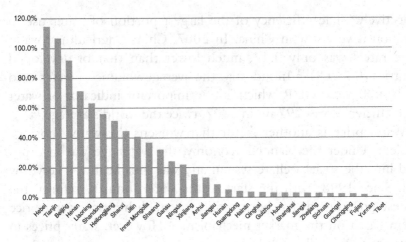

Fig. 7. Groundwater exploitation rate in China's provinces (municipalities) in 2008.
Source: China Statistical Yearbook 2009.

Existing measures to increase sources of water supply (especially in northern China) mainly include groundwater exploitation (Figure 7) and large-scale water transfer projects. However, both methods are faced with dilemmas. Overexploitation of groundwater has caused serious problems. Many cities, especially those in northern China, rely on exploiting groundwater to increase the water supply. Consequently, groundwater in those areas is overexploited, resulting in earth sinking. In 2008, groundwater constituted around 18% of China's total water supply. More than 400 cities exploit groundwater as part of their water supply. Among them, around 60 cities mainly rely on groundwater for their water supply. Overexploitation of groundwater has led to earth sinking in over 50 cities, with a total sinking area of 94,000 km² and cones of groundwater depression covering 190,000 km².[15] Another problem of overexploiting groundwater is pollution. The groundwater in around 136 cities is polluted.[16]

---

[15] "More than 50 Cities Suffer from Earth Sinking Disaster", 10 October 2006, http://www.geoenv.cn/lrm_article/5f/5120.html, accessed on 17 May 2010.

[16] Among them the most serious are Baotou, Changchun, Zhengzhou, Anshan, Taiyuan, Shenyang, Harbin, Beijing, Xian, Lanzhou, Urumqi, Shanghai, Wuxi, Changzhou, Hangzhou, Hefei, Wuhan, etc.

Realizing that groundwater exploitation cannot solve the water shortage problem and will cause other serious problems, China has turned to the large-scale *nanshui beidiao gongcheng*, which includes three lines, namely the Eastern, Central and Western Lines. However, each line of the project has had its own difficulties in the course of construction.[17]

The Eastern Line Project has encountered the problem of pollution at the source. Started in 2003, the Eastern Line Project was planned to be completed at the end of 2007. Yet the completion date is now postponed to 2013.[18] The crucial problem is pollution along the line, especially in the Shandong part. Numerous paper mills, chemical plants, coal plants and pharmaceutical factories are located along the line in Shandong. Take Jining as an example. Since the Eleventh Five-Year Plan, 351 polluting enterprises have been shut down and 223 new projects rejected. Besides industrial pollution, agriculture and shipping are also the main sources of pollution. Only two lakes in Jining have Class III water quality, while the rest are Class IV or Class V. Despite the serious pollution, projects to solve the problem lagged behind. In Shandong, among the 13 wastewater treatment plants, 5 of them have established water recycling and renewing projects. Yet, to date, only the one in Zoucheng is effective.[19]

The Central Line Project faces the problem of resettling local residents. Before the Eastern Line Project, the completion date of the Central Line Project was announced to be postponed from 2010 to 2014. The major reason for the deferment lies in resettling residents along the line. To finish the project, the dam body of Danjiangkou Reservoir needs to be heightened. In the area, 330,000 residents, including 210,000 in Henan and 120,000 in Hubei, have to be resettled.[20] Although the government has promised 25 billion RMB to

---

[17] See Yang Mu and Teng Siow Song, "China Struggling to Cope with its Water Crises", EAI Background Brief No. 387, 12 June 2008, for more information on this project.

[18] "*Nanshui beidiao gongcheng* Postponed by Five Years Due to Various Factors", *21 Century Business Herald*, 5 February 2010.

[19] Ibid.

[20] Kong Pu, "330,000 People in the Danjiangkou Reservoir District Have to Move", *The Beijing News*, 23 February 2010.

build the new villages and implemented some favourable policies for the residents,[21] the compensation is not satisfactory for them. Many residents in this area were forced to relocate when the government decided to build the reservoir in 1965. Now, due to the *nanshui bei-diao gongcheng*, they have to move again. Moreover, since the announcement of the project, economic and social developments in the area have stagnated. People have long suffered from extreme poverty.[22]

The Western Line Project is the most controversial due to environmental concerns and is still in the planning stage.[23] Moreover, the project has also aroused the uneasiness of neighbouring countries such as India.[24] On 10 August 2009, Brahma Chellaney, an analyst at India's Centre for Policy Research, published an article, "Water Bomb: China Controls the Source of Most Major Rivers in Water-Scarce Asia", in the *South China Morning Post*. He asserts that China's project to transfer water from Tibet to northern China may reduce the volume of India's international rivers, and this project is a "water bomb" to India. The Voice of America also published an article addressing the same issue, asserting that China is trying to use water source as a "political weapon" to deal with the downstream countries.[25] The tension between China and its southwestern neighboring countries on water source is a critical obstacle to the project.

Facing so many complicated problems, the *nanshui beidiao gongcheng* can hardly solve China's water crisis. Even if the project were completed, it may encounter the same problem as the *yin-luan rujin* (阳光能源) project. Due to the year-long drought in the Luan River Basin, in 2000, the Panjiakou Reservoir had to use

---

[21] For instance, children of the first generation of immigrants in Danjiangkou enjoy 5 bonus points in their college entrance examination.

[22] Kong Pu, "330,000 People in the Danjiangkou Reservoir District Have to Move".

[23] "As Water Vanishes, Chinese City Booms", *International Herald Tribune*, 28 September 2007.

[24] *The Times of India* published an article expressing the India government officials' worry about China's water transfer project. http://news.163.com/06/1024/09/2U6JTC210001121M.html.

[25] "Indian Scholars Worry about Water Interception By China", 14 August 2009, http://www.sinonet.net/news/world/2009-08-14/36354.html, accessed on 18 May 2010.

dead storage to supply water to Tianjin. Yet the supply from the *yinluan rujin* project is far from enough to meet Tianjin's demand. Since 2000, Tianjin has had to transfer water from the Yellow River to deal with emergent water shortages.[26] In the end, Tianjin still suffers from serious water shortages. Thus, the water transfer project is not a sustainable way to solve China's water shortage problem.

CHINA'S POLICY TOWARD RECYCLED WATER: LOOKING FOR A MORE SUSTAINABLE SOURCE OF WATER SUPPLY

Since groundwater exploitation and large-scale water transfer projects are not sustainable in the long run, China has to reconsider the problem from a more macro and more sustainable perspective. According to the developed countries' experience, there are several ways to increase water supply, including collecting rainwater and, more importantly, using recycled water.

Recycled water is increasingly recognized as one of the important sources of water supply in the globe. Countries like the US, Israel, Japan and Singapore have developed advanced technology to produce recycled water. In Singapore, 100% of wastewater is collected and treated. The NEWater produced by the Public Utilities Board (PUB) has reached such a good quality that it is safe to drink.[27] At present, China's recycled water industry is still in its infancy — only a small number of cities have started to use recycled water in recent years.

At the beginning of the 21st century, facing the looming water crisis, the Chinese government turned its attention to the use of recycled water. In 2001, the International Conference and Exhibition on Developmental Strategy of Urban Sewage Treatment and Reutilization in the 21st Century, co-organized by the Ministry of

---

[26] "Luanhe River", 9 September 2007, http://blog.sina.com.cn/s/blog_4e62959301000bz7.html, accessed on 17 May 2010.

[27] Cecilia Tortajada, "Water Management in Singapore", *Water Resource Development* 22 (June 2006), 230.

Construction, the World Bank and the United Nations Industrial Development Organization (UNIDO), was held in Beijing. At the conference, Zheng Yijun, Deputy Minister of Construction, stated that reutilization of wastewater was the inevitable way to realize sustainable use of water resources. Zheng claimed that China would comprehensively launch sewage reutilization projects and strengthen international technology cooperation. China would also welcome foreign financial institutions and enterprises to invest in such projects.[28]

To effectively recycle urban sewage and guarantee the quality of sewage treatment, in recent years, the Ministry of Construction and the Standardization Administration of the PRC have established a series of standards on sewage treatment and recycling. These standards provide a technical basis for municipal wastewater treatment engineering.[29]

In 2006, China's Ministry of Construction and Ministry of Science and Technology co-issued the City Wastewater Renewable Technology Policy. The policy proposes that the government provide support to the recycled water industry in various areas, including urban planning, water price, fiscal policy and taxation. According to this policy, by the end of 2010, the direct use rate of recycled water from discharged urban sewage in northern cities will be 10–15%, and in southern coastal cities 5–10%. In 2015, the rates will be 20–25% and 10–15% respectively.[30] In June 2009, the Ministry of Finance announced an adjustment in value-added tax in

---

[28] Speech by the Deputy Minister of Construction on the "International Conference and Exhibition on Developmental Strategy of Urban Sewage Treatment and Utilization in the 21st Century", http://www.hnccic.com/web/html/jzxw/200112%5C200112094.html, accessed on 31 May 2010.

[29] These regulations include "Standards for Inspection of the Quality of Urban Sewage Treatment Plant Engineering", "Standards for the Design of Wastewater Recycle and Reutilization Project", "Standards for the Design of Graywater Use in Buildings" and "Quality of Urban Sewage".

[30] "Status of Recycled Water in China", 18 Febuary 2010, http://www.91wisdom.com/index.aspx?menuid=15&type=articleinfo&lanmuid=57&infoid=180&language=cn, accessed on 17 May 2010.

favour of the new water industry. With the effect of the adjustment, the sale of recycled water and wastewater treatment services are free from value-added tax.[31]

The coming Twelfth Five-Year Plan will include construction of facilities for recycling water for the first time. A considerable amount of investment in this area is expected during the planning period. Wastewater treatment, including water recycling, in towns will be one of the focuses in the Plan. A new scheme will be introduced to build wastewater treatment plants in county-level towns and major towns. There are more than 30,000 county-level towns and over 10,000 major towns in China. The total amount of investment needed is estimated to be 153.969 billion *yuan*.[32]

STATUS OF WASTEWATER TREATMENT INDUSTRY/RECYCLED WATER INDUSTRY IN CHINA

In the past two decades, the wastewater treatment industry in China's urban areas has developed rapidly. From 1991 to 2007, the number of wastewater treatment plants increased from 87 to 883, and the capacity increased from 3,170,000 m³/day to 71,460,000 m³/day (Figure 8). By October 2009, China had 1817 units of wastewater treatment plants in operation, with a daily capacity of over 99.58 million m³, 3.8 times and 4.5 times of those in 2000, respectively.[33]

The wastewater treatment rate has also increased significantly, from 14.86% in 1991 to 62.87% in 2007 (Figure 9). However, the rate is still far less than those in developed countries such as the US and the Netherlands, which are over 90%. Furthermore, while the wastewater treatment rate in cities reached 62.8% at the end of 2007,

---

[31] "Notice of Exempting Value Added Tax for Recycled Water Industry", 29 June 2009, http://www.wssbw.com/zhengcefagui/1799.html, accessed on 10 May 2010.
[32] "Recycled Water Facility Construction Receiving 150 Billion *Yuan* Investment Package", 9 April 2010, http://news.hexun.com/2010-04-09/123282105.html, accessed on 17 May 2010.
[33] "GUOSEN Report on Water Industry", 5 January 2010.

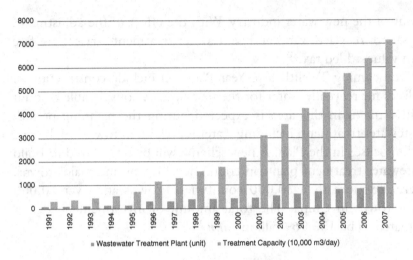

Fig. 8.   China's wastewater treatment has increased.

Source: China Urban Construction Statistical Yearbook 2007.

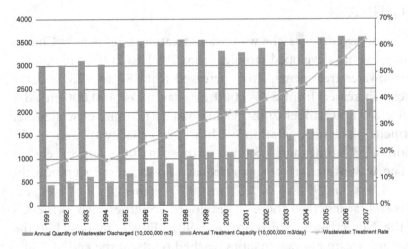

Fig. 9.   Wastewater treatment rate in China.

Source: China Urban Construction Statistical Yearbook 2007.

the rate in counties was much less, only 22.60%.[34] According to the Eleventh Five-Year Plan, at the end of 2010, the average wastewater treatment rate in cities and towns will be above 60%, with 80% for provincial capitals, 60% for prefecture-level cities, 50% for county-level

---

[34] "Bright Perspective for Water Industry", 9 October 2008, http://stock.588588.com/2008/10/091447120744-2.shtml, accessed on 12 May 2010.

cities, and 30% for counties.[35] Therefore, there is much room for the expansion of wastewater treatment services.

The level of marketization of the wastewater treatment industry is much higher than that of the water supply industry. In 2007, 50–70% of total wastewater services in China was provided by international companies, while the percentage was 15–20% in water supply. Build-operate-transfer/transfer-operate-transfer (BOT/TOT) is the main method of attracting social capital. By March 2008, among all 1321 wastewater treatment plants in operation, 414 units, or 31%, were established through the BOT/TOT method. Among the 771 units under construction, 306, or 40%, were based on BOT/TOT.[36]

However, wastewater treatment in current China is just to treat sewage to meet the quality standards for discharge. The rate of water recycled is rather low. In 2007, the national average wastewater recycle rate[37] was about 5% and the ratio of wastewater recycled to wastewater discharged was only 2.7%.[38] With the efforts to encourage water recycling, the rates increased to 15% and 5% in 2009 respectively.[39] Yet the ratio of wastewater recycled to wastewater discharged is still far from the target (10–15%) set by the Eleventh Five-Year Plan.

In recent years, recycled water has been popularized and used in some northern cities which are experiencing serious water shortages. In cities like Beijing, Tianjin and Qingdao, recycled water is used for agricultural irrigation, industrial cooling, urban landscape, municipal use, car washing and toilet flushing. Beijing is the leading city in using recycled water. In 2009, recycled water surpassed surface water

---

[35] "SYWG Research & Consulting Report", 24 January 2009.
[36] "GUOSEN Report", 5 January 2010.
[37] Wastewater recycling rate = amount of wastewater recycled/amount of wastewater treated.
[38] "Guotai Junan Securities Report", 23 February 2009.
[39] "Status of Recycled Water in China", http://www.91wisdom.com/index.aspx?menuid=15&type=articleinfo&lanmuid=57&infoid=180&language=cn, accessed on 17 May 2010.

and became the second largest water source for Beijing.[40] With the construction of the Eastern Line Project of *nanshui beidiao gongcheng*, the use of recycled water has increased along the line in Shandong.

Yet in most cities, recycled water is not widely used or simply does not exist. The capacity and use of recycled water among different provinces and cities vary dramatically (Figures 10 and 11). Utilization of recycled water in most provinces is still underdeveloped. There is much room for improvement to meet the target set by the government as mentioned above.

Besides recycling sewage, desalination is also an important method to increase water supply. By the end of 2006, there were 41 desalination facilities in operation in China, most of which were located in Shandong, Liaoning, Zhejiang, Hebei and Tianjin (see Table 1). The total production capacity was 120,394 m³/day. However, the actual volume of water produced was only 50,000 m³/day, less than half of the capacity.[41] To date, China's total desalination capacity has been improved significantly to 600,000 m³/day.[42] Yet to meet the target set by the government, as shown in Table 2, the potential for future development is still significant.

MAJOR CORPORATIONS IN CHINA'S WASTEWATER TREATMENT/RECYCLED WATER MARKET

At present, there are three main types of water corporations that have business in wastewater treatment and/or recycled water in China,

[40] "Beijing Uses More Recycled Water than Surface Water", *Caijing*, 26 March 2010, http://www.caijing.com.cn/2010-03-26/110404143.html, accessed on 18 May 2010.
[41] Compass Information Consulting Co. Ltd., *Report and Forecast of China's Desalination Industry in 2009–2013*, September 2009, 38.
[42] "Tianjin Gains Great Achievement in Desalination", 24 March 2010, http://news.enorth.com.cn/system/2010/03/24/004557447.shtml, accessed on 20 May 2010.

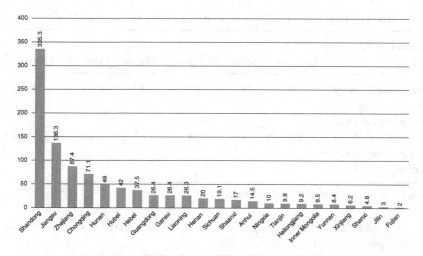

Fig. 10. Recycled water production in provinces (municipalities) in 2007 (10,000 m³/day).

Note: Data for some provinces and municipalities such as Beijing and Shanghai are missing.
Source: China Urban Construction Statistical Yearbook 2007.

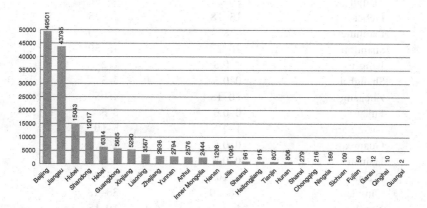

Fig. 11. Annual quantity of recycled water used in provinces (municipalities) in 2007 (10,000 m³).

Note: Data for some provinces and municipalities are missing.
Source: China Urban Construction Statistical Yearbook 2007.

including multinational corporations, restructured state-owned enterprises (SOEs) and domestic private companies. Different kinds of corporation vary from one another in their social background, resources possessed, technology and equipment, and human capital.

Table 1. Desalination facilities in coastal provinces and cities in 2006

Provinces/ Cities	Zhejiang	Hebei	Shandong	Tianjin	Liaoning	Others
Desalination capacity as a percentage of the national total (%)	38	25	14	14	9	0
Desalination facilities as a percentage of the national total (%)	29	5	34	7	20	5

Source: Compass Information Consulting Database.

Table 2. Development goal for desalination in China and its provinces/cities (10,000 m³/day)

Provinces/Cities	2010	2020
China	80–100	250–300
Tianjin	20–25	45–50
Hebei	15–18	20–25
Liaoning	6–8	15–20
Shandong	20–25	45–50
Jiangsu	0–0.5	1–2
Shanghai	0–0.5	3–5
Zhejiang	10–15	45–50
Fujian	0–0.5	3–5
Guangdong	1–2	5–10
Guangxi	0–0.5	1–2
Hainan	0–0.5	3–5
Dalian	8–10	15–20
Qingdao	18–20	35–43
Ningbo	1–2	10–15
Xiamen	0–0.5	3–5
Shenzhen	1–2	3–5

Source: Compass Information Consulting Database.

Since 2002, a number of foreign companies have been encouraged to enter China. To date, there are six major multinational water corporations in China, namely Veolia Water, Suez Environment Group (Sino-France Water Investment Co. Ltd.), Biwater Plc Group, Western

Water Group (China), Hong Kong and China Gas Co., and Jinzhou Environment. These multinational corporations have advanced technology and equipment and enjoy favourable policies from the government. By the end of 2008, these six companies had signed over 50 water supply projects in China, with a total supply capacity of more than 20 million m^3/day (8% of China's total supply capacity).[43]

Many SOEs in the water industry have been restructured to be more efficient and competitive in the market. The main water SOEs include Shenzhen Water Group (深圳水务集团), Beijing Water Group (北京排水集团), Shou Chuang Holdings (首创股份), Chuang Ye Huan Bao (创业环保), General Water of China (海通集团), and China Water Investment (中环保水务). SOEs have extensive social resources and stable funding guarantees of operation. Private water companies such as Shunde Huanbao (中国水务投资) and Guozhen Huanbao (国祯环保) are flexible and active in business. Yet due to limited capital resources, the operations and markets are limited to the medium and small cities and towns.

Before the global financial crisis, multinational corporations were very active in China's water market. However, since the financial crisis, the expansion speed of these companies has significantly slowed down. The Chinese society's criticisms and suspicion about foreign companies' aggressive acquisitions in China's water market also contributed to the slowdown. At the 4th Annual China Water Congress 2010, the Vice CEO of Suez Environment (China) complained that they could not find any project to bid on in China's water market now.[44]

In the meantime, large-scale SOEs have become the major competitors in China's water market since the financial crisis. Among the 4 trillion *yuan* investment package initiated by the Chinese government, over 200 billion *yuan* was for environment protection

---

[43] Fu Tao, "On China's Water Price", 10 August 2009, http://blog.h2o-china.com/html/62/251662-10219.html, accessed on 18 May 2010.

[44] Hua Yan, "The Surge of Acquisitions in Water Market, SOEs become Major Competitors", 25 May 2010, http://news.h2o-china.com/html/2010/05/671274748834_1.shtml, accessed on 28 May 2010.

and development. The SOEs thus gained great financial support from the central government. Seizing the opportunities, large-scale water SOEs have been very active in expanding and integrating their market at the provincial level.[45]

Among the 13 listed water companies, only 2 of them have business in recycled water. These are Chuang Ye Huan Bao (创业环保) and Shou Chuang Holdings (首创股份). In 2009, Chuang Ye Huan Bao sold 3.46 million m^3 of recycled water with a sales revenue of 8.64 million *yuan*. Sales revenue of recycled water contributed 0.7% of its total sales revenue in 2009.[46] Recycled water is not one of Shou Chuang Holdings's main businesses. Yet the company holds 22.4% of shares in Beijing Jingcheng Zhongshui Co. Ltd. (北京京城中水有限责任公司), whose business is recycled water.[47]

Recycled water plants face various constraints in current China, including high treatment costs, lack of supporting facilities like pipe networks, low quality of treatment, and people's habits of water usage. Due to the constraints, the utilization rate of recycled water facilities is about 10%, and most recycled water plants are under deficit.[48]

Singapore's water companies, with their advanced technology and management, have advantages in China's wastewater treatment and recycled water industry. The main Singapore water companies having business in China include Hyflux, Keppel Seghers Environment Engineering (China), Salcon Group and SembCorp Industries. Among these companies, Hyflux has the largest share of wastewater treatment market in China (0.144% in 2008).[49] To date, Hyflux has built 10 wastewater treatment plants in China. Another 34 plants are under construction. In 2007, Hyflux's water business in China constituted 80% of the company's total revenues and 50% of its profits.[50]

---

[45] Ibid.

[46] *Company Report of Chuang Ye Huan Bao 2009.*

[47] *Company Report of Shou Chuang Holding 2009.*

[48] SYWG Research & Consulting, "Report on Water Industry", 27 April 2009, 9.

[49] http://www.shenguang.com/news/2009-12/984508245893.html, accessed on 12 May 2010.

[50] "Singapore's Water Tycoon Favors Chinese Market", 26 April 2010, http://news.h2o-china.com/html/2010/04/671272247175_1.shtml, accessed on 18 May 2010.

Since 2009, newly signed wastewater treatment projects have constituted a major part of total water investment projects in China. These new water treatment projects are on smaller scales than before and the speed of business expansion has decreased (Appendix 2). One possible reason is that the wastewater treatment rate in cities is quite satisfactory and there is less room left for business expansion. In the following years, the focus will be on counties and towns, where the wastewater treatment rate is rather low. At the same time, as the rate of capacity utilization in existing wastewater treatment companies was only 74% on average in 2008, future development will be transferred to improve operation capacity.

The wastewater industry in China is quite dispersed (Figure 12). There are more than 2000 water plants located in China's 669 cities. Every city has its own water plant(s).[51] The largest two company market shares are only 3.02% (Chuang Ye Huan Bao) and 2.33% (Shou Chuang Holdings). In France, Veolia Water, Suez Environment Group, and SAUR have a 96% share of the national market. Since the concentration level is very low in China's wastewater treatment market, mergers and acquisitions will be the main theme in the long run.

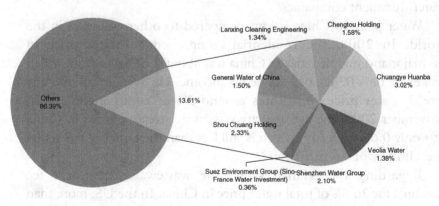

Fig. 12. Major water companies' market share in the wastewater treatment industry in China.

Source: GUOSEN Securities.

---

[51] "GUOSEN Report", 5 January 2010.

INSTITUTIONAL OBSTACLES OF THE DEVELOPMENT OF WASTEWATER TREATMENT/RECYCLED WATER INDUSTRY IN CHINA

The major institutional obstacle to the development of China's wastewater treatment and recycled water industry is water price. The government found itself in a dilemma over its policy of water price reform. As water price is relevant to people's daily life and thus social stability, under the current situation of increasing inflation, the government has had to postpone its water price reform several times.

Currently, water price in China consists of three parts, namely water resource fee, tap water fee, and wastewater treatment fee. Water resource fees go to the government. Tap water fees belong to water supply companies. Wastewater treatment fees are first collected by the government and then paid back to the wastewater treatment companies. The wastewater treatment fees are decided through negotiation between water treatment companies and the government. Thus, the wastewater treatment fee has a direct impact on the profitability of water treatment companies.

Water price in China is low, compared to other countries in the world. In 2008, the residential comprehensive water price in 36 major and middle cities in China was about 2.38 *yuan*/ton, which makes up only 0.98% of a resident's income. On average, all over the world, water price constitutes around 2% of family income.[52] In November 2009, the average city wastewater treatment fee in China was only 0.66 *yuan*/m^3, which is still less than the target of 0.8 set by the Ministry of Construction.[53]

Regarding the relative value, the wastewater treatment fee accounts for 26.6% of total water price in China. In the US, more than 55% of tap water tariffs are wastewater treatment fees. The percentage

---

[52] SYWG Research & Consulting, "Report on Water Industry", 27 April 2009.
[53] Ibid.

in the UK is 51%, which is also much larger than the 26.6% in China.[54] Hence, there is much room for a water price increase in China.

Many water treatment enterprises have found it difficult to make profit given the low water price in China. The French company Suez Ondeo is an example. In 1994, when Suez Ondeo entered China's water market, it expected the increase in water price to make profit. However, water price didn't increase as fast as Suez expected. Failing to make profit, Suez Ondeo withdrew from China's water market in 2002.[55]

Low water price not only constrains foreign companies but also limits domestic water companies. Shenyang Water is a typical example. In 1997, Shenyang Water was listed in the Hong Kong Exchange. Before the listing, the Shenyang government promised either to give the company subsidies or increase water price. However, after listing, the Shenyang government didn't keep its promise. Since the water price was too low for Shenyang Water to make profit, without the support of the government, the company had to be delisted in 1999.

The water price structure in China is another disincentive. In 2002, the Chinese government required all province-administered municipalities to establish progressive pricing, for domestic water use by the end of 2003, and other cities by the end of 2005. Yet, to date, only 80 cities have initiated progressive water pricing among selected residences.[56] Beijing and Shanghai failed to establish progressive water pricing in the past years. Chengdu is among the few cities that has announced progressive water pricing

---

[54] "Donghai Securities Water Industry Report", 14 January 2010.

[55] "Foreign Water Companies Occupy 30% of Water Market Shares in Major Cities", 23 August 2009, http://www.fjnpiz.gov.cn/html/ShowArticle.asp?ArticleID=922, accessed on 17 May 2010.

[56] "List of Further Price Reform for Water, Electricity, Oil and Gas", 30 April 2010, http://jjckb.xinhuanet.com/gnyw/2010-04/30/content_219360.htm, accessed on 7 June 2010. The 80 cities include Nanjing, Shenzhen, Wuhan, Xiamen, Ningbo, Dongguan, Foshan, etc.

Table 3. Water prices in Singapore (S$)

Tariff Category	Consumption Block (m³/mth)	Tariffs (cents/m³)	Water Conservation Tax (% of tariff)	Water-Borne Fee (cents/m³)	Sanitary Appliance Fee
Domestic	1 to 40	117	30	30	$3/fitting per mth
Domestic	Above 40	140	45	30	$3/fitting per mth
Non-domestic	All units	117	30	60	$3/fitting per mth
Shipping	All units	192	30	—	—
Industrial	All units	43	—	—	—

Source: Public Utilities Board Singapore, 2008.

throughout the city by the end of 2010.[57] Singapore has effectively practiced progressive water pricing (Table 3), which China has a lot to learn from.

Despite the dilemma, the Chinese government did make efforts to increase the price. Table 4 shows the laws and regulations on water price established by the Chinese government in the past decade. The decade saw a steady increase in domestic water prices and wastewater treatment fees in China's 120 major and medium-sized cities. After adjusting for the inflation rate, the growth rate of wastewater treatment fees is higher than that for the domestic water prices.[58] In 2009, among the 36 large and medium-sized cities, 11 have actually increased the total water price and wastewater treatment fees. Six cities have held hearings on the issue, while the remaining five cities were preparing for price increase (Table 5).

---

[57] "Chengdu Plans to Practice Progressive Water Price for Nondomestic Use", 22 March 2010, http://www.sc.xinhuanet.com/content/2010-03/23/content_19315376.htm, accessed on 7 June 2010.

[58] Fu Tao, "On China's Water Price: Its Nature, Components, and Status", 10 August 2009, http://blog.h2o-china.com/html/62/251662-10211.html, accessed on 18 May 2010.

Table 4. Laws and regulations on water price in China

Publication Date	Laws/Regulations
1998	Measures for the Administration of Urban Water Supply Pricing (城市供水价格管理办法)
2002	Notice of Furthering Price Reform of Urban Water Supply (关于进一步推进城市供水价格改革工作的通知)
2003	Regulation on Collection and Usage of Pollutant Discharge Fees (排污费征收使用管理条例)
	Measures for the Administration of the Charging Rates for Pollutant Discharge Fees (排污费征收标准管理办法)
2004	Measures for the Administration of the Pricing of Water Supplied by Hydraulic Engineering (水利工程供水价格管理办法)
2005	Price Law of the People's Republic of China (中华人民共和国价格法)
2006	Measures for the Supervision and Examination of the Government's Pricing Costs (政府制定价格成本监审方法)
	Measures for the Supervision and Examination of the Pricing Costs of Water Supplied by Hydraulic Engineering (tentative) (水利工程供水定价成本监审办法（试行）)
2007	General Technological Standards for the Supervision and Examination of Pricing Costs (定价成本监审一般技术规范)
2009	Notice of Several Problems in the Administration of Urban Water Supply Pricing (关于做好城市供水价格管理工作有关问题的通知)
2010	Opinions on Major Tasks to Deepen the Economic System Reform in 2010 (关于 2010 年深化经济体制改革重点工作的意见)

Source: Compiled by the authors.

As price management by the National Development and Reform Commission (NDRC) is the focal point of China's industry policy, reforms of resource prices including water price will continue. The Pricing Department of NDRC is working on revising regulations on water price management. On 30 April 2010, the State Council passed the Opinions on Major Tasks to Deepen Economic System Reform in 2010, which emphasizes that the NDRC will push for water price reform

Table 5. Progress in water price increase in selected major cities in 2009

City	Time	Progress	Tap Water Price	Amount Increased	Percentage Increased	Wastewater Treatment Fees	Amount Increased	Percentage Increased
Beijing	2009-11-19	Increased	4.12	0.22	6%	1.68	0.18	12%
Shanghai	2009-6-20	Increased	1.33	0.3	30%	1.08	0.18	20%
Tianjin	2009-4-1	Increased	3.9	0.5	15%			
Nanjing	2009-4-1	Increased	2.8	0.3	12%			
Shenyang	2009-7-1	Increased	1.8	0.4	29%	0.6	0.1	20%
Kunming	2009-6-1	Increased	2.45	0.4	20%	1	0.1	20%
Lanzhou	2009-11-1	Increased	1.75	0.3	21%			
Guiyang	2009-8-1	Increased						
Ningbo	2009-12-1	Increased	2.1	0.4	24%	0.65	0.15	30%
Nanchang	2009-9-1	Increased	1.18	0.3	34%			
Yinchuang	2010-1-1	Increased	1.74	0.3	21%			
Harbin	2009-12-8	Hearing	2.4	0.6	33%			
Chongqing	2009-11-25	Hearing	2.5	0.4	19%	1	0.3	43%
Nanning	2009-11-21	Hearing	1.45	0.4	38%			
Jinan	2009-12-10	Hearing	2.25	0	0%	0.9	0.2	29%
Fuzhou	2009-12-16	Hearing	1.5	0.3	25%	0.85		
Shenzhen	2009-12-30	Hearing	1.9			0.9		
Average					24%			25%
Qingdao	2009-11-18	In preparation	1.8			0.7		
Changsha	2009-11-7	In preparation	1.21			0.65		
Huhehaote	2009-8-1	In preparation	1.95			0.45		
Chengdu		In preparation	1.35			0.8		
Lhasa	2009-11-11	In preparation	0.6					

Source: GUOSEN Securities.

this year. One of the main tasks of this year's reform will be enforcing progressive water pricing for urban household consumption.[59]

It is important to note that the on-going pricing reform discussed here is limited to household consumption. There is still no mechanism to reform agricultural and industrial water prices. The major difficulty in agricultural water pricing reform lie in protecting vulnerable peasants and securing food supply. Large variation in factors like geography, climate, and technology among different regions is also a main obstacle for agricultural water price reform. As for the industrial-use water price reform, local governments face with a policy dilemma. Higher water prices would lead to higher production costs, which weakens the competitiveness of local industries. Lower water prices, on the other hand, would discourage water conservation which worsens water shortage and other environmental problems. As agricultural and industrial water use constitutes about 88% of total water use in China, there is still a long way to go in China's water pricing reform.

APPENDIX 1

Recycled Water in Beijing

Recycled water has become the second largest water source in Beijing since 2008. Taking the Olympics as an opportunity, Beijing has made significant progress in constructing its drainage facility system, which includes drainage pipeline networks, wastewater treatment plants, water recycling facilities and sludge treatment facilities. In 2009, the volume of recycled water used in Beijing was 650 million m^3, constituting 18% of total water use in the city.

To improve management of drainage and recycled water, the Beijing government published the Measures for the Administration of Drainage and Recycled Water in Beijing on 1 January 2010. According to the regulation, recycled water in Beijing is mainly used in industry, agriculture, environmental protection, and urban miscellaneous consumption.

---

[59] "List of Further Price Reform for Water, Electricity, Oil and Gas".

Recycled water is supplied for industrial use in Beijing. For example, the Beijing Gaobeidian wastewater treatment plant supplies recycled water to Huaneng Heating Plant, Sanhe Thermal Power Plant, and some other industrial enterprises in Beijing every day. The supply capacity is more than 40,000 tons per day.

In 2007, among the 495 million m^3 recycled water used in Beijing, 60 million m^3 was used in supplementing water in urban landscape and environmental protection. Beijing has also built 20 automatic water filling machines that can supply 20 million m^3 of recycled water for environmental and urban administration use.

Beijing is one of the cities that first introduced recycled water for daily miscellaneous water consumption. In 1987, the Beijing administration published Measures for the Construction and Administration of Recycled Water in Beijing to push the construction and application of recycled water facilities. Till 2007, there were more than 160 recycled water facilities in operation in Beijing, most of which were in hotels, restaurants and universities. Water for daily miscellaneous use such as bathing water is recycled and reused in toilet flushing, car washing, road cleaning and other daily water consumption. The capacity of these facilities was 40,000 ton/day in 2007.

Recycled water has been increasingly used in agriculture irrigation. In 2007, the recycled water irrigation area in the suburban districts of Beijing, including Daxing and Tongzhou, was 1.8 million acres. The total volume of recycled water used in agriculture was 230 million m^3 in Beijing in the same year. Using recycled water for irrigation can save 60 million m^3 of groundwater every year.

Sources:
1. "Beijing Uses More Recycled Water than Surface Water", *Caijing*, 26 March 2010, http://www.caijing.com.cn/2010-03-26/110404143. html, accessed on 18 May 2010.
2. Qian Xin, "Status and Outlook of Urban Recycled Water Use in China", 14 December 2009, http://www.lrn.cn/zjtg/societyDiscussion/ 200712/t20071214_178605.htm, accessed on 18 May 2010.

APPENDIX 2

Business Locations of Major Singapore Water Corporations in China

Company	Business Location
Hyflux	Tianjing, Jiangsu, Jiangxi, Hebei, Henan, Liaoning, Shandong, Yunnan, Guangdong, Shanghai, Heilongjiang
Keppel Seghers	Guangdong, Hebei, Macau
Salcon Group	Shanghai, Jiangsu, Henan, Guangdong, Tianjin, Beijing, Yunnan, Chongqing, Shaanxi, Hubei, Fujian, Liaoning, Sichuang
Semb Corp Industries	Shanghai, Jiangsu, Tianjin, Liaoning

Source: China Water Net (http://www2.h2o-china.com/report/singapore/index.htm).

APPENDIX 3

Major Trans-Regional Mergers and Acquisitions in China'sWater Industry in 2009

Date	M&A Acquiring Company	M&A Target Company/Project	Location	M&A Pattern	Capacity (10,000 ton/day)
Oct	上海联合水务	宿迁第二水厂	Suqian (Jiangsu)	BOT	12
	钱江水利	婺城区金西西畈水厂	Jinhua (Zhejiang)	BOT	5
Sep	中持环保	河北正定县污水厂	Shijiazhuang (Heibei)	Entrusted Operation	6
	创业环保	合肥十五里河污水厂	Hefei (Anhui)	Entrusted Operation	5
Aug	新加坡凯发集团	天津北辰一污水项目	Tianjin	BOT	4
	新加坡三达集团	吉林白城市污水处理厂	Baicheng (Jilin)	BOT	10
	首创股份	南阳市污水处理厂二期工程	Nanyang (Henan)	BOT	10
Jul	亚洲环保	河南周口市沙北污水处理工程	Zhoukou (Henan)	BOT	5
	北控水务	锦州城市污水及再生水股权项目	Jinzhou (Liaoning)	Joint Venture	10/20
Jun	中山公用	济宁水务（供水/污水）	Jining (Guangdong)	Stock Right Transfer	30/20
	新加坡联邦环境与能源有限公司	新津化工园区工业生产用水供水工程	Chengdu (Sichuan)	BOT	6
May	国祯环保	东川污水处理厂	Kunming (Yunnan)	Entrusted Operation	2
	北控水务	齐齐哈尔市富拉尔基区污水处理厂项目	Heilongjiang	BOT	10
	中国水务控股	都匀城市污水厂	Duyun (Guizhou)	TOT	6
Apr	国祯环保	江门污水处理	Jiangmen (Guangdong)	BOT	10
	光大国际	济南市西客站污水处理项目	Jinan (Shandong)	BOT	3
	北控水务	贵州清镇污水厂（朱家河污水处理厂一期、二期、百花湖乡污水厂、站街镇污水厂）	Qingzhen (Guizhou)	TOT + BOT	2.5/2.5/0.05/0.2

(*Continued*)

(*Continued*)

Mar	碧水源	MBR水处理工程		TOT	11
	首创股份	湖南醴陵污水项目	Liling (Hunan)	BOT	5
	国祯环保	湖南汨罗市污水处理项目	Miluo (Hunan)	BOT	3
Feb	加拿大ECO公司	湖北黄梅污水项目	Huanggang (Hubei)	BOT	6
	苏伊士环境	重庆供水	Chongqing	BOT	20
	重庆水务集团	重庆市东部新城（鱼嘴组团）项目	Chongqing	BOT	5
Jan	北控水务	贵州污水处理	Guiyang (Guizhou)	TOT + BOT	5.3
	首创股份	湖南攸县、吉首污水处理项目	Zhuzhou, Jishou (Hunan)	BOT\TOT	2.5/7
	金州集团	南京城北污水处理厂	Nanjing (Jiangsu)	TOT	30
	武汉控股	沙湖污水处理厂二、三期资产	Ningxia	Tender Offers	10

Source: GUOSEN Securities.

APPENDIX 4

Wastewater Treatment Projects between Singapore Companies and Jiangsu

Company	Project	Investment (10,000 yuan)	Waste-water Treatment Capacity (m³/day)
SembCorp Industries (新加坡胜科工业集团)	张家港保税区胜科水务有限公司二期改扩建项目	9,848	15,000
SembCorp Utilities (新加坡胜科公用事业公司)	南京胜科水务:1A工程	8,000	12,500
	南京胜科水务:1B工程	9,225	12,500
	南京胜科水务:II期工程	11,000	30,000
	南京胜科水务预处理装置	1,260	3,000
	南京化学工业园水业有限公司一期工程	20,000	100,000
Asia Environment Holdings (新加坡亚洲环保控股有限公司)	南京江宁开发区污水处理项目	-	80,000
	南京溧水污水处理项目	-	40,000
	丹阳市乡镇污水处理工程	43,000	55,000
	南通西北片引江区域供水项目	-	200,000
Asia Water (亚洲水务投资私人控股有限公司)	苏州汾湖经济开发区污水处理项目	-	30,000
Hyflux (新加坡凯发集团)	常熟东南（古里镇）污水处理厂	20 million US dollars	60,000
	扬州青山污水处理厂	7.5 million US dollars	20,000
Salcon Group (新加坡盛康集团（宝德集团成员）)	吴江市盛泽镇印染废水深度处理工程	300	12,000

(*Continued*)

(*Continued*)

China-Singapore Suzhou Industrial Park Development Group (中新苏州工业园区开发有限公司)	中新-苏通生态科技园	-	-
Hang Lung Water (新加坡恒隆水务私人有限公司)	连云港经济技术开发区大浦工业区污水处理厂	8,000	48,000
Wanxiang International (新加坡万香国际有限公司)	有机废水无害化处理	2,800	3,000
Joint Environmental Technology (新加坡联合环境技术有限公司)	大丰市海洋开发区污水处理厂	3,500	20,000

Source: Environmental Protection Department of Jiangsu Province.

APPENDIX 5

Listed Water Companies in China: An Overview

Company	Location	Total Assets (RMB b.)	Distribution of Business		Production Capacities (10,000 tons/day)			Revenue Composition (%)			
			Region	%	Raw Water	Tap Water	Wastewater Treatment	Raw Water	Tap Water	Wastewater Treatment	Others
中原环保	Zhengzhou (Henan)	0.74	Zhengzhou	100			40			55	45
合加资源	Yichang (Hubei)	2.67	Central China	81		12	60		2	15	83
			Beijing & Inner Mongolia	15							
			Jiangsu & Zhejiang	4							
首创股份	Beijing	14.45	Beijing	53		403	399		39	40	21
			Anhui	14							
			Hebei	12							
			Tianjin	6							
			Jiangsu	5							
			Zhejiang	5							
武汉控股	Wuhan (Hubei)	3.49	Wuhan	100		130	5		67	5	28
钱江水利	Hangzhou (Zhejiang)	2.79	Zhejiang	80		100			62		38
			Others	20							
南海发展	Foshan (Guangdong)	2.13	Foshan	100		126	14		87	8	5
洪城水业	Nanchang (Jiangxi)	0.70	Nanchang	86		120	19		86	14	
			Jiujiang	6							
			Wenzhou	5							
			Pingxiang	3							
城投控股	Shanghai	20.24	Shanghai	98	348	63	154	17	5	9	69
			Jiangsu	1							
			Zhejiang	1							
创业环保	Tianjin	7.20	Tianjin	78		20	288		4	85	11
			Hangzhou	10							
			Qujing	4							
			Guizhou	3							
			Fuyang	3							
重庆清党	Chengdu (Sichuan)	2.15	Chengdu	100			130			100	

Source: Company Reports, SYWG Research & Consulting.

APPENDIX 6

Water Tariffs in China's 36 Large and Medium-Sized Cities in May 2010

City	Tap Water Price (Wastewater Treatment Fee excluded) (yuan)					Wastewater Treatment Fee (yuan)					Renewed Water
	Domestic	Industry	Administration	Service	Special Industry	Domestic	Industry	Administration	Service	Special Industry	
Beijing	2.96	4.44	4.12	4.66	60	1.04	1.77	1.68	1.55	1.68	1
Changchun	2.5	4.6	4.6	8	16	0.4	0.8	0.8	0.8	2	
Changsha	1.21	1.38	1.21	2.2	4.2	0.65	0.8	0.7	1.28	1.18	
Chengdu	1.35	2.9	2.9	2.9	5	0.8	1.4	1.4	1.4	1.7	
Chongqing	2.7	3.25	2.7	3.25	3.25	1	1.3		1.3	1.3	
Dalian	2.3	3.2	3.2	5	20	0.6	0.9	0.9	0.9	1.1	
Fuzhou	1.2	1.35	1.2	1.5	2	0.85	1.1	0.85	1.5	1.1	
Guangzhou	1.32	1.83	1.61	2.71	3.38	0.9	1.4	1.2	1.4	2	
Guiyang	2	2.5	2.5	3.3	10	0.7	0.8	0.8	0.8	0.8	10
Haikou	1.6	2.5	1.8	2.5	2.5	0.8	1.1	1.1	1.1	1.1	
Hangzhou	1.35	1.75	1.9	2	4	0.5	1.8	1.5	1.5	1.5	
Harbin	2.4	4.3	4.3	4.3	16.4	0.8	1.1	1.1	1.1	1.1	0.9
Hefei	1.29	1.41	1.5	1.93	5.12	0.51	0.59	0.59	0.77	0.77	
Huhehaote	2.35	3.5	3.5	4	20	0.65	0.95	0.95	0.95	0.95	
Jinan	2.6	2.9	2.6	4.3	16	0.9	1.1	1.1	1.1	1.1	
Kunming	2.45	4.35	3.6	4.35	14.1	1	1.25	1.25	1.25	1.25	
Lahsa	0.6	1.4	1	1.2	1.5						
Lanzhou	1.75	2.53	2.5	2.8	15	0.5	0.8	0.8	0.8	0.8	
Nanchang	1.18	1.45	1.45	1.65	6	0.8	0.8	0.8	0.8	1	
Nanjing	1.5	1.85	1.7	1.85	2.95	1.3	1.55	1.5	1.55	1.65	
Nanning	1.48	2.23	2.23	2.23	5	0.8	0.8	0.8	0.8	0.8	
Ningbo	2.1	3.5	3.5	3.5	9	0.65	1.8	1.8	1.8	1.8	
Qingdao	1.8	2.2	1.8	2.1	2.6	0.7	0.8	0.7	0.9	0.9	
Shanghai	1.03	2	2	2	10.6	1.08	1.7	1.7	1.7	1.7	0.9
Shenyang	1.8	2.5	2.6	3	10.2	0.6	1	1	1	1	
Shenzhen	1.9	2.25	2.3	2.95	7.5	0.9	1.05	1.1	1.2	2	
Shijiazhuang	2.5	3	2.8	3.5	24	0.8	1	1	1	1	1.5
Taiyuan	2.4	2.7	2.7	3.5	14	0.5	0.8	0.5	1.2	1	
Tianjin	3.08	6.3	6.3	6.3	20.7	0.82	1.2	1.2	1.2	1.2	5.7
Urumqi	1.36	1.48	1.48	2.44	8.7	0.7	0.7	0.7	0.7	0.7	0.1
Wuhan	1.1	1.65	1.5	2.35	4.8	0.8	0.8	0.8	0.8	0.8	
Xiamen	1.8	1.8	1.8	1.8	2.8	1	1.2	1.8	1.2	1.5	1.2
Xian	2.25	2.55	2.95	3.4	16.1	0.65	0.9	0.9	0.9	0.9	1.1
Xining	1.3	1.38	1.65	2	4.5	0.52	0.63	0.57	0.95	1.15	
Yinchuang	1.6	2.28	1.75	2.28	18.08	0.7	1	1	1	2	
Zhengzhou	1.6	2	2	3	9.2	0.65	0.8	0.8	0.8	1	

Source: China Water Net (http://www.h2o-china.com/).

Harvesting Sunlight: Solar Thermal Industry in China

Mu YANG and Rongfang PAN

The Chinese government is now taking concrete steps to increase the share of non-fossil energies in its primary energy consumption. As one of China's emerging industries of strategic importance, the solar thermal industry for the utilization of solar heat is expected to play a significant role in the green campaign. Based on its core technology which is leading in the world, China has always been the largest market for solar thermal applications and the largest producer of solar heat collectors in the world. In addition to the traditional household applications, building integrated solar systems and other solar thermal technologies in industrial and agricultural production are the huge potential markets to be opened. Despite the rosy outlook, a variety of challenges facing the industry have to be addressed to ensure a healthy development.

SUNRAY BOOSTS CHINA'S GREEN CAMPAIGN

The Chinese central government is now accelerating its pace in boosting a low-carbon economy. During the first plenary meeting of the National Energy Commission on 22 April 2010, Premier Wen Jiabao emphasized that China "must accelerate the development and use of renewable energies to ensure the country's energy security and better cope with climate change".[1] It has been officially announced that China aims to increase the proportion of non-fossil, renewable energies in the total primary energy consumption from 9.9% in 2009 to 15% in 2020.[2] Taking the long construction period into consideration, the building of renewable energy infrastructure is going to be included in the Twelfth Five-Year Plan for national economic development (2011–2015).[3]

To meet the target, billions of *Renminbi* will be invested to promote the application and research and development (R&D) of clean energies including wind, solar, biomass, geothermal and nuclear energy. Solar energy, or the radiative energy from the sun, will play a significant role in the green campaign. Similar to wind energy, it enjoys inexhaustible access to the pollution-free source and has great potential to power daily life and economic activities.

China has enormous solar energy resources which demonstrate variety in geographic distribution. In its vast territory of 9.6 million square kilometers, over two-thirds annually receive utilizable sunshine in excess of 2,200 hours and a radiation of more than 5,000 megajoules per square metre (MJ/m^2) (see Appendix 1).[4] The annual total solar

---

[1] "Chinese Premier Wen Jiabao Urges Development of Renewable Energy", *News of the Communist Party of China*, 23 April 2010, online edition, http://english. cpc.people.com.cn/66102/6960466.html.

[2] Ibid.

[3] "China to Develop Low-Carbon Economy", *China Daily*, 1 March 2010, online edition, http://www.chinadaily.com.cn/china/2010-03/01/content_9521265.htm.

[4] The megajoule (MJ) is equal to one million joules. Li-qun Liu, Zhi-xin Wang, Hua-qiang Zhang and Ying-cheng Xue, "Solar Energy development in China — A Review", *Renewable and Sustainable Energy Reviews* 14 (2010), 301–311.

energy absorbed by ground surface, or theoretical storage volume, is tantamount to 1.7 trillion tons of standard coal, which is an astronomical figure in comparison to China's annual energy consumption of 3.1 billion tons of coal equivalent in 2009.[5] In particular, north Ningxia, north Gansu, south Xinjiang and the Qinghai-Tibet tableland receive the most radiation.[6]

Application of the rich solar energy resources is divided into two broad types of technologies: solar thermal energy (STE) for the utilization of solar heat, and solar photovoltaic (PV) for electric power generation.[7] Solar thermal technologies, particularly solar water heating (SWH), have been broadly commercialized and currently take up a much greater role in China's energy consumption than solar PV (Figure 1). Even when compared with the fastest growing wind power industry, the development of SWH in China is nonetheless spectacular. In comparison, total installed capacity of SWH was four-fold that of wind power by 2009.

In addition, China has been the largest market for solar thermal applications and the largest producer of solar heat collectors in the world, accounting for nearly two-thirds of the global total capacity (Figure 2), excluding unglazed collectors for swimming pool heating (for more details, see Appendix 2). Therefore, this Chapter will mainly examine solar thermal industry in China.

As for solar thermal applications, the contribution of installed solar heat collectors to the energy supply and CO_2 emission reduction is

---

[5] "2050 Energy Plan Revealed", *China Daily*, 7 December 2009, online edition, http://www.chinadaily.com.cn/bw/2009-12/07/content_9127229.htm.

[6] "我国太阳能热能资源分布", China Renewable Energy Industries Association (CREIA), available at http://www.creia.net/html/200810916711179.html.

[7] Solar thermal can be utilized in water heating, space heating, cooling, and ventilation, water treatment (solar desalination), solar cooking, process heat, and drying; solar photovoltaic applications include street lighting system, water pump, grid-connected photovoltaic power generation, building-integrated photovoltaic (BIPV), wind-solar hybrid system etc.

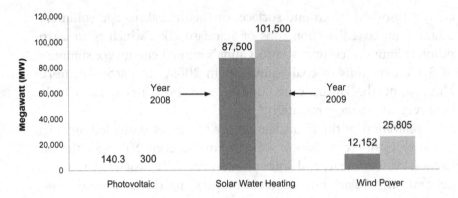

Fig. 1. Comparative total capacity in China.

Source: NDRC; GWEC; Chinese Solar Industry Information (中国太阳能产业资讯), 2010–02.

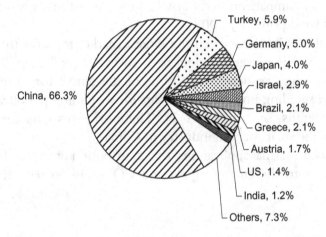

Fig. 2. Share of world solar water heating capacity by 2007.

Notes: Sum of glazed flat-plate and evacuated tube collectors, not including unglazed collectors.
Source: International Energy Agency (IEA).

significant. By the year 2007, China's total solar thermal capacity in operation contributed to energy savings with 6.6 million tons of oil equivalent per annum and an annual avoidance of 21.5 million tons of CO_2, accounting for 1.5% of China's annual CO_2 emission reduction

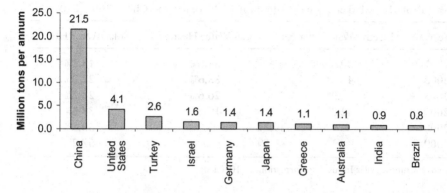

Fig. 3. Global leaders in CO_2 reduction by solar thermal applications by 2007.
Source: International Energy Agency (IEA).

target of 1.5 billion tons by 2010 (see Appendix 3).[8] In addition, China is also the global leader in emission reductions by solar thermal applications (Figure 3).

SOLAR THERMAL APPLICATIONS IN CHINA

Solar water heating (SWH) is the most widely used solar thermal technology in the world. China's solar water heating utilization dates back to the 1980s, with its market initially focused on low-income families in the rural areas. In the 1990s, the SWH technologies developed and the market expanded to small and medium cities. Since the late 1990s, the SWH application has witnessed broader awareness among the population, which therefore facilitated further technological innovations, and steady market expansion nationwide, including metropolises. A greener trend can be observed in the overall water heating market: the share of solar water heaters outperforms that of electric and gas water heaters, rising from 15.2% in 2001 to 57.2% in 2009 (Table 1).

---

[8] "World Development Report 2010: Development and Climate Change", World Bank, 192, available at http://siteresources.worldbank.org/INTWDR2010/Resources/5287678-1226014527953/WDR10-Full-Text.pdf.

Table 1.   Market share of water heaters (by output) in China, 2001–2009

Year	Electric Water Heaters	Gas Water Heaters	Solar Water Heaters
2001	30.0%	54.8%	15.2%
2003	44.2%	33.6%	22.2%
2005	45.2%	26.6%	28.2%
2007	42.3%	19.2%	38.5%
2008	49.2%		50.8%
2009	42.8%		57.2%

Source: Chinese Solar Industry Information, 2010–01.

Table 2.   Cost comparison of different types of water heaters

Comparison	Electric Water Heaters	Gas Water Heaters	Solar Water Heaters
Hot Water Supply (Litre per day)	100	100	100
Equipment Cost (*yuan*)	1,200	1,000	1,800
Annual Operational Cost (*yuan*)	500	350	5
Operational Lifetime (Year)	8	8	10
Annual Cost (*yuan*)	650	560	185
Cost Comparison Index (SWH as 100)	350	300	100

Source: Chinese Solar Industry Information, 2010–01.

The expansion can be explained from two aspects. On the demand side, along with the improvement of living standards in China, safe hot water has become indispensible to people's daily life. Second, a comparison of household investment in different types of water heaters shows that a solar water heater is the most cost-efficient among the three (Table 2). The annual costs of electric and gas water heaters within operational lifetime are more than threefold that of solar water heaters. Third, it is energy saving: each year, 1 m² of solar water heater can save 150 kilograms (kg) of standard coal, equivalent to 417 kilowatt hours (kWh) of electricity. On the supply side, government subsidies to newly established technology-based firms and fierce competition among small and medium manufacturers contribute to the great expansion.

Table 3. China's solar water heating capacity, 1998–2009

Year	Annual Output			Operating Capacity		
	million m²	Megawatt Thermal (MWth)	Y-o-Y Growth (%)	million m²	Megawatt Thermal (MWth)	Y-o-Y Growth (%)
1998	3.5	2,450	—	15.0	10,500	—
1999	5.0	3,500	42.9%	20.0	14,000	33.3%
2000	6.4	4,480	28.0%	26.0	18,200	30.0%
2001	8.2	5,740	28.1%	32.0	22,400	23.0%
2002	10.0	7,000	22.0%	40.0	28,000	25.0%
2003	12.0	8,400	20.0%	50.0	35,000	25.0%
2004	13.5	9,450	12.5%	62.0	43,400	24.0%
2005	15.0	10,500	11.1%	75.0	52,500	21.0%
2006	18.0	12,600	20.0%	90.0	63,000	20.0%
2007	23.0	16,100	27.8%	108.0	75,600	20.0%
2008	31.0	21,700	34.8%	125.0	87,500	15.7%
2009	42.0	29,400	35.5%	145.0	101,500	16.0%

Source: Chinese Solar Industry Information, 2010–01.

Over the past decade, China's production of solar water heaters grew at an average rate of 25% per year. The total operating solar collecting area increased from 15 million m² in 1998 to over 145 million m² in 2009 (Table 3). Annual capacity has exceeded the target of 20 million m² previously planned in the Eleventh Five-Year Renewable Energy Development Plan by the National Development and Reform Commission (NDRC).[9]

In the Medium and Long-Term Development Plan for Renewable Energy in China,[10] the NDRC called for an increase in the total installed solar collecting area to 150 million m² by 2010 and

---

[9] For details, see the "Eleventh Five-Year Renewable Energy Development Plan", available at http://www.sdpc.gov.cn/nyjt/nyzywx/W02008031839087398136.pdf.

[10] English version: the Chinese Renewable Energy Industries Association (CREIA), available at http://www.creia.net/cms/upload_file/news/01f519da551602d6 bdf82bdda36bc92a.doc; Chinese version: National Development and Reform Commission (NDRC), available at http://www.ndrc.gov.cn/zcfb/zcfbtz/2007 tongzhi/W020070904607346044110.pdf.

Table 4. China's solar water heating capacity, forecast 2010–2020

Year	The National Development and Reform Commission (NDRC) Installed Capacity (m²)	Solar Thermal Utilization Committee, China Rural Energy Industry Association Installed Capacity (m²)	Area per 1,000 Inhabitants (m²)
2010	150 million	150 million	136
2015	—	379 million	260
2020	300 million	657 million	437

Source: http://www.ndrc.gov.cn/zcfb/zcfbtz/2007tongzhi/W020070904607346044110.pdf. *China New and Renewable Energy Statistical Yearbook* (2009).

300 million m² by 2020 (Table 4). In comparison, officials from the China Rural Energy Industry Association are more optimistic and estimate that total solar water heaters in operation will reach 190 million m² by 2010 and 657 million m² by 2020.[11] In the meantime, total operating capacity per 1,000 inhabitants will increase from 83.1 m² in 2007 to 437 m² in 2020.[12]

Despite the development of China's solar hot water over the past decades, per capita installation of solar hot water systems remains low, with the market penetration in most provinces below 10%. The low market penetration is indicative of a huge growth potential in China for the years to come. It is estimated that 20 to 30% of households in China will use solar hot water systems by 2015.[13] As for rural areas

---

[10] English version: the Chinese Renewable Energy Industries Association (CREIA), available at http://www.creia.net/cms/upload_file/news/01f519da551602d6 bdf82bdda36bc92a.doc; Chinese version: National Development and Reform Commission (NDRC), available at http://www.ndrc.gov.cn/zcfb/zcfbtz/2007 tongzhi/W020070904607346044110.pdf.

[11] Luo Zhentao, Huo Zhichen, Solar Thermal Utilization Committee, China Rural Energy Industry Association. *China New and Renewable Energy Statistical Yearbook (2009)*, 186–187.

[12] Ibid.

[13] Former State Economic and Trade Commission (SETC 原国家经济贸易委员会), "Key Points of 2000–2015 New and Renewable Energy Industry Development Plan (2000–2015 年新能源和可再生能源产业发展规划要点)", *China Economic and Trade Herald* 21 (2001), 25–28.

and townships, the availability of SWH will account for 60% by the year 2020.[14]

In this sense, a prefecture-level city in Shandong Province, Rizhao, meaning "City of Sunshine" in Chinese, takes the lead with a penetration of close to 100% of urban housing and 30% of rural homes.[15] In 2008, Rizhao joined the Climate Neutral Network[16] and was recognized by the United Nations Environmental Programme (UNEP) as one of the "trailblazers on the route to zero emission" cities.[17] In terms of air quality, Rizhao is consistently among the top ten cities in China. The example shows that it is possible to push forward with a full coverage by SWH systems in cities endowed with rich solar energy resources.

A fairly new trend in the development of solar water heating system is its integration into buildings (太阳能热水利用系统与建筑一体化). Thanks to the joint efforts of SWH manufacturers, building design institutions, real estate developers, and to the strong political will of central and local governments, China has gained remarkable achievement in the integration of SWH and buildings for nearly ten years. Since 2000, more and more civil buildings, hotels, schools, hospitals and factories have been equipped with solar hot water systems for environmental protection and lower running costs. In the foreseeable future, the integration will be a promising arena for China's solar energy engineering.

---

[14] "Background Paper: Chinese Renewables Status Report October 2009", REN21: Renewable Energy Policy Network for the 21st Century, available at http://www. ren21.net/pdf/Background_Paper_Chinese_Renewables_Status_Report_2009.pdf.

[15] "UNEP Unveils the Climate Neutral Network to Catalyze a Transition to a Low Carbon World", United Nations Environment Programme (UNEP), available at http://www.unep.org/climateneutral/News/UNEPNews/UNEPunveilstheClimate NeutralNetwork/tabid/195/Default.aspx.

[16] The Climate Neutral Network (CN Net) is an initiative of UNEP that promotes national, regional and global action and involvement in climate neutrality at all levels of society. The CN Net gives participants a platform to present their strategies in climate neutrality to the world, providing visibility and inspiring others.

[17] "Climate Change: The Role of Cities", the UNEP, available at http://www. unhabitat.org/downloads/docs/2226_alt.pdf.

Olympic Village SWH system is an exemplary project of the application and a pivotal element of China's "Green Olympics" concept in 2008. The 6,000 m² SWH system was installed on rooftops as a unified entity, supplying hot bathing water for 16,800 athletes during the Beijing Olympic Games. It has thereafter been used to cover the daily hot water needs of all the 2,000 households in the village. The system annually saves 10 million kWh of electricity, 2,400 tons of standard coal and 8,000 tons of CO_2 emissions.[18] The most recent large-scale installation of SWH in China is a 5,450 m² of SWH mounted on 20 dormitory buildings of Zhongshan University in Guangdong for the use of over 8,000 students.[19]

For industrial applications, so far the world's largest solar water heating system in operation is in Changshu (Jiangsu Province, China). It was recently completed to supply industrial hot water for a textile-dyeing factory. The system of over 10,000 units of solar water heaters has a thermal collecting area of 15,000 m². It is estimated that it will annually reduce 3.9 million *yuan* in energy cost, 3,500 tons of standard coal and 9,000 tons of CO_2 emission for the company.[20] As shown by the residential and industrial applications, building-integrated SWH systems, if popularized nationwide, will contribute immensely to energy conservation and emission reduction.

Apart from solar hot water, building-integrated space heating, ventilation and air-conditioning (HVAC) technologies have been promoted as another promising area for solar thermal utilization. The most widely applied solar air-conditioning technology in China today is solar space heating. Figure 4 reveals that space heating fuelled by coal in north China alone takes up as high as 45% of the total national urban building energy consumption (for more details, see

---

[18] "Green Olympics Boosts China's Solar Energy Industry", *Economic Information Daily* (经济参考报), 30 July 2008, online edition, available at http://jjckb. xinhuanet.com/wzpd/2008-07/30/content_110554.htm.

[19] "Southern China: Large-Scale Installations of Flat Plate Collectors", Global Solar Thermal Energy Council, 7 January 2010, available at http://www.solarthermal world.org/node/1007.

[20] "The World's Largest Solar Water Heating System Starts Operation in Changshu", *China Economic News Net*, 15 March 2010, available at http://www.jjxww.com/ html/show.aspx?id=163873&cid=211.

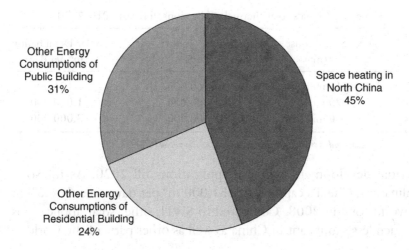

Fig. 4. Urban building energy consumption in China, 2009.

Source: W. G. Cai, Y. Wu, Y. Zhong and H. Ren, "China Building Energy Consumption: Situation, Challenges and Corresponding Measures". *Energy Policy* 37 (2009), 2054–2059.

Appendix 4). Seeing that the consumption of coal can be partly replaced by solar energy, it is expected that China's space heating will see enhanced energy efficiency to a great extent.

The solar cooling technology to cool buildings is another eye-catcher. It is most appropriate for cities with high intensity of solar radiation in summer. With its multiple functions of air heating in winter and cooling in summer, the application has great market potential in China. Successful examples of the pilot projects include Tianpu New Energy Demonstration Building and Beiyuan Solar Energy Pilot Project. Moreover, adsorption chillers jointly developed by Shanghai Jiao Tong University (SJTU) and Jiangsu Shuangliang Air Conditioner Equipment Co., Ltd. are commercially available.[21]

In addition to solar water heating and solar air-conditioning, other solar thermal technologies have also been in use, such as solar house, solar cooking (solar cooker) and solar distillation (desalination of seawater for human consumption or irrigation). Table 5 shows the

---

[21] D.W. Wu and R.Z. Wang, "Combined Cooling, Heating and Power: A Review", *Progress in Energy and Combustion Science* 32 (September–November 2006), 459–495.

Table 5. China's solar thermal applications, forecast 2010–2020

Year	Solar House (m^2)	Solar Cooker (unit)	Solar Desalination (m^3 per day)
2008	15 million	2,960,000	151,000
2010	20 million	4,000,000	1,000,000
2020	30 million	5,000,000	3,000,000

Source: *China New and Renewable Energy Statistical Yearbook* (2009).

potential development of these applications till 2020. As for solar desalination, China's capacity of 151,000 m^3 per day was only 0.3% of the world total in 2008. Compared to SWH, other solar applications are much less significant in China as well as other parts of the world.

GOVERNMENT POLICIES, REGULATIONS AND STANDARDS

The Chinese government had been active in the initial stage of the development of the SWH industry, including R&D and trial production. The first National Experience Sharing Session on Solar Energy Utilization held in 1975 marked the starting point of China's strategic development of the SWH technology. Since then, SWH R&D has been incorporated into the state plan, namely the Sixth, Seventh and Eighth Five-Year Plans (1981–1985; 1986–1990; 1991–1995), and has received special funding and material support.

After SWH production was commercialized and the Energy Conservation Law took effect in the watershed year of 1998, the Chinese government left development of the industry mainly to the mercy of the market (Table 6). However, it established the Innovation Fund to provide finance at zero or discounted interest rates to those technology-based firms at their infant stage.[22] The years after 2005 saw a new round of government involvement in the application but financial support was restricted to pilot projects of building-integrated

---

[22] The Innovation Fund is a special government fund set up upon the approval of the State Council in 1999. It aims to support technological innovations by technology-based firms at infant stage by providing various types of financial support.

Table 6. Solar thermal development in China

Phase	Year	Milestones
R&D (Government subsidies)	1975	The first National Experience Sharing Session on Solar Energy Utilization was held in Anyang, Henan Province
	1979	Beijing Solar Energy Research Institute (BSERI) was founded
	1980	The first issues of *Solar Energy Learning Paper* and *Solar Energy* (journals)
	1985	Solar-selective absorbing coating for all-glass evacuated heat-collecting tubes was successfully developed
Pilot Run (Government subsidies; Discount bank loans)	1989	Tsinghua University finished the development and application of glass evacuated-tube SWH technology with trial production
	1993	Tsinghua Solar Systems Ltd started small-scale production
	1995	The 9th Five-Year Plan and Plan through 2010 on Building Energy Conservation
	1998	China started commercialization of SWH
Commercialization (Market competition; Innovation Fund for technology-based firms at infant stage)	1998	The Energy Conservation Law was put into effect on 1 January 1998 (amended in 2008)
	2001	The 10th Five-Year Plan on New and Renewable Energy Industry
	2001	Outlines and Technical Guidelines for the Construction of Green Ecological Residential Quarter by the former Ministry of Construction
	2006	The Renewable Energy Law was enacted
Large-scale Promotion and Building-Integration (Market competition; Government subsidies for pilot projects of building-integrated solar systems)	2006	The 11th Five-Year Plan on Renewable Energy Development by the NDRC
	2006	Technical Specification for Application of SWH in Civil Buildings
	2006	Green Building Evaluation Criteria
	2007	The Enforcement Plan to Promote Solar Thermal Utilizations Nationwide
	2008	The Ordinance on Energy-Saving of Civil Buildings
	2008	The Solar Energy Standardization Committee was founded
	2009	2009 Tasks for Energy Conservation and Emission Reduction by the State Council
	2009	Household Appliances to Rural Areas

Source: Authors' compilation.

solar systems. The application was listed as one of the most important technologies to be promoted during the Eleventh Five-Year plan (2006–2010).[23] Accordingly, a number of standards, technical specifications and programs were successively announced in recent years.

The revolutionary Renewable Energy Law in 2006 also requires real estate enterprises to provide necessary conditions for the utilization of solar energy in the design and construction of buildings.[24] In the same year, the Ministry of Housing and Urban-Rural Development (MOHURD, former Ministry of Construction) published the Technical Specification for Application of SWH in Civil Buildings, which set standards for building-integrated SWH systems.[25]

The following year witnessed a new round of energy saving and emission reduction campaign launched nationwide. In April 2007, the NDRC and the MOHURD jointly organized a National Solar Thermal Utilization Conference and issued the Enforcement Plan to Promote Solar Thermal Utilizations Nationwide. The plan encouraged local governments to push forward with the construction of solar energy integrated buildings and make SWH compulsory.[26] Thereafter, a number of local governments mandated that all newly built and rebuilt residential buildings at 12 stories or below must be installed with SWH systems.[27] At present, provinces like Jiangsu, Hainan, cities like Beijing, Dalian, Shenyang, Wuhan, Kunming, Nanjing, Xiamen,

[23] '建设部十一五' 可再生能源建筑应用推广技术目录", Ministry of Housing and Urban-Rural Development, 5 September 2007, available at http://www.mohurd.gov.cn/zcfg/jswj/jskj/200709/P020080423544718280874.xls.
[24] The Renewable Energy Law, approved by the Standing Committee of the National People's Congress (NPC) of the People's Republic of China in the 14th Session on 28 February 2005 and put into effect on 1 January 2006.
[25] Ministry of Housing and Urban-Rural Development, Circular No. 394, 5 December 2005, available at http://www.bjjs.gov.cn/publish/portal0/tab1647/info43816.htm.
[26] "Recommendations for Improving the Effectiveness of Renewable Energy Policies in China", *REN21* (Renewable Energy Policy Network for the 21st Century), October 2009, available at www.ren21.net/pdf/Recommendations_for_RE_Policies_in_China.pdf.
[27] Eric Martinot and Li Junfeng, "Powering China's Development: The Role of Renewable Energy", *Worldwatch Institute*, November 2007, Worldwatch Report 175.

Zhengzhou, Shijiazhuang, Shenzhen, Jinan, Yantai, Guangzhou, Jining, and prefecture-level cities like Rizhao, Dezhou, are among the local governments implementing the mandate.[28]

The most aggressive plan to promote SWH integrated buildings is in Hainan. According to the Several Opinions of the State Council on Promoting the Construction and Development of the International Tourist Island in Hainan, one of the six "strategic orientations" is to build Hainan into a pilot eco-province (eco-friendly province) of the nation.[29] From 2010, the Hainan government will extend fiscal support to promote the construction of SWH integrated buildings. It aims to have a total of 45 million m² of such buildings by the year 2015.[30]

In 2008, the State Council released the Ordinance on Energy-Saving of Civil Buildings. For all regions rich in solar energy resources, local government should encourage and support organizations, companies or individuals to make use of SWH, solar space heating and cooling systems in existing and newly built buildings. Governments at or above the county level should subsidize the SWH building integration. Any real estate developers in violation of the ordinance or specifications related to the construction of green civil buildings are subject to penalties, penal liabilities, or revocation of the qualification certificate.[31]

Government subsidies and special funds in favour of solar thermal applications were also in place. In terms of subsidies for rural end-users, the most recent initiative is the Household Appliances to Rural Areas in early 2009, the first national rebate program for installing solar water heaters in China's rural areas.[32] The government program,

---

[28] *China New and Renewable Energy Statistical Yearbook* (2009).

[29] The State Council, No. 44, 31 December 2009, available at http://www.gov.cn/zwgk/2010-01/04/content_1502531.htm.

[30] Ministry of Housing and Urban-Rural Development, 14 January 2010, available at: http://www.mohurd.gov.cn/dfxx/201001/t20100114_199284.htm.

[31] Decree of the State Council, No. 530, 1 August 2008, available at http://www.gov.cn/zwgk/2008-08/07/content_1067038.htm.

[32] "First National Rebate Programme in China", Global Solar Thermal Energy Council, 30 April 2009, available at http://www.solarthermalworld.org/node/559.

with a 13% subsidy, encouraged rural use of household electric appliances, including solar water heaters. The move further promoted the expansion of SWH market in China.

Another circular jointly issued by the Ministry of Finance and MOHURD in 2009 (No. 305) states that China will subsidize renewable energy utilizations in urban cities.[33] The central government would allocate financial grants to local governments for the installation of renewable energy facilities, particularly building-integrated solar systems, to residential houses, schools, hotels, and other public buildings. Cities with no less than 2 million m² of such applications are classified as pilot eco-cities. In each province, up to three eco-cities will each receive a subsidy of 50 to 80 million *yuan*.[34] A similar circular by the two ministries (No. 306) promotes renewable energy applications, particularly solar houses and solar public bathing houses in rural areas. Counties with no less than 300,000 m² of such applications are pilot eco-counties. The government will subsidize 15 *yuan* per m² to SWH applications and 60% of the newly added investment into the construction of solar houses in these counties.[35]

SOLAR WATER HEATING TECHNOLOGIES, MANUFACTURING, AND EXPORT

In the manufacturing of solar collectors and solar water heaters, China developed its core technology which is leading in the world.

---

[33] "China to Subsidize Renewable Energy Buildings and Projects in Pilot Areas", 9 July 2009, Chinese Government Official Website, available at http://www.gov.cn/english/2009-07/09/content_1361321.htm.

[34] The Ministry of Finance and MOHURD, Circular No. 305: "*Jia kuai ke zai sheng neng yuan jian zhu ying yong cheng shi shi fan shi shi fang an de tong zhi* (加快可再生能源建筑应用城市示范实施方案的通知)", 9 July 2009, available at http://www.gov.cn/zwgk/2009–07/09/content_1360900.htm.

[35] The Ministry of Finance and MOHURD, Circular No. 306: "*Jia kuai tui jin nong cun di qu ke zai sheng neng yuan jian zhu ying yong de shi shi fang an de tong zhi* (加快推进农村地区可再生能源建筑应用的实施方案的通知)", 9 July 2009, available at http://www.gov.cn/zwgk/2009-07/09/content_1360930.htm.

The technology has been broadly commercialized, and the industrial chains for raw material processing, engineering design, product development and manufacturing, and marketing services are well established. It has promoted the production of related materials such as glass, metal, insulation materials, and vacuum equipment, etc. Solar thermal industry is one of the few industries in which the production is mostly based on China's in-house R&D.

As previously shown in Table 5, China has conducted its own R&D from 1979 when the first solar energy research institute, Beijing Solar Energy Research Insittute (BSERI) was established.[36] The following six years till 1985 witnessed a breakthrough in the government-funded R&D of heat collectors: the core technology of all-glass evacuated heat-collecting tubes, solar-selective absorbing coating was successfully developed by Tsinghua University. From 1986, Tsinghua University has started to work on the trial production based on its patent and established a company, Tsinghua Solar in 1993, which together with the BSERI finally led China's SWH industry into the new era of commercialization in 1998.[37]

Since then, China has already established a large, mature, and commercialized solar thermal industry. By the year 2009, there were more than 3,000 manufacturers of solar collectors and solar water heaters, employing over 2.5 million people.[38] Fifty of the manufacturers had an output value of over 50 million *yuan*, with a market share of 46.9%; and 25 had an output value of over 100 million *yuan*, with a market share of 31.2%.[39] The two largest manufacturers, Himin and

---

[36] Beijing Solar Energy Research Institute was later transformed into Beijing Sunda Solar Energy Technology Co., Ltd. in 1995. It is currently the seventh largest SWH manufacturer in China (see Appendix 5).

[37] Tsinghua Solar Systems Ltd. is a subsidiary of Tsinghua Holding Co., Ltd. run by Tsinghua University. It is the trailblazer of the SWH industry in China and currently the third largest SWH manufacturer domestically (see Appendix 5).

[38] "Development and Prospects of Solar Thermal Utilization in China (中国太阳能热利用行业发展状况与前景)", Chinese Solar Industry Information (中国太阳能产业资讯), 2010–01.

[39] "Background Paper: Chinese Renewables Status Report October 2009", REN21.

Sunrain, have an output value of over 1.5 billion *yuan* (top ten listed in Appendix 5). It is estimated that the market share of the leading manufacturers with an annual revenue of over 50 million *yuan* will hit 50% soon from 20% in 2001.[40]

Most Chinese SWH manufacturers are privately owned enterprises and have not received any form of government subsidies. Himin Group, the world's largest manufacturer with 6,500 employees, is one of them. Founded in 1995, Himin has established the world renowned "China Solar Valley" in Dezhou, Shandong Province, which beat British university town Oxford and Australia's Adelaide as host of the 2010 International Solar Congress (see Appendix 6).[41] In terms of the production of core components, Linuo Group is the world's largest manufacturer of solar-evacuated tubes. It raised production output by 70% in 2008 and sold the largest portion of it to the solar thermal industry.[42]

Overall, China's sales of solar collectors have been expanding at a steady pace domestically and globally. The domestic sales revenue of solar water heaters increased from 32 billion *yuan* in 2007 to 43 billion *yuan* in 2008, a growth of 34.3%, and increased by 46.5% to 63 billion *yuan* in 2009. In the global market, Chinese-made solar water heaters have been exported to more than 80 countries around the world, with the total export value rising by 20 times from US$10 million in 2001 to US$200 million in 2009 (Figure 5). The accelerating growth rate from 17.6% to no lower than 60% reflects the effectiveness of the Chinese government's active promotion of solar energy and other renewable energies since 2006. As a whole, the total export value accounts for merely 2.1% of China's total SWH sales in 2009.

---

[40] Ibid.

[41] "2010 4th International Solar Cities Initiative World Congress, Dezhou, China; September 16–19, 2010", available at http://www.chinasolarcity.cn/Html/dezhou/151113424.html.

[42] "China: Linuo Solar runs five Solar Glass Tubing Factories", 28 July 2009, available at http://www.solarthermalworld.org/node/764.

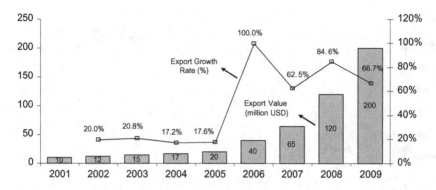

Fig. 5. China's export value of SWH, 2001–2009.

Source: The Renewable Energy Policy Network for the 21st Century.

PRODUCTION STRUCTURE AND INDUSTRY TRENDS

The unique production structure in China has to be taken into consideration. Among the two major types of collectors, evacuated-tube and flat-plate (glazed and unglazed), the former dominates China's domestic SWH markets, with a market share of 90% in comparison to the latter of 10%. In 2009, the newly added area of evacuated-tube collectors was around 40 million m^2 while that of flat-plate collectors was only 2 million m^2.[43]

In this sense, China has followed its own way in the international market. While almost all other countries focus on flat-plate SWH, China assumes almost all the productions of evacuated-tube collectors in the world (Figure 6). As for flat-plate SWH, China has nearly no unglazed collectors, while the United States and Australia take up the largest part of production for unglazed collectors. Due to the distinct focus of each country, major competitors in the world market are largely complementary to each other.

The imbalanced global production structure is attributed to two different technologies developing on different tracks. As shown in

---

[43] "Development and Prospects of Solar Thermal Utilization in China", Chinese Solar Industry Information.

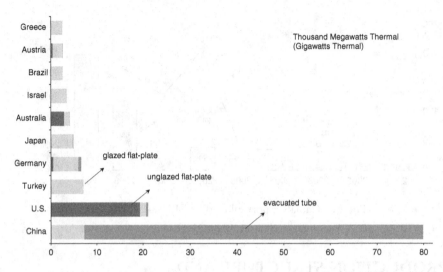

Fig. 6. World top ten SWH producers by types of collectors, 2007.

Source: International Energy Agency (IEA).

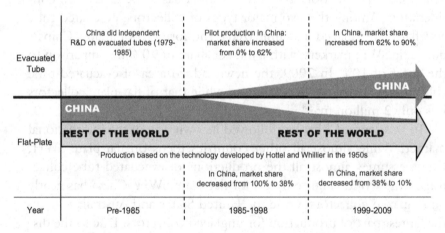

Fig. 7. Dual-track development of SWH in the world.

Source: Authors' compilation.

Figure 7 and Table 6, China followed the rest of the world in the production of flat-plate collectors till 1985 before diverging to the production of evacuated-tube collectors. This is mainly due to a dramatic drop in the cost of producing evacuated tubes, and the

Table 7. Evacuated-Tube vs. Flat-Plate

Evacuated Tube Collectors	Flat-Plate Collectors
Vacuum between concentric tubes to reduce heat loss	A network of piping through which water is circulated
Adaptable to a wide range of ambient temperatures; anti-freezing, high efficiency in cold areas	High efficiency of heating process in full sunshine conditions
Aside from solar water heating, can also be used for solar space heating and cooling	High absorber plate area to gross area ratio
	High pressure bearing, long lifetime

Source: Authors' compilation.

isolation mechanism to prevent heat loss, making such solar heat collectors applicable in cloudy, windy, cold conditions and even in freezing winter.

Despite the aforementioned advantages, the performance of evacuated-tube collectors cannot rival flat-plate collectors in various aspects (Table 7). Most importantly, flat-plate is more efficient in the integration of SWH into buildings than evacuated tubes. The reason is that flat-plate has a much higher absorber plate area to gross area ratio, which means it takes less space. In addition, it withstands pressure and is more reliable when combined into a large unified piece of collector, which itself can be a rooftop. Therefore, flat-plate, SWH and buildings can be harmoniously integrated at a comparatively lower cost, and installation and construction can be carried out at the same time.

Since the integration of solar energy into buildings is the future trend of China's solar thermal industry, China may need to rethink on its single-minded development of evacuated-tube collectors. Either increasing scientific research and technological input or a transition to a balanced production structure is required to overcome the mismatch between production and strategic planning so as to ensure a healthy development of the SWH industry in China. In addition to low-temperature SWH technologies at household level, middle- and high-temperature SWH systems should be developed to broaden the use of solar thermal in industrial (process heating for textiles, chemicals, desalination) and agricultural (food desiccation) production. Moreover, solar air-conditioning, solar house, and solar cooking are the major areas for the R&D of solar thermal technologies to be carried out in the future.

CHALLENGES AND RECOMMENDATIONS

Over the past three decades, the Chinese government has played a key role in R&D and implementation of quality control standards. However, because multiple departments for the administration of planning, design, construction and installation are involved, there is a lack of effective communication and coordination between solar thermal manufacturers and the building industry. Therefore, government institutions with integrated management functions should take the lead in addressing the problem.[44]

Second, low-quality products proliferate in the Chinese market, particularly in rural markets. Due to the low threshold in terms of start-up capital and technology, it is easy for unregulated small businesses to enter the market and cause fierce market competition. Some fake and shoddy products without after-sales services have flooded the Chinese countryside along with the Household Appliances to Rural Areas program. It is imperative for the government to strengthen market regulations, enhance product quality testing and establish market order for fair competition. On safety risks resulting from unprofessional installations, professional training and industry standards are indispensible to regulating the installation companies.

---

[44] "Background Paper: Chinese Renewables Status Report October 2009", REN21.

APPENDIX 1

China's Solar Energy Resource Distributions

Category	Annual Sunshine (hours/ year)	Annual Radiation (megajoule/m²)	Regions	Solar Energy Resources
I	3200–3300	6680–8400	North Ningxia, North Gansu, South Xinjiang, West Qinghai, West Tibet	Rich area of solar energy resources
II	3000–3200	5852–6680	Northwest Hebei, North Shanxi, South Inner Mongolia, South Ningxia, Central Gansu, East Qinghai, Southeast Tibet, South Xinjiang	Good
III	2200–3000	5016–5852	Shandong, Henan, Southeast Hebei, South Shanxi, North Xinjiang, Jilin, Liaoning, Yunnan, North Shaanxi, East Gansu, South Guangdong	Moderate
IV	1400–2200	4180–5016	Hunan, Guangxi, Jiangxi, Zhejiang, Hubei, North Fujian, North Guangdong, South Shaanxi, South Anhui	Poor
V	1000–1400	3344–4180	Sichuan, Guizhou	Poorest

Source: China Renewable Energy Industries Association (CREIA).

APPENDIX 2

Total Solar Water Heating Capacity in Operation by the Year 2007

Country	Water Collectors Megawatts Thermal (MWth)			Air Collectors Megawatts Thermal (MWth)		Total Megawatts Thermal (MWth)
	Unglazed flat-plate	Glazed flat-plate	Evacuated tube	Unglazed flat-plate	Glazed flat-plate	
China		7,280.0	72,618.0			79,898.0
United States	19,347.6	1,329.2	404.9	0.1	160.8	21,242.5
Turkey		7,105.0				7,105.0
Germany	525.0	5,448.9	604.8			6,578.7
Japan		4,777.2	89.0	304.1	8.8	5,179.0
Australia	2,849.0	1,162.0	16.1			4,027.1
Israel	16.9	3,455.8				3,472.8
Brazil	68.2	2,511.3	0.3			2,579.7
Austria	426.2	2,064.7	30.1			2,521.0
Greece		2,496.3	4.8			2,501.1
India		1,505.0	23.1		11.9	1,516.9
France	73.2	991.6				1,087.8
Switzerland	148.7	303.4	17.8	586.6		1,056.5
Taiwan		795.8	82.9			878.7
Spain	2.1	814.9	31.9			848.9

(Continued)

(*Continued*)

Country	Water Collectors Megawatts Thermal (MWth)			Air Collectors Megawatts Thermal (MWth)		Total Megawatts Thermal (MWth)
	Unglazed flat-plate	Glazed flat-plate	Evacuated tube	Unglazed flat-plate	Glazed flat-plate	
Italy	18.4	611.5	72.0			701.9
Mexico	327.3	310.7				638.0
Canada	466.1	57.2	3.3	91.0	0.1	617.8
South Africa	440.0	173.4				613.4
Jordan		588.2	5.0			593.3
Cyprus		556.3	0.7			557.0
Netherlands	240.5	230.7				471.1
Denmark	15.0	275.7	2.4	2.4	13.1	308.6
Sweden	56.0	156.1	20.3			232.4
United Kingdom		194.5	18.9			213.4
Portugal	0.4	193.2	3.8			197.5
Poland	0.9	138.5	25.7	2.1	1.8	169.0
Tunisia		151.6	1.0			152.6
Belgium	34.2	93.6	8.7			136.5
Czech Republic	10.7	68.0	10.8			89.5
New Zealand	4.4	72.0	7.0			83.4
Slovenia		81.1	0.8			81.9
Slovak Republic		61.8	6.9			68.8

(*Continued*)

(*Continued*)

Country	Water Collectors Megawatts Thermal (MWth)			Air Collectors Megawatts Thermal (MWth)		Total Megawatts Thermal (MWth)
	Unglazed flat-plate	Glazed flat-plate	Evacuated tube	Unglazed flat-plate	Glazed flat-plate	
Barbados		58.0				58.0
Thailand		49.0				49.0
Romania		48.7				48.7
Albania		35.0	0.2			35.1
Hungary	2.0	28.9	1.8			32.7
Ireland		19.4	5.5			24.9
Malta		20.6				20.6
Bulgaria		19.3				19.3
Macedonia		13.4	0.1			13.5
Luxembourg		13.2				13.2
Finland	0.4	10.9	0.9			12.2
Norway	1.1	7.9	0.1		0.8	9.9
Namibia		4.2	0.1			4.3
Lativa		3.8				3.8
Lithuania		2.4				2.4
Estonia		1.0				1.0
Total	25,074.1	46,390.8	74,119.8	986.2	197.3	146,768.2

Source: International Energy Agency (IEA). Werner Weiss, Irene Bergmann and Roman Stelzer, "Solar Heat Worldwide: Markets and Contribution to the Energy Supply 2007 (2009 Edition)".

APPENDIX 3

Oil Equivalent and CO_2 Reduction of Solar Thermal Applications by the Year 2007

Country	Total collector area [m²]	Total capacity [MWth]	Collector yield [GWh/a]	Collector yield [TJ/a]	Energy savings — oil equivalent [t/a]	CO_2 reduction [t/a]
China	114,140,000	79,898	49,217	177,182	6,596,379	21,467,451
United States	30,116,580	21,082	8,848	31,854	1,275,576	4,143,322
Turkey	10,150,000	7,105	6,051	21,782	807,694	2,626,236
Israel	4,961,100	3,473	3,644	13,118	492,169	1,597,153
Germany	9,398,077	6,579	3,457	12,445	420,310	1,365,272
Japan	6,951,638	4,866	3,317	11,939	418,424	1,359,003
Greece	3,573,000	2,501	1,883	6,779	331,672	1,078,740
Australia	5,753,000	4,027	2,192	7,892	323,918	1,052,261
India	2,150,000	1,505	1,929	6,943	271,352	881,500
Brazil	3,685,291	2,580	1,598	5,753	238,859	775,847
Austria	3,601,431	2,521	1,205	4,336	152,307	494,756
Jordan	847,532	593	595	2,141	103,247	335,330
Taiwan	1,255,340	879	630	2,266	93,586	304,420
Spain	1,212,764	849	739	2,662	93,614	304,089
France	1,554,000	1,088	516	1,859	76,850	249,321
Cyprus	795,710	557	499	1,797	71,911	233,427
Mexico	911,473	638	436	1,569	69,380	225,359
Italy	1,002,650	702	424	1,528	56,450	183,336

(Continued)

(Continued)

Country	Total collector area [m²]	Total capacity [MWth]	Collector yield [GWh/a]	Collector yield [TJ/a]	Energy savings — oil equivalent [t/a]	CO_2 reduction [t/a]
South Africa	876,290	613	227	815	32,345	105,018
Tunisia	218,000	153	145	524	27,010	87,800
Canada	752,422	527	183	659	25,187	81,813
Portugal	282,109	198	177	637	24,275	78,848
Switzerland	671,310	470	196	705	23,664	76,853
Netherlands	673,033	471	163	586	18,809	61,072
Denmark	418,630	293	141	506	16,681	54,178
United Kingdom	304,920	213	102	366	12,211	39,670
Sweden	332,000	232	125	449	11,976	38,887
Barbados	82,794	58	68	243	10,119	32,848
Poland	235,897	165	77	275	9,795	31,795
Thailand	70,000	49	48	172	9,937	31,483
Belgium	194,946	137	65	233	7,824	25,412
Slovenia	116,965	82	42	152	5,205	16,898
Romania	69,600	49	32	116	5,086	16,530
Slovak Republic	98,215	69	39	142	4,950	16,075
Czech Republic	127,810	90	40	144	4,795	15,509
New Zealand	119,177	83	35	127	4,723	15,346
Malta	29,360	21	9	33	2,818	9,153
Hungary	46,700	33	16	57	2,511	8,162

(Continued)

(*Continued*)

Country	Total collector area [m²]	Total capacity [MWth]	Collector yield [GWh/a]	Collector yield [TJ/a]	Energy savings — oil equivalent [t/a]	CO₂ reduction [t/a]
Bulgaria	27,600	19	12	43	2,075	6,734
Ireland	35,567	25	12	42	1,300	4,215
Macedonia	19,270	14	7	26	1,251	4,061
Albania	50,176	35	7	25	1,153	3,745
Luxembourg	18,900	13	7	24	762	2,481
Finland	17,385	12	5	20	602	1,956
Namibia	6,169	4	3	11	599	1,932
Norway	12,970	9	4	15	452	1,467
Lativa	5,350	4	2	7	208	677
Lithuania	3,450	2	1	4	135	439
Estonia	1,470	1	1	2	52	171
Total	207,978,070	145,585	89,168	321,004	12,162,209	39,548,052

Notes: MWth = megawatt thermal; GWh/a = gigawatt hour per annum;
  TJ/a = terajoule per annum; t/a = tons per annum.

Source: International Energy Agency (IEA). Werner Weiss, Irene Bergmann and Roman Stelzer, "Solar Heat Worldwide: Markets and Contribution to the Energy Supply 2007 (2009 Edition)".

APPENDIX 4

Urban Building Energy Consumption in China

Category	Building area (billion m^2)	Energy consumption efficiency (kWh/m^2)	Building energy consumption per year (billion kWh)	Percentage
Urban area for space heating (North China)	6.5	57	370	45%
Urban area exc. space heating				
Residential	10.0	10–30	200	24%
Commercial	6.0	20–300	260	31%
Total	22.5	25	830	100%

Reproduced from: W. G. Cai, Y. Wu, Y. Zhong and H. Ren, "China Building Energy Consumption: Situation, Challenges and Corresponding Measures", *Energy Policy* 37 (2009), 2054–2059.

APPENDIX 5

Top Ten in China's SWH Industry

Ranking	Manufacturer	Ownership	Brand
1	Himin Solar Energy Group Co., Ltd. 皇明太阳能集团有限公司	Private	Himin 皇明
2	Jiangsu Sunrain Solar Energy Co., Ltd. 江苏太阳雨太阳能有限公司	Private	Sunrain 太阳雨
3	Tsinghua Solar Systems Ltd. 清华阳光公司	State	Tsinghua Solar 清华阳光
4	Beijing Tianpu Solar Energy Group 北京天普太阳能工业有限公司	Private	Tianpu 天普
5	Beijing Sijimicoe Solar Energy Co., Ltd. 北京四季沐歌太阳能技术有限公司	Private	Sijimicoe 四季沐歌
6	Jiangsu Sunshore Solar Energy Industry Co., Ltd. 江苏桑夏太阳能产业有限公司	Private	Sunshore 桑夏
7	Beijing Sunda Solar Energy Technology Co., Ltd. 北京市太阳能研究所有限公司	State	Sunpo 桑普
8	Jiangsu Huayang Solar Energy Co., Ltd. 江苏省华扬太阳能有限公司	Private	Huayang 华扬
9	Guangdong Five Star Solar Energy Co., Ltd. 广东五星太阳能有限公司	Private	Five Star 五星
10	Zhejiang Meida Solar Energy Co., Ltd. 浙江美大太阳能工业有限公司	Private	Meida 美大

Source: Chinese Solar Industry Information Net.

APPENDIX 6

Himin: I Have a Dream

"...I have a dream that one day throughout the whole world, renewable energy resources will take the dominant position..."

"...I have a dream that one day the solar industry will be as advanced as the IT industry, as mature as the electric home appliances industry, and as large-scale and automatic as the automobile industry..."

— Himin Group

Chairman

Huang Ming, Chairman of the Himin Solar Energy Group, is reported as the leader of the 56 deputies to the National People's Congress to bring forward the bill of the Renewable Energy Law in 2003. He has even given a speech on the "Himin Model" during the 14th session of United Nations Commission on Sustainable Development (CSD-14) in May of 2006 and was elected Vice President of an UN-accredited NGO, the International Solar Energy Society (ISES), in 2008. He was also invited by UNESCAP* to attend the Asia-Pacific Business Forum 2010: Business Opportunities and Low-Carbon Economy (April 2010) held in Kunming, China.

China Solar Valley

Himin started the construction of "China's Solar Valley" since 2004 because the concept of a solar valley "demonstrates to the international community everything that solar energy can do". According to Huang Ming, the decision was part of the company's strategy to transform Solar Valley from an R&D centre into an area of eco-friendly residential buildings covering a wide range of solar technologies. The cluster in Dezhou covers an area of over 330 hectares and will be developed as the country's centre of solar thermal production, logistics, research and quality testing.

Sun-Moon Mansion: Landmark of World Solar Energy

The headquarters of Himin Group, Sun-Moon Mansion, is also located in the valley. It's the largest single solar architecture in the world with an energy conservation rate of up to 88%. With a floor area of 75,000 m², the building functions include display, working, R&D, meeting, training, hotel, recreation, etc. Technologies of solar air collectors, seasonal heat storage, solar heating and cooling, ceiling radiation, intelligent control and geothermal system provides hot water, cooling in summer and heating in winter, while those of PV power generation, PV lighting, building-integrated PV (BIPV) brightens the building in the evening. Besides, Winpin energy-saving glass, sun-shading panels, external wall insulation, roof gardens, rain-water collection and water treatment systems reduce energy consumption of this building. It can save 2,640 tons of standard coal, 6,600,000 kWh of electricity and reduce pollution by 8,672.4 ton. Furthermore, integrating solar technologies with architecture has enlightened the way of modern construction.

Sources:

1.   Himin Solar Energy Group.
2.   Global Solar Thermal Energy Council.
3.   "2010 4th World Congress, Dezhou, China; September 16–19, 2010", available at http://www.chinasolarcity.cn/Html/dezhou/151113424.html.

*UNESCAP: United Nations Economic and Social Commission for Asia and the Pacific.

8

Harvesting Sunlight: Solar Photovoltaic Industry in China

Mu YANG and Rongfang PAN

While China has been successful in the utilization of solar energy in terms of solar thermal applications, solar photovoltaics (PV) for electric power generation is only a fledgling industry in China. Despite the fact that China is the world's largest solar cell producer, the development of China's solar PV market has been sluggish. It was only in recent years that the installed capacity saw a moderate growth in the country. In the meantime, the focus is now undergoing a transition from off-grid to grid-connected applications, including building-integrated PV systems and large-scale PV power stations. In the future, the domestic market has to be explored and the cost of solar electricity has to be reduced by developing the research and development of solar PV technologies.

SUNNY DAYS AHEAD FOR CHINA'S SOLAR PHOTOVOLTAIC INDUSTRY

China is rich in solar energy resources. In its vast 9.6 million km^2 territory, over two-thirds annually receive annual sunshine in excess of 2,200 hours and a radiation of over 5,000 megajoules per square metre (MJ/m^2).[1] At present, only a drop in the ocean of the energy has been utilized throughout human history. So far the exploration of solar energy is mainly divided into two categories, solar thermal for the use of solar heat and solar photovoltaic (PV) for electric power generation.

While China has been successful in the utilization of solar energy in terms of solar thermal applications, solar PV for electric power generation is currently a fledgling industry in China. Photovoltaic, with "photo" meaning light and "voltaic" meaning electricity, literally refers to generating electricity from light.

Solar PV is one of the most promising technologies in the strategic development of renewable energies domestically and internationally. Like solar thermal utilization, solar PV produces no noise, harmful emissions or polluting gases; it can be quickly installed and requires minimal maintenance; and most importantly, the fuel, solar energy, is free. As fossil energies are now being depleted worldwide, solar PV is considered a future substitute for fossil-fired electric power generation.

Although solar PV currently only takes up a tiny share of electric power generation in the whole world, it is likely to dominate primary energy supply in the long run. According to a projection by the European Commission Joint Research Center, solar PV and thermal power generation is expected to account for over 10% of world electricity supply by the year 2030, 20% by the year 2040, and 60% by the end of the 21st century.[2] Similarly, a newly released roadmap by the

---

[1] China Renewable Energy Industries Association.
[2] European Commission Joint Research Centre (2004) "European Roadmap for PV R&D", p. 11.

International Energy Agency (IEA) estimates that solar electricity, including solar PV and solar thermal electricity, will represent up to 20 to 25% of global electricity by 2050.[3]

The insignificant proportion of solar PV in power supply is mainly due to the high cost of producing the core component part — solar cells. In comparison to traditional power generation, the cost is high enough to impede the development of solar PV if it simply relies on market force (Table 1). Solar power generation is also more costly than other types of new energy power, such as wind and nuclear power. Solar PV power generation only saw larger market shares in countries receiving government financial support for development of the industry.

Table 1. Comparison of on-grid power prices in China, 2009

Power Generation	Investment Cost (*yuan* per kilowatt)	On-grid Power Price (*yuan* per kilowatt hour)
Coal-fired Electricity	4,500	0.2749 ~ 0.4792
Hydro Electricity	7,000	0.14 ~ 0.40
Wind Power	7,000 to 9,000	0.51 ~ 0.61
Nuclear Power	12,000	0.414 ~ 0.471
Solar PV	35,000	4.0 (205 kW PV power plant in Inner Mongolia and 1 MW PV power plant in Shanghai)
		1.09 (10 MW PV power plant in Gansu)
		1.15 (four PV power plants in Ningxia)

Sources: All China Marketing Research (ACMR), "2008–2009 China Solar PV Industry Report"; NDRC, *Fa gai jia ge* [2010] No. 653, 2 April 2010.
kW: kilowatt, equal to one thousand watts.
MW: megawatt, equal to one million watts.
kWh: kilowatt hour is a unit of energy equal to one thousand watt hours. Energy in watt hours is the multiplication of power in watts and time in hours.

---

[3] "IEA sees Great Potential for Solar, Providing up to a Quarter of World Electricity by 2050", International Energy Agency (IEA), 11 May 2010, available at: http://www.iea.org/press/pressdetail.asp?PRESS_REL_ID=301.

In this respect, most of the top ten solar PV markets in the world benefit from fiscal incentives (see Appendix 1 and Table 2). Various types of subsidies such as fixed asset investment and subsidies for grid-connection or distribution of solar electricity were adopted by different countries. The feed-in tariff adopted by many European countries such as Germany, Spain and Italy has proved its efficiency in developing the solar electricity market. Similarly, a reduction in the tax liability for solar PV investment in the United States, namely the Investment Tax Credit (ITC), and a government subsidy policy covering the capital cost of PV system installations in Japan have helped to make them leaders in PV development worldwide.

Table 2.   World top ten solar PV installed capacity, 2008–2009

Rank 2009	Country	2009			2008		
		Total Installed Capacity (MW)	Growth Rate %	Share of World Total %	Total Installed Capacity %	Growth Rate %	Share of World Total %
1	Germany	3,800	90	52.7	2,002	81	31.9
2	Italy	730	116	10.1	338	383	5.4
3	Japan	484	110	6.7	230	10	3.7
4	USA	477	39	6.6	342	65	5.4
5	Czech Republic	411	706	5.7	51	1600	0.8
6	Belgium	292	484	4.0	50	178	0.8
7	France	185	302	2.6	46	318	0.7
8	China	160	256	2.2	45	125	0.7
9	Spain	69	−97	1.0	2,605	365	41.5
10	Greece	36	227	0.5	11	450	0.2
	Rest of the World	572	2	7.9	563	154	9.0
	World Total	7,216	15	100.0	6,283	159	100.0

Source: European Photovoltaic Industry Association, "Global Market Outlook for PV until 2014".

In comparison, China's share in the world's solar PV market was relatively insignificant due to a variety of reasons, including backward technologies and a lack of feed-in tariff. Since the application of the first solar cells in the "No. 2 East Red Satellite" in 1971, the development of China's solar PV applications has been sluggish. It is only after 2002 when the National Development and Planning Commission (NDRC) initiated a number of programs to solve power supply problems in rural areas that a real solar PV market has been gradually developed, albeit small in size. Since 2006, China's domestic PV market growth has picked up pace dramatically (Figure 1).

The Renewable Energy Law enacted in 2006 has provided a legal framework underpinning solar power generation. Referring to its provisions, grid companies are required to buy all of the electricity generated by solar PV systems within the coverage of their power grid, and provide grid-connecting services. The grid power price for renewable energy power generation projects shall be determined by the pricing authorities of the State Council according to the principle

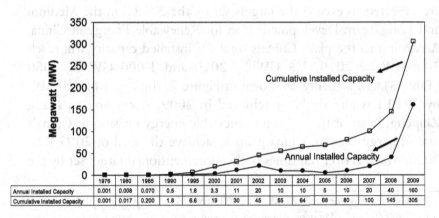

	1976	1980	1985	1990	1995	2000	2001	2002	2003	2004	2005	2006	2007	2008	2009
Annual Installed Capacity	0.001	0.008	0.070	0.5	1.6	3.3	11	20	10	10	5	10	20	40	160
Cumulative Installed Capacity	0.001	0.017	0.200	1.8	6.6	19	30	45	55	64	68	80	100	145	305

Fig. 1. Solar PV Installed capacity in China (1976–2009).

Sources: Renewable Energy Policy Network for the 21st Century (REN21); The European Photovoltaic Industry Association (EPIA).

of being "beneficial to the development and utilization of renewable energy and being economical and reasonable". In addition, the cost difference between the renewable energy power and traditional power should be shared in the national grid network by levying additional tariffs on electricity users. Amended at the end of 2009, the law has worked as a shot in the arm to the development of grid-connected solar PV in China.

China's solar PV industry witnessed a dramatic change in 2009, which is hailed as "the Dawn of a New Era".[4] For the first time, China's share in the world's solar PV market exceeded 1%, ranking among the top ten in the world (Table 2). In this single year, China's solar PV market experienced an expansion of 160 MW, which is larger than the cumulative installed capacity of 140 MW over the past three decades. A number of organizations estimate that the coming years will see an explosion of growth in China's solar PV market. This is mainly attributed to the spate of government incentive policies and programs aiming to boost the industry. Furthermore, lowering cost as a result of technological improvement and economy of scale also plays a pivotal role.

Under such circumstances, solar PV power installations in China are expected to exceed the targets set by the NDRC in the Medium and Long-Term Development Plan for Renewable Energy in China. According to the plan, China's total PV installed capacity will reach 300 MW by 2010, 1.8 GW by 2020 and 1,000 GW by 2050 (Table 3).[5] In actuality, as shown in Figure 2, the target of 300 MW by 2010 has already been achieved in 2009. According to Liang Zhipeng, head of the new and renewable energy division in China's State Energy Bureau, China plans to achieve the goal of 20 GW by 2020, which is over ten times of the aforementioned target set by the

---

[4] The Green Leap Forward, 27 March 2009, available at http://greenleapforward.com/2009/03/27/dawn-of-a-new-era-the-gansu-solar-concession-and-landmark-solar-roofs-program/.

[5] MW, short for megawatt, equals one thousand kilowatts; GW, short for gigawatt, equals one million kilowatts.

Table 3. Targets of solar PV installation in China (2010–2020)

Year	NDRC in 2007 (MW)	NDRC in 2009 (MW)	CREIA in 2009 (MW)	SEMI in 2009 (MW)
2010	300	500	1,000	745
2020	1,800	20,000	20,000	28,000

Sources: National Development and Planning Commission (NDRC); Chinese Renewable Energy Industry Association (CREIA); and Semiconductor Equipment and Materials International (SEMI).

NDRC in 2007.[6] Similarly, a white paper issued by the PV group of the Semiconductor Equipment and Materials International (SEMI) suggests that the targets for China's solar power capacity by 2010 and 2020 should respectively be adjusted to 745 MW and 28 GW.[7]

SOLAR PHOTOVOLTAIC APPLICATIONS IN CHINA

The PV technology is used in a variety of applications, which are categorized mainly under two types of system: grid-connected and off-grid (for more details, see Appendix 2). Due to a lack of access to national power grid in remote areas, off-grid applications dominate the PV market in China. Before 2008, off-grid PV systems accounted for as high as 94% of the market whilst that of grid-connected applications took only 6% (Table 4). However, the market share of grid-connected PV systems increased to 18% in 2008 due to a strategic shift to the construction of large-scale grid-connected PV (LSPV) power plants and building-integrated photovoltaic (BIPV) systems.

---

[6] "China's Solar Power Capacity Will Reach 20 mln KW in 2020", *People's Daily*, 7 December 2009, online edition, available at http://english.peopledaily.com.cn/90001/90778/90860/6834016.html.

[7] "China's Solar Future — A Preliminary Report on a Recommended China PV Policy Roadmap", Semiconductor Equipment and Materials International (SEMI), May 2009, available at http://www.pvgroup.org/cms/groups/public/documents/web_content/CTR_029841.pdf.

Table 4.   Market share of PV applications in China 2006–2008; forecast for 2010 and 2020

Types	Applications	Cumulative Installed Capacity (MW)					Market Share (%)				
		2006	2007	2008	2010	2020	2006	2007	2008	2010	2020
Off-grid	Rural Electrification	33	42	47	80	200	41	42	34	32	12.5
	Communication and Industrial Applications	27	30	35	40	100	34	30	25	16	6.3
	Electrical Appliances	16	22	33	30	100	20	22	24	12	6.3
On-grid	BIPV*	4	6	25	50	1,000	5	6	18	20	62.5
	LSPV*				50	200				20	12.5
	Total	80	100	140	250	1,600	100	100	100	100	100

Sources: China Renewable Energy Society (2006–2008) and National Development and Planning Commission (forecast for 2010 and 2020).
BIPV: building-integrated photovoltaic, which means grid-connected solar PV systems in buildings.
LSPV: large-scale grid-connected power plants.

According to the NDRC, grid-connected solar PV systems, particularly BIPV, will dominate the future development of the industry. As Table 4 shows, the market share of BIPV is estimated to increase to 20% in 2010 and 62.5% in 2020. As for LSPV, the share may first increase to 20% in 2010 but fall back to 12.5% in 2020.

Rural electrification takes up the largest share of solar PV applications in China. This is mainly attributed to the national Brightness Program launched by the NDRC (former State Development Planning Commission) in response to the World Solar Summit in 1996. It was designed to make electricity available in remote areas where there was no access to electricity. Using renewable technologies, it aims to provide electricity for 23 million people with an average capacity of 100 W per person by the end of 2010. Pilot projects include 30,000 household-scale solar PV systems and 40 village-scale solar PV systems in Inner Mongolia, Gansu, Tibet, Xinjiang, and Qinghai. This "brightness" initiative, focusing on the western provinces, has been progressing in stages.

The first is an ambitious plan known as the Township Electrification Program (*song dian dao xiang*) launched in 2002. By 2005, it ended up providing renewable electricity to 1.3 million people (around 300,000 households) in 1,065 townships in western provinces: Gansu, Inner Mongolia, Shaanxi, Sichuan, Xinjiang, Qinghai and Tibet, etc.[8] A mix of small hydro, solar PV, wind power, and PV-wind hybrid systems was used. As the world's largest rural electrification program, it involved a government investment of 1.6 billion *yuan* and financial support from the World Bank (WB) to subsidize the capital costs of equipment for a total installation of 15.5 MW (see Table 5 and Appendix 3).[9]

The program is being succeeded by a similar but larger China Village Electrification Program (*song dian dao cun*), which plans to electrify 3.5 million households in 10,000 villages with renewables by 2010 and to achieve full rural electrification by 2015.[10] By providing electricity service to rural areas, the two programs help develope the

Table 5. PV installed capacity in the Township Electrification Program

Province	Number of Townships	Installed Capacity (kilowatts)	Total Investment (million *yuan*)	NDRC grant (%)	Provincial grant (%)
Xinjiang	48	1,932	177	50	50
Qinghai	86	2,600	266	80	20
Gansu	12	1,230	113	50	50
Inner Mongolia	39	1,362	68	50	50
Shaanxi	10	70	8	50	50
Sichuan	51	1,600	180	50	50
Tibet	350	6,700	800	100	0
Total	596	15,494	1,612	—	—

Source: NREL, "Renewable Energy in China: Township Electrification Program".

---

[8] *China Solar PV Report 2007*, China Environmental Science Press.
[9] Ibid.
[10] "Renewables Global Status Report 2006", Renewable Energy Policy Network for the 21st Century, available at http://www.ren21.net/pdf/RE_GSR_2006_Update.pdf.

solar industry, promote local economic development, as well as improve living conditions. Implementation of the two programs accounts for a large proportion of rural electrification in China's installations of solar PV systems.

In terms of on-grid PV systems, building-integrated photo-voltaics (BIPV) and large-scale PV power plants (LSPV) have been underdeveloped in China compared to most other countries. While grid-connected systems are the most popular type of applications in the world PV market, the market share of on-grid systems in China was only 18% by 2008 (Table 4). Since the Ninth Five-Year Plan (1996–2010), pilot projects partly financed by the central and local governments have played a key role in promoting BIPV and LSPV.

National-level projects include on-grid PV applications in international extravaganzas such as the Beijing 2008 Olympic Games and the Shanghai 2010 World Expo, which are respectively labelled "green" and "better life". While the 2008 Olympics was characteristic of thermal applications of solar energy, the World Expo 2010 is a showcase of solar power generation, particularly BIPV technology (see Appendix 4).

At the same time, some local governments, including Shanghai, Beijing, Jiangsu, Zhejiang, Guangdong also launched BIPV pilot projects in their urban areas. Among the projects, Shanghai's 100,000 Solar PV Roof Plan from 2006 to 2010 is the most remarkable one, with an estimated total installed capacity of 400 MW.[11] Amazingly, the world's largest stand-above BIPV project started transmitting power to the grid in Shanghai on 18 July 2010.

In 2009, the Chinese government demonstrated its commitment to expediting BIPV applications nationwide. A number of policies were issued and two large-scale BIPV programs, known as the Solar Rooftop Plan and the Golden Sun Program, were initiated within the year (Table 6). By unveiling the two programs, China plans to subsidize building-integrated PV pilot projects in the following two to three years (2009–2011). Financial subsidies, R&D support, and market exploration are combined to promote commercial application

---

[11] *China Solar PV Report 2007.*

Table 6. Government policies and programs for BIPV, 2009

Date	Policy	Program	Government Subsidy
23 March 2009	The Opinion of Speeding up BIPV Application (Caijian [2009] No. 128)	The Solar Rooftop Plan	RMB20/Wp for BIPV systems;
23 March 2009	Circular on Subsidizing BIPV Application (Caijian [2009] No. 129)		In 2009, total 111 BIPV projects with installed capacity of 91 MW were subsidized
16 July 2009	Circular on Implementing the Golden Sun Pilot Projects (Caijian [2009] No. 397)	The Golden Sun Program	50% of total cost in on-grid PV projects; 70% for independent systems in remote areas

Notes: Wp means watt-peak units, the power output of photovoltaic systems.
Source: Ministry of Finance, Ministry of Housing and Urban-Rural Development.

and development of PV technology. Infrastructure capacity building projects are subsidized mainly through government loans at discount rate.

On the other hand, the development of large-scale on-grid PV stations is supposed to be the biggest potential solar PV market. By issuing a circular on promoting grid-connected PV pilot projects in November 2007, the NDRC began to develop LSPV stations each with a capacity of no less than 5 MW in solar energy-rich areas of western China, particularly Ningxia, Gansu, Xinjiang, Qinghai, Tibet, and Inner Mongolia.[12] Similar to the Town Electrification Program, the initiative is also part of the Western Development strategy (*xibu da kaifa*) launched in 2000 to facilitate the social and economic development in western China.

---

[12] "The Circular of Requirements on the Construction of Large Scale Grid-Connected PV Projects", NDRC, *Fa gai ban neng yuan* [2007] No. 2898, 22 November 2007, available at http://www.sdpc.gov.cn/zcfb/zcfbtz/2007tongzhi/t20090123_258060.htm.

The unprecedented plan targets the 2.5 million km² of desert, a quarter of the country's land area.[13] If merely 1% of the desert could be used for PV stations, a total capacity of 2,500 GW could be installed to generate over 3,000 TWh of electricity each year, which roughly covers the whole nation's power consumption of 3,700 TWh in 2009.[14]

Under the initiative, investors are selected through a competitive bidding process. The first round of concession bidding resulted in a 10 MW program in Dunhuang, Gansu, which is now in operation at a fixed on-grid power price (Table 1). According to the NDRC, the second round of bidding was launched early in 2010, which will push China's development of LSPV into the fast track in a phase-wise manner. The government is now tendering for bids to develop 13 LSPV projects with a combined capacity of 280 MW in the western regions.

Aside from the government-financed applications discussed above, the commercial use of solar PV, i.e. applications without government subsidies, has developed steadily. Applications such as telecommunications, industrial uses and solar PV products accounted for nearly half of the total cumulative installed capacity (Table 4). Solar PV use in this category is mainly driven by the competition mechanism of the market.

As for PV applications in electrical appliances, China has now become the largest producer of PV-powered products in the world. These widely used products include solar street lights, traffic signals, garden lamps, solar-powered vehicles, LED indication boards, advertising boards, calculators and solar toys. Public lighting for highways is perceived to be the most promising area for off-grid PV applications. In 2009, the Ministry of Transport (MOT) issued a circular to

---

[13] *China Solar PV Report 2007*, China Environmental Science Press.

[14] TWh is short for terawatt hours, equal to 10^{12} watt hours. The power consumption in 2009 is based on the "Statistical Communiqué of the People's Republic of China on the 2009 National Economic and Social Development" issued by the National Bureau of Statistics of China on 25 February 2010, available at http://www.stats.gov.cn/tjgb/ndtjgb/qgndtjgb/t20100225_402622945.htm.

promote "energy saving and environmental friendly development of public transport" in China with a target of highway construction to reach 3 million km by the end of 2020.[15]

In brief, a huge domestic market remains to be opened for solar PV applications in China. Considering the enormous demand of power supply, grid-connected power generation applications such as LSPV and BIPV will be the major arenas for future development. In view of the high PV power prices, whether the potential can be realized depends mainly on the government's decisions on feed-in tariff. It is reported that the NDRC is now working on a policy to subsidize solar electricity with a premium tariff per generated kWh.[16]

CHALLENGES IN THE INDUSTRIAL CHAIN OF PV MANUFACTURING

There has been an asymmetry in the industrial chain of China's PV manufacturing. Known as the "both ends out" (*liang tou zai wai*) problem, China imported 95% of its PV raw materials due to a lack of advanced technologies producing crystalline silicon and exported 95% of its finished products due to an underdeveloped domestic market.[17] In other words, China is weak in the upstream of the PV industrial chain, namely silicon production, while it is very strong in the labour-intensive downstream, including cell production and PV module encapsulation etc (see Appendix 5).[18]

---

[15] The figure does not include rural roads. See "*Guan Yu Yin Fa Zi Yuan Jie Yue Xing Huan Jing You Hao Xing Gong Lu Shui Lu Jiao Tong Fa Zhan Zheng Ce De Tong Zhi*", *Jiao ke jiao fa* [2009] No. 80, 9 March 2009, Ministry of Transport. Available at: http://www.moc.gov.cn/zizhan/siju/kejiaosi/guanlipindao/guanli-wenjian/200903/t20090309_563598.html.

[16] "Solar & Renewable Energy Sources", China Solar Energy, 2010-04, p. 10, available at: http://www.chinaygny.cn/pdf/阳光能源2010-04.pdf.

[17] "Solar & Renewable Energy Sources", China Solar Energy, 2010-02, 38, available at http://www.chinaygny.cn/pdf/2010能源02.pdf.

[18] Solar PV industrial chain includes production of crystalline silicon, silicon ingot and wafer, solar cells, modules, and arrays.

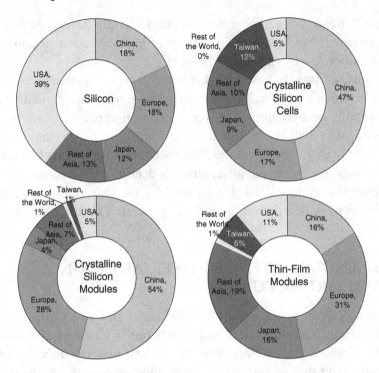

Fig. 2. Global distribution of production capacity, 2009.

Reproduced from European Photovoltaic Industry Association (EPIA) (2010) "Global Market Outlook Until 2014", 22.

As shown in Figure 2, China can only manufacture 18% of the global silicon material in the upstream while it accounts for 47% and 54% of the global production capacity respectively for cells and modules in the downstream. In this sense, the heavy reliance on cells and module export means that the development of China's PV industry was to some extent financed by foreign governments, which extended subsidies to China's overseas market.

In the long term, the structural problem poses a big threat to the healthy development of China's PV industry. First, it relies too much on the overseas market. A declining foreign demand, as in the 2008 global economic slowdown, is likely to create great pressure on domestic production. Second, import of crystalline silicon makes cost control difficult. Despite comparatively lower costs in the downstream manufacturing, the price of solar cells remains high due to the massive input in the initial stage of production.

As the basic feedstock of solar cells, production of high purity polycrystalline silicon has been the bottleneck in the whole industrial chain.[19] In the international market, over 90% of solar cells are made of high purity polycrystalline silicon. China is lagging behind the international level in the processing of silicon purification. Ironically, its high energy consumption and emission of poisonous waste due to backward technologies and low threshold of market entry have posed major problems for the industry labelled as green. Though some of the problems are common around the world, the case of China is much worse than those in other countries.

In recent years, China's silicon production saw an easing of the situation because of a multiplication in silicon manufacturers and hence a surge in production growth, which are largely driven by attractive returns (see Figure 3 and Appendix 6). However, quantitative changes did not come along with qualitative changes: challenges such as low efficiency and pollution still persist. Along with the growing demand,

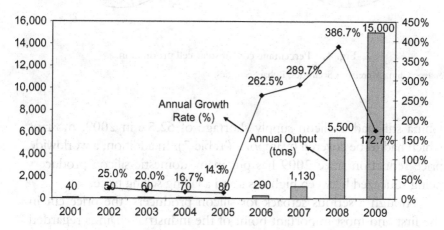

Fig. 3. China's polycrystalline silicon production, 2001–2009.

Source: The National Development and Planning Commission.

---

[19] "Background Paper: Chinese Renewables Status Report October 2009", The Renewable Energy Policy Network for the 21st Century.

Table 7. Polycrystalline silicon supply and demand in China, 2005–2009

Type	2005	2006	2007	2008	2009
Output (tons)	80	290	1,130	4,729	15,000
Demand (tons)	1,652	4,686	10,597	23,190	40,000
Shortage (tons)	1,572	4,396	9,467	18,461	25,000
Percentage of Shortage (%)	95.2%	93.8%	89.3%	79.6%	62.5%

Source: China Renewable Energy Society.

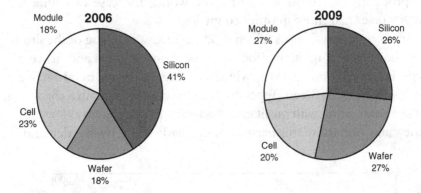

Fig. 4. Percentage cost in solar cell production.

Source: China Merchants Securities; Bohai Securities.

China still had a silicon supply shortage of 62.5% in 2009, most of which had to be covered by imports (Table 7). In addition, a worldwide price reduction since 2009 has put many domestic silicon producers being squeezed between high costs and a falling selling price.

Though a serious setback for silicon producers, the price cut in the first and most important point of the industrial chain is regarded by many as a favourable turn. A falling cost in this stage means a brighter future for solar PV to gradually replace traditional fossil-fired power generation. As Figure 4 shows, the cost of producing silicon as a share of the total cost of producing solar cell modules had decreased from 41.0% in 2006 to 26.7% in 2009. Nevertheless, the cost is not low enough to make solar PV competitive in comparison to traditional types of electricity generation.

As the second stage of the industrial chain, the status of silicon ingot and wafer production is largely dependent on the silicon feedstock. Accompanied by a dynamic expansion of silicon production in recent years, wafer manufacturing in China also experienced rapid growth, at an annual average rate of 100% between 2004 and 2008.[20] As for the core technology of wafer production, China's silicon ingot slicing is relatively mature at the international level. It is reported that lower cost has been achieved in wafer production because thinner wafers were developed and therefore less silicon feedstock is needed.[21] In addition, a structural change in wafer production from monocrystalline to polycrystalline silicon indicates that China's ingot industry is becoming increasingly mature.

Solar cell manufacturing is the third step in the industrial chain. As the world's largest manufacturer of crystalline silicon solar cells, China took nearly half of the world's solar cell production capacity in 2009 (Figure 3). Its production has sustained rapid growth of over 100% since 2003, with the exception of 2009 when the industry was hit by the global economic crisis (Figure 5). In 2008, top ten domestic producers accounted for 75% of the national total output, whilst the largest one, Suntech, took nearly 20% of the national total output (Appendix 7). In terms of thin-film solar cells, China's development is relatively insignificant due to its backward technology and lower efficiency rates.

As mentioned earlier, China is particularly strong in the downstream of the industrial chain: to incorporate clusters of PV cells into a unit, namely module encapsulation. In 2009, China's share in the world's module production capacity was as high as 54% (Figure 2). This stage is featured by the highest localization rates for its equipments, the lowest technological threshold, the largest number of small and medium-sized businesses, and the greatest expansion in the

---

[20] "Solar & Renewable Energy Sources", China Solar Energy, 2009–12, 38, available at: http://www.chinaygny.cn/pdf/我国太阳🔆12期.pdf.

[21] Ibid. The average thickness of wafers has been reduced from 0.32 mm to 0.18 mm.

whole PV industry. Low labour costs in China makes possible a larger annual output from the labour-intensive module encapsulation than that from solar cell production, with some cells imported for encapsulation (Figures 5 and 6).

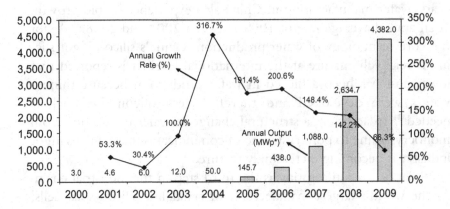

Fig. 5.   Silicon solar cell production in China, 2000–2009.

Note: MWp is the power output of photovoltaic systems described in megawatt-peak units, equal to one million watt-peak units.

Source: China Renewable Energy Society.

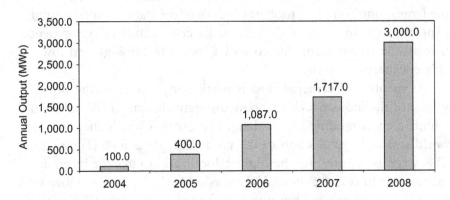

Fig. 6.   Module encapsulation in China, 2005–2008.

Note: MWp is the power output of photovoltaic systems described in megawatt-peak units, equal to one million watt-peak units.

Source: "Solar & Renewable Energy Sources", China Solar Energy, 2009–12, 39, available at: http://www.chinaygny.cn/pdf/我国太阳能12期.pdf.

CHALLENGES AND POLICY IMPLICATIONS

In summary, the problems and challenges discussed in the previous sections have to be addressed to ensure sustainable development of the solar PV industry in China. The biggest challenge facing China's solar PV industry comes largely from the demand side. Its overdependence on overseas markets may become a constraint to its development in the long run. Demand from the domestic market could be further explored through the construction of grid-connected PV systems such as building-integrated and large-scale PV power stations in the coming years. In this respect, the Solar Rooftop Plan and the Golden Sun Program have to be encouraged for the sake of energy conservation and emission reduction. This could also boost domestic demand and therefore stimulate the economy.

On the supply side, the high cost of solar electricity compared to traditional power has been the major stumbling block to the growth of the solar PV market. A policy on implementing feed-in tariff could be considered by the government to subsidize solar power generation. Government subsidies for only a few pilot projects are not enough to popularize solar electricity nationwide. Foreign experiences from European countries, the United States and Japan can be taken into account to suit China's actual conditions. Furthermore, the government also needs to enhance related technical standards, entry criteria and regulations to create a healthy solar PV market.

Last but not least, the "both ends out" problem is rooted in China's weakness in the technology-intensive part of manufacturing and its competitiveness in labour-intensive part of production. Investment in the R&D of solar PV technologies is necessary to realign the asymmetric industrial chain and to cut down the production cost. If China plans to develop the world's largest renewable energy market in the next decade, it has to overcome its weakness in terms of R&D.

APPENDIX 1
Government Subsidies in Top PV Markets
The Feed-In Tariff: Driver of Europe's Solar Success Story

The basic idea behind a feed-in tariff is that producers of solar electricity 1) have the right to feed solar electricity into the public grid; 2) receive a premium tariff per generated kWh reflecting the benefits of solar electricity compared to electricity generated from fossil fuels or nuclear power; 3) receive the premium tariff over a fixed period of time. Extending such feed-in tariff mechanisms beyond Germany is a cornerstone of the European Photovoltaic Industry Association's strategy for promoting the uptake of solar electricity in Europe. The simplicity of the concept, and its low administrative costs, mean that it is a highly effective tool for boosting the contribution of solar electricity in national energy mixes.

Solar America Initiative (SAI) and Investment Tax Credit (ITC) in the United States

Launched in 2006, the Solar America Initiative (SAI) activities focused on making solar electricity cost competitive with conventional forms of electricity by 2015. SAI was part of the President's Advanced Energy Initiative. The main features are: investment in R&D projects targeted at reducing costs, improving efficiency and PV reliability; support for new solar cell companies that have the potential to transfer from the laboratory to the commercial stage; facilitating the establishment of partnerships between power companies in the same state to jointly stipulate regulations and incentive policies, etc.

As part of the Emergency Economic Stabilization Act of 2008, the solar investment tax credit (ITC) was extended for eight years, with the following key provisions: extension of the 30% federal investment tax credit for both residential and commercial solar installations for eight years through 31 December 2016; elimination of the $2,000 cap on the investment tax credit for residential solar electric installations placed into service after 31 December 2008; and public utilities are now eligible to claim the solar investment tax credits.

New Sunshine Project in Japan

Japan started implementation of the New Sunshine Project in 1993, with the aim of accelerating the development and utilization of solar PV, hydrogen and geothermal energy. Till 2005, a user subsidy policy had been implemented which means that a subsidy is paid towards the capital cost of installing a PV system. There is an annual reduction from the original 50% subsidy to zero over ten years. In 2008, 5 billion *yen* in PV promotion funds were allocated to subsidize one-third of the capital cost and 70,000 *yen* to each household.

Sources:

1. "Solar Generation V — 2008," European Photovoltaic Industry Association and the Greenpeace, available at: http://www.greenpeace.org/raw/content/international/press/reports/solar-gene-ration-v-2008.pdf.
2. "Solar Photovoltaic Cell/Module Manufacturing Activities 2008," US Energy Information Administration, available at: http://www.eia.doe.gov/cneaf/solar.renewables/page/solarreport/solarpv.html.
3. US Department of Energy.
4. "2008–2009 China Solar PV Industry Report", All China Marketing Research (ACMR).

APPENDIX 2

Solar Photovoltaic Applications

Grid-Connected Domestic Systems

This type of solar PV system is for homes and businesses in developed areas. Connection to the local electricity network allows any excess power produced to feed the electricity grid and to be sold to the utility. Electricity is then imported from the network when there is no sun. An inverter is used to convert the direct current power produced by the system to alternative power for running normal electrical equipments.

Grid-Connected Power Plants

These systems, also grid-connected, produce a large quantity of photovoltaic electricity in a single point. The size of these plants range from several hundred kilowatts to several megawatts. Some of these applications are located on large industrial buildings such as airport terminals or railways stations. This type of large application makes use of already available space and compensates for part of the electricity produced by these energy-intensive consumers.

Off-Grid Systems for Rural Electrification

Where no mains electricity is available, the system is connected to a battery via a charge controller. An inverter can be used to provide AC power, enabling the use of normal electrical appliances. Typical off-grid applications are used to bring access to electricity to remote areas (mountain huts, developing countries). Rural electrification means either a small solar home system, covering basic electricity needs in a single household, or larger solar mini-grids, which provide enough power for several homes.

Off-Grid Industrial Applications

Use of solar electricity for remote applications is very frequent in the telecommunications field, especially to link remote rural areas to the rest of the country. Repeater stations for mobile telephones powered by PV or hybrid systems also have a large potential. Other applications include traffic signals, marine navigation aids, security phones, remote lighting, highway signs and wastewater treatment plants. These applications are cost competitive today as they enable power to be brought into areas far away from electric mains, avoiding the high cost of installing cabled networks.

Consumer Goods

Photovoltaic cells are used in many daily electrical appliances, including watches, calculators, toys, battery chargers, professional sunroofs for automobiles. Other applications include power for services such as water sprinklers, road signs, street lights and phone boxes.

Source: European Photovoltaic Industry Association (EPIA).

APPENDIX 3

The World Bank's Renewable Energy Development Program

International programs such as the World Bank's Renewable Energy Development Program also provided subsidies for solar PV installation and other small-scale renewable energy in remote areas of China. Since 1993, the World Bank (WB) and the Global Environmental Facility (GEF) have supported projects to improve commercial markets and financing for renewable energy technologies in developing countries. In China, from 1999 to 2007, the WB and the GEF provided US$40 million in grants and loans to fund market surveys, key capital investments, and the development of product standards and certification. This effort played an important role in supporting the installation of PV systems to approximately 400,000 rural households and institutions during the eight-year period, and helped make China the top producer of solar equipment and components in the world today.

Source: "Technology Roadmap: Solar Photovoltaic Energy", *International Energy Agency*, 11 May 2010, available at: http://www.iea.org/papers/2010/pv_roadmap.pdf.

APPENDIX 4

Solar PV in Shanghai 2010 World Expo

The Shanghai 2010 World Expo sees the greatest use of solar energy in the event's history. With the theme "Better City, Better Life", the Shanghai Expo will incorporate visitors into environmentally friendly and environmentally sensitive urban systems that are not only equipped with the latest life-facilitating gadgets, but are also prepared for sustainable urbanization.

In line with the expo theme, four building structures in the Expo Park have taken up the building-integrated photovoltaic (BIPV) technology, in which photovoltaic materials are used to replace conventional building materials on the rooftop. They are incorporated into the construction of the buildings as a principal or ancillary source of electrical power. In total, the installed capacity of solar PV in the four buildings reaches 4.6 MW, which is going to supply 4 million kWh of electricity and reduce 3,400 tons of carbon dioxide emissions per year. Technologies used are developed independently by China.

The solar panels installed on the China Pavilion and the Theme Pavilion cover 31,100 m^2 of roof space, with a combined power output of 3.1 MW. At present, the PV system in the Theme Pavilion is Asia's largest BIPV project integrated in a single building. It is estimated that the system will generate 2.8 million kWh of electricity per year — enough for 2,500 Shanghai households for a year. It will annually save 1,000 tons of standard coal, 2,500 tons of carbon dioxide emissions, 84 tons of sulfur dioxide, 42 tons of nitrogen oxide and 762 tons of dust.

An interesting foreign PV application in the Expo Park is the Japanese Pavilion, which is compared to a giant purple silkworm cocoon. Other types of PV applications and renewable energies also feature in the Expo Park: solar street lights, solar tourist cars, and even newsstands, etc. are widely used.

Sources:

1. "Suntech Powers Shanghai World Expo with 3MW Solar Systems", 14 January 2010, available at: http://phx.corporate-ir.net/phoenix.zhtml?c=192654&p=irol-newsArticle&ID=1374977&highlight=.
2. The official website of the Expo 2010 Shanghai China, 14 September 2009, available at: http://www.expo2010.cn/a/20090914/000010.htm.
3. World Expo Shanghai 2010, "Solar Application at Shanghai Expo", 21 February 2010, available at: http://www.expo2010china.hu/index.phtml?module=hir&ID=1155.

APPENDIX 5

Solar PV Industrial Chain

Industrial Chain	Silicon	Ingot/Wafer	Cells	Modules	PV Arrays
Features	Capital intensive; High technical threshold; Long payback period; High energy consumption; Poisonous emissions	High technical barrier; Decrease in the thickness of silicon wafers is an effective way to reduce cost of PV cells	Large-scale production is most important; Certain capital and technical threshold	Low capital and technical threshold; Labour-intensive; Short payback period; Fierce competition	Low technical threshold but comprehensive use of combined technologies is required
Manufacturing in China	Weak	Medium	Strong	Strong	Strong

Source: "2008–2009 China Solar PV Industry Report", All China Marketing Research (ACMR), p.11.

APPENDIX 6

Polycrystalline Silicon Production by Company (Tons), 2005–2008

	2005		2006		2007		2008	
Company	Cap.	Prod.	Cap.	Prod.	Cap.	Prod.	Cap.	Prod.
Ermei Semiconductor	100	80	100	105	200	155	700	500
Luoyang Zhonggui	300	—	300	185	1,000	520	3,000	1,000
Sichuan Xinguang	—	—	—	—	1,260	230	1,260	800
Xuzhou Zhongneng	—	—	—	—	1,500	150	4,000	1,800
Wuxi Zhongcai	—	—	—	—	300	55	300	200
Shanghai Lengguang	—	—	—	—	50	20	40	40
Chongqing Daquan	—	—	—	—	—	—	2,000	60
Total	400	80	400	290	4,310	1,130	20,000	5,500

Note: Cap. is short for capacity (tons); Prod. is short for production (tons).
Source: The Renewable Energy Policy Network for the 21st Century.

APPENDIX 7

Top Ten Solar Cell Producers in China, 2008

Company Name	MWp Produced	Percentage
Suntech Power	497.5	19.3%
Yingli Green Energy	281.5	10.9%
JA Solar	277.0	10.8%
Trina Solar	209.0	8.1%
Solarfun Power	189.0	7.3%
China Sunergy	110.9	4.3%
Canadian Solar	108.0	4.2%
Eging Photovoltaic	99.7	3.9%
Ningbo Solar	97.0	3.8%
Jiangyin Jetion S&T	65.0	2.5%
Top TEN Total	1,934.6	75.2%
National Total	2,574.0	100.0%

Note: MWp is the power output of photovoltaic systems described in megawatt-peak units, equal to one million Wp.

Source: "Solar & Renewable Energy Sources", China Solar Energy, 2009–12, 38, available at: http://www.chinaygny.cn/pdf/阳光能源12期.pdf.

Chapter

9

China Enters the Age of High-Speed Rail

Hong YU and Mu YANG

The fast pace of industrialization and economic development has greatly spurred on domestic high-speed railway construction over the last decade. China's vast geographical area and its population of 1.3 billion have naturally created a high demand for freight and passenger travel. Developing an efficient and reliable system of railway transportation based on the high-speed railway network is crucial for China. The construction of high-speed rail represents China's scale of technological progress. From design and construction through to management, China is seeking to become the world's leader in the high-speed railway sector. The appeal of high-speed rail lies in its environmental friendliness. A substantial reduction of greenhouse gas (GHG) output can be achieved through the development of high-speed railways. However, huge challenges still remain for China in building a highly efficient and reliable railway network in the coming years. Low efficiency and high operational costs are pressing issues.

INTRODUCTION

This paper attempts to provide an illuminating and detailed analysis of China's high-speed railway industry over the last decade. The structure of this paper is as follows. Section One offers a general review of railway development in China. Section Two focuses on an overview of the development of high-speed railways. The government's 4-trillion-*yuan* stimulus package announced last year has further boosted the construction of high-speed railways. Moreover, the Medium and Long-Term Railway Network Plan, which is expected to be the principal government document for designating and implementing the policies on railway development, is addressed in this section. Section Three focuses on an analysis of the background to the fast development of the high-speed railway sector in China. Section Four analyses the major challenges facing the domestic railway sector. Section Five draws conclusions.

RAILWAY DEVELOPMENT IN CHINA: AN OVERVIEW

The start of China's railway construction can be traced back to the establishment of the Shanghai-Wusong railway in 1876 during the Qing dynasty. From a historical angle, Huenemann[1] conducted an important study of railroad development in China before 1949. Huenemann's research suggests that railway construction has benefited Chinese economic development; particularly in the interior regions without access to water transport. Liang's empirical study[2] shows that the railroad has stimulated agricultural growth in China. Chih[3] gives some detailed discussion regarding railroad construction

---

[1] R. W. Huenemann, *The Dragon and the Iron Horse: The Economics of Railroads in China 1876–1937* (Massachusetts: Harvard University Press, 1984).

[2] Liang E.P. "China: Railways and Agricultural Development, 1875–1935" Department of Geography, Research Paper No. 203 (Chicago: University of Chicago, 1982).

[3] Chih Chung, *An Outline of Chinese Geography* (Peking: Foreign Languages Press, 1978).

development in China and its significance in stimulating inter-regional commercial interaction and regional economic growth. For example, the regions along the line of the Lanzhou-Xinjiang railway (*Lanxin line*) have enjoyed the benefits contributed by this railway. Before the construction of this railway, many regions, such as Yumen and Urumqi, were very difficult to access and suffered from geographical remoteness. The importance of the Baotou-Lanzhou railway in stimulating the economic development in Inner Mongolia should not be underestimated. The construction of this railway has rendered the rich metal resources in Baotou exploitable, and transformed this place into a crucial iron and steel production centre in China. The traditionally underdeveloped Hetao Area located in Inner Mongolia also shares the economic benefits brought by railway construction.

Sun's study[4] suggests that the construction of the Yingtan-Xiamen railway linked inaccessible regions with the rest of Fujian. Rich forest resources in Fujian became exploitable. Sun discusses the role played by transportation in boosting Chinese economic growth; in particular, he highlights the effect of railroad construction on transportation of raw agricultural and industrial materials to the place where they are required, more quickly and at lower cost. The building of railways has already brought enormous economic benefits to China's vast mountainous and interior regions along the rail lines, as is evident in Guizhou, Sichuan and Yunnan. Before 1949, the lack of a rail network hindered the commercial communication of these southwest provinces with the outside world. However, the situation has improved substantially since 1949 due to the construction of Chengdu-Chongqing and Baoji-Chengdu, two key railways.[5]

The remote and landlocked regions enjoy economic benefits from the railway effect; the railway reduces the geographical isolation of

---

[4] Sun Jingzhi, *The Economic Geography of China* (Hong Kong: Oxford University Press, 1988).

[5] Chih Chung, *An Outline of Chinese Geography* (Peking: Foreign Languages Press, 1978).

these regions and provides more opportunities for commercial links with other regions. In particular, many underdeveloped regions would be able to benefit from the spread effects brought about by high-speed railways construction in the future. Construction of high-speed railways could also introduce competitive advantages, such as low labour costs, to the remote and underdeveloped regions and local economic growth in these regions could be stimulated. Failure to provide sufficient and good infrastructure will inevitably cause slow economic growth and industrial development and industrialization might never be achieved.

The length of operational railways jumped to 79,000 kilometres (km) in 2008 from 53,000 km in 1980 while that of national electrified railways increased to 25,000 km in 2008 from only 2,000 km in 1980 (Figure 1). China was ranked third in the world for railway mileage by 2007, after the United States and Russia. According to the data given by the World Bank Report (2007), China had become the world's largest passenger carrier, accounting for 26% of the world's rail passenger traffic by 2005. Also, China held second

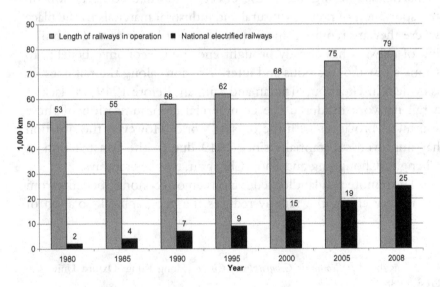

Fig. 1.   Length of railways in operation in China.

Source: China Statistical Yearbook 2009.

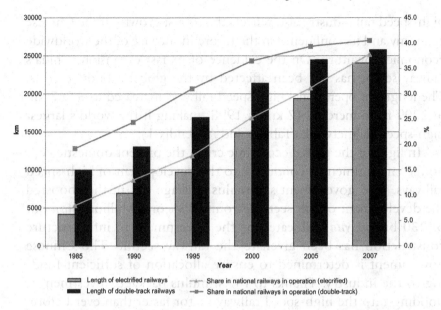

Fig. 2. Technical development of national railways in China.

Source: *China Statistical Yearbook* 2008.

position worldwide in terms of rail freight traffic in 2005, with its share of 23% exceeded only by the United States. According to the figures presented in Figure 2, the shares of electrified and double-track railways in total national rail length had increased substantially from 8% and 19.2% in 1985 to 37.8% and 40.5% respectively in 2007.

FAST EXPANSION OF HIGH-SPEED RAIL IN CHINA

The boom in the Chinese economy and the country's speedy industrialization has greatly spurred domestic high-speed railway[6] construction over the last decade. The rapid development of China's

---

[6] In this paper, the definition of high-speed rail is public transport which is able to handle trains travelling at over 200 km per hour.

high-speed rail industry also reflects the robust growth of the Chinese economy and its confidence in the future in the face of the worldwide economic downturn. On the evidence of its fast expansion, China's railway sector has not been affected by the global economic crisis. The length of operational high-speed railways increased to 3,753 km in 2009 from merely 147 km in 1998, making it the world's largest high-speed rail network (Table 1 and Appendix 1).

In light of the global economic crisis, the present domestic economic environment is conducive to the development of high-speed railways. The government's stimulus package has further boosted the development of this sector. Around 13% or 30 billion *yuan* out of 230 billion *yuan* allocated by the government to infrastructure construction has been given to the railway sector.[7] The Chinese government is determined to ensure allocation of sufficient funding to the industry. Thanks to the stimulus package, investment is flooding into the high-speed railway sector faster than ever before. The railway sector is set to become the biggest beneficiary of this

Table 1.   World comparison of operational high-speed railways

Country	Rank	Total Network Length (km)	Maximum Speed[a] (km/h)	Average Speed (km/h)
China	1	**3,753**	**350**	**236**
Japan	2	2459	320	256
France	3	1700	320	272
Germany	4	1290	300	226
Spain	5	1272	300	236
Italy	6	814	300	178
Russia	7	650	210	144
Belgium	8	326	300	237
South Korea	9	240	300	200
United Kingdom	10	109	300	219

Note: [a]The maximum speed is the fastest speed at which a train is able to run.
Source: The data is based on the authors' calculations using a variety of information; wikipedia

---

[7] *Beijing Review* 52 (4 June 2009).

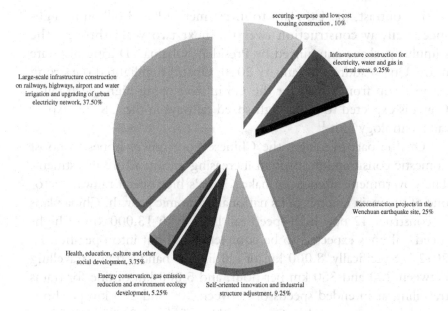

Fig. 3. The planned distribution of the central government's 4 trillion-*yuan* stimulus package.

Source: Ministry of Finance, People's Republic of China, 2009.

huge stimulus package to increase domestic consumption and boost economic growth. In total, the construction of transportation and other infrastructure projects took 37.5% (1.5 trillion *yuan*), which is the lion's share of the 4-trillion-*yuan* state investment (Figure 3).

The Wuhan-Guangzhou passenger-dedicated railway reached a top speed of 394 km per hour during a test run. It was put into operation in December 2009.[8] The travelling time between these two cities has been cut to only three hours, making it the fastest locomotive in the world currently.

---

[8] "The Top Speed of the Wuhan-Guangzhou Passenger-Dedicated Line is up to 394 km/h", *Xinhua*, http://news.southcn.com/z/2009-12/09/content 6957117.htm, 9 December 2009.

In contrast, the US plans to invest merely US$8 billion in high-speed railway construction over the next two years through the stimulus package announced by President Obama.[9] During his State of the Union address in January 2010, Obama highlighted the strong competition from China for the US in developing high-speed rail.[10] China is expected to build high-speed railways in the US and export rail technology to it.[11]

On the part of China, the Chinese government hopes to boost domestic consumption through increasing infrastructure investment. The government intends to make China's high-speed railway sector one of the main engines of its national economic growth. China plans to construct 42 new high-speed rail lines, with 13,000 km of high-speed rail lines expected to be completed and put into operation by 2012.[12] Specifically, 8,000 km of rail line to handle trains travelling between 200 and 350 km per hour, and 5,000 km of line for trains travelling at intended speeds of between 200 and 250 km per hour would be constructed.[13] Construction of the 1,318 km Beijing-Shanghai high-speed railway is expected to be completed in 2010. The travelling time between these two most important cities in China would be cut to only 4 hours from 12 hours.

According to the Medium and Long-Term Railway Network Plan (referred to as the Plan) (see Appendix 2), China is to build an inter-city passenger railway system to cover all the densely populated, economically advanced regions within the Bohai Bay Region (BBR), Yangtze River Delta (YRD) and Pearl River Delta (PRD). The high-speed

---

[9] "High-Speed Rail", *The New York Times*, http://topics.nytimes.com/topics/reference/timestopics/subjects/h/high_speed_rail_projects/index.html, 13 May 2010.

[10] "Building Infrastructure and Creating Jobs at Home", State of the Union, White House, USA, January 2010.

[11] "China Anticipates Bidding to Build High-Speed Rail Lines in the US", *The New York Times*, 17, 15 March 2010.

[12] "China Unveils High-Speed Railways", *BBC News*, http://news.bbc.co.uk/2/hi/asia-pacific/8246600.stm, 13 May 2010.

[13] "China to have World's Fastest Train by 2012", *China Daily*, online edition, http://www.chinadaily.com.cn/china/2009-03/06/content_7549048.htm, 6 March 2009.

Table 2. The four horizontals and verticals railway network planned for China

The "Four Horizontals"	The "Four Verticals"
1 The 1,318 km-long Beijing-Shanghai railway connecting the two major economic municipalities around the BBR and YRD	The 1,400 km-long Xuzhou-Zhengzhou-Lanzhou railway
2 The 2,260 km-long Beijing-Wuhan-Guangzhou-Shenzhen railway	The 880 km-long Hangzhou-Nanchang-Changsha railway connecting central and east China
3 The 1,700 km-long Beijing-Shenyang-Harbin railway	The 770 km-long Qingdao-Shijiazhuang-Taiyuan railway linking eastern and northern China
4 The 1,600 km-long Hangzhou-Ningbo-Fuzhou-Shenzhen railway, connecting areas within the YRD, the southeast coastal region and PRD	The 1,600 km-long Nanjing-Wuhan-Chongqing-Chengdu railway linking eastern and southwest China

Source: Ministry of Railways, 2008.

railway network will consist of four north-south and four west-east rail lines (Four Verticals and Four Horizontals) (Table 2). The rapid development of high-speed railway is anticipated to gradually change the unequal industrial distribution and economic imbalance between the eastern, central and western regions. Such a network would help the prosperous eastern region to generate more economic spillover effects to the underdeveloped western region.

Indeed, this state plan is ambitious and if successfully implemented, it is expected that China's high-speed railway sector will lead the world and leave competitors in its wake. Besides addressing existing challenges, the Plan has set ambitious goals for upgrading technological levels for the high-speed railway, raising the percentage of domestically made parts in the China's high-speed railway (CRH) trains and increasing research and development (R&D) spending.

The two largest domestic railway builders, namely China Railway Construction Corp. (CRCC) and China Railway Group Ltd. (CRG) are expected to benefit enormously from the state stimulus package and seek numerous opportunities to construct high-speed rail lines over the next decade. From design and construction through to management, China is seeking to become the world's leader in the high-speed railway sector.

China's high-speed railway sector has adopted the "going out" strategy to strengthen its global competitiveness. In August 2009, the CRG won a contract from the Venezuela Railway Authority to build a $7.5 billion 468 km-long railway in Venezuela.[14] Historically, this could be the biggest overseas railway construction order that Chinese railway construction companies have ever won. In March 2009, the CRCC won a contract for part of a $1.8 billion 450 km-long high-speed railway project in Saudi Arabia.[15] During a recent visit to China made by Russian Prime Minister Vladimir Putin, China and Russia signed a memorandum of understanding on the development of high-speed railways in Russia.[16] It paves the way for China to export railway technologies and build high-speed railways on Russian territory and in other Western countries. These events represent a major breakthrough for China and its global competitiveness is dramatically rising. It appears that high-speed rail has increasingly become a new promotion brand for China.

The development of high-speed railways also has the capability of helping the government cope with high unemployment caused by the global economic crisis. A huge number of construction-related jobs would be generated by high-speed railway projects. Many new permanent jobs in railway maintenance and passenger service are expected to be generated as well. According to the estimation made

---

[14] "China Railway Gets $7.5b Global Order", *China Daily*, online edition, http://www.chinadaily.com.cn/bizchina/2009-08/04/content_8514924.htm, 4 August 2009.

[15] "China Railway Construction Wins Part of $1.8b Saudi Deal", *China Daily*, online edition, http://www.chinadaily.com.cn/bizchina/2009-03/04/content_7536677.htm, 4 March 2009.

[16] "Russia, China to Sign Deals on Missiles and High-Speed Trains", *France 24*, http://www.france24.com/en/20091011-russia-china-sign-deals-missiles-high-speed-trains-vladimir-putin-wen-jiabao, 13 May 2010.

by the Ministry of Railway (MOR), six million jobs are expected to be created in 2009 and 2010 as a result of 600 billion *yuan* of planned state investment in railway construction projects.[17]

FACTORS UNDERLYING THE RAPID DEVELOPMENT OF CHINA'S HIGH-SPEED RAILWAYS

Transportation Sector Struggles to Meet Increasing Demand

For China as a fast-developing country, the spread of its key raw materials and energy resources over such a large area means that railway freight services are crucial to industrial production and foreign trade. Along with highway passenger traffic, the railway lines form a key part of the national transportation system. However, the domestic railway sector has been struggling to keep up with the fast economic growth over the past several decades. Railway transport capacity for both cargo and passenger traffic has been lagging behind real demand. Railway capacity inadequacy has caused a bottleneck in goods transport and Chinese economic development.

During the reform period, industrial distribution was unequal among regions of China. Industrial development of the eastern region was robust and industrial agglomeration has gradually taken shape in this region. Rail transport forges a key means of transferring millions of western migrants to work in the eastern region.

China's dramatic economic development is largely driven by industrial growth, which requires a reliable and continuous supply of raw materials and energy resources. The rail services are also important to foreign trade in providing effective and reliable means for the transportation of international shipping containers arriving or departing from ports. The development of high-speed railways is badly needed for long-term sustainable development.

---

[17] *Beijing Review* 52 (4 June 2009).

Table 3.   National railway freight by main category of cargo, 2007

Item	Freight Traffic (million tons)	Share in National Freight Traffic (%)
Coal	1220	46.7
Metal Ores	275	10.5
Steel and Iron, and Non-Ferrous Metal	215	8.2
Petroleum	127	4.8
Grain	104	3.9
National Total	2612	100

Source: China Statistical Yearbook 2008.

Along with highway traffic, the railway lines form a key part of the national transportation system. The dominance of the railway sector over cargo transportation since the beginning of the 1950s has been illustrated especially by the movement of strategic freight such as coal, metal ores, iron ore and petroleum. The share of coal in national freight traffic was 46.7% in 2007 (Table 3). Although the railway has been the key transportation mode for transferring coal from the north to the southern region since the early 1950s,[18] the inadequacy of rail capacity has caused a bottleneck, hampering goods transportation and Chinese economic development. For instance, Shanxi, China's key coal-producing region, could not deliver sufficient coal to the major coal-consuming regions due to the poor capacity of railway transportation.

The number of people using the railways has increased substantially since 1980. Railway usage increased to 777.8 billion passenger-km in 2008 from 138.3 billion passenger-km in 1980. However, the share of railways in national passenger-km had actually demonstrated a sharply declining trend, from 60.6% in 1980 to merely 33.5% in 2008. Compared to a more than seventeen-fold

---

[18] In China, coal production is mainly concentrated in the northern region, while the main areas for coal consumption are located in the southern coastal region.

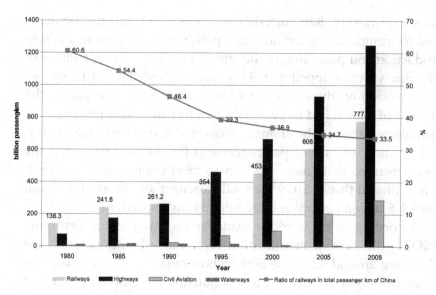

Fig. 4. Passanger-km for transportation modes in China.
Source: China Statistical Yearbook 2008.

growth in road passenger-km, the growth of railway passenger traffic
was much slower during the same period (Figure 4).

Due to the lack of seating capacity, the railway sector is unable to
accommodate all the travellers, particularly during the annual Chinese
Lunar New Year, when millions of people are on the way home for
family reunions. Capacity strain is a common phenomenon in domestic railway transportation. In terms of kilometers of railway track per
million people, China's achievement was relatively poor at 815, ranking
only 73rd in the world. The US was 7th with 14,195 km of railway
track per million people.[19]

The snow disaster in 2008, which resulted in many cargo trains
being out of service for several days, proved the importance of railway
transportation to the Chinese economy and society as a whole as well

---

[19] Russell Pittman, "Chinese Railway Reform and Competition: Lessons from the
Experience in other Countries", *Journal of Transport Economics and Policy* 38
(2004), 309–32.

as its vulnerability. Raw materials and resources could not be delivered to manufacturing factories and power stations, causing a halt in production and panic among the affected regions. Worse, millions of passengers were trapped at railway stations and this led to serious social tension on the eve of the Chinese New Year. Wen Jiabao, the Premier of China, had to personally comfort the angry passengers at the railway stations. The dramatic economic development has intensified the flow of railway passengers and freight, and pressured the government to build more rail lines to meet the increasing demand. It is estimated that in 2010 the total passenger and freight traffic will reach 1.5 billion persons and 3.5 billion tons respectively.[20]

According to the forecast made by the Ministry of Transport (MOT), the current urbanization level and urban population for China are around 41% and 500 million respectively. However, the urbanization rate and total urban population are expected to exceed 50% and 740 million by 2020, whilst the average number of annual journeys for the urban population could be eight to nine times higher than that of the rural population.

China's vast geographical area and its population of 1.3 billion have naturally created a high demand for freight and passenger travel and, in particular, for an efficient and reliable system of railway transportation based on the high-speed railway network. If the railway industry fails to modernize and expand, lack of railway capacity could become a fatal constraint for the sustainable growth of the Chinese economy. China must accept the reality of rail transport inadequacy and tackle this difficulty. Thus, the development of a mass transit public system is an essential policy requirement for the government.

Two workable solutions to capacity inadequacy are the construction of more high-speed railways and raising train running speeds. China is taking both options. Before 1997, the average speed for domestic trains was just 48 km per hour. However, China has raised train speeds by up to six times over the past ten years. The national average speed for rail

---

[20] The Eleventh Five-Year Plan for the Railway Sector, The Ministry of Railways.

cargo transportation has increased to 120 km per hour. These increases in train running speeds have also allowed the industry to conduct research and gradually learn high-speed railway technologies. These are the lab tests for China's CRH railways.

Zhang Shuguang, Vice Chief Engineer of the Ministry of Railways (MOR), predicts that the total passenger traffic on the railways could be up to 7 billion persons in 2012 when the high-speed railway network is completed.[21] Such rapid urbanization will inevitably lead to an increase in demand for railway transportation in the coming decade. Also, rail transportation has always been a popular means of long-distance travel for ordinary people in China. The establishment of advanced high-speed railway infrastructure should be welcomed. Waterway transportation for the landlocked regions is simply not possible, and air transportation is very expensive. Although road transportation is relatively cheap and convenient, for many agricultural and industrial products, it just takes too long to deliver the goods to the consumer market. Moreover, the increasing cost of fuel and serious road traffic congestions are the two important factors drawing Chinese passengers back to railway transportation.

The construction of high-speed rail lines for the principal truck railways would greatly ease rail travel strains and enhance the efficiency of national railway transportation. For example, the 120 km-long inter-city CRH running at a speed approaching 350 km per hour between Beijing and Tianjin has cut travel time to 30 minutes from 90 minutes in the past. This high-speed railway has greatly increased communication and commercial interaction between these two large municipalities; Beijing and Tianjin might become highly integrated in the near future. During the first month of operation, from August 2008, the passenger traffic recorded for this railway was

---

[21] A report delivered by Zhang Shuguang entitled "The Self-Dependent Innovation of China's High-Speed Railways Sector" to the 2009 annual meeting of China Association for Science and Technology available at *People's Net*, http://scitech.people.com.cn/GB/25509/56813/166862/166864/10013564.html, 13 May 2010.

18.3 million, which represented a growth of 128.4% compared to the corresponding figure in the previous year.[22]

When the national network of high-speed railways comes into operation in 2012, the bottlenecks in both cargo and passenger transportation are expected to be eased. For ordinary people, obtaining a train ticket during peak travel times, such as national holiday weeks and the spring festival, would no longer be a frustrating experience. A key focus of the state in developing high-speed railways is to enhance the capacity and quality of passenger mobility in China.

Riding on Technological Progress

The construction of high-speed railways represents China's scale of technological progress and showcases the nation's overall power and demonstrates its socioeconomic development status. Technological development in the high-speed railway sector has been impressive over the past few years. The development of this industry is not confined to fast trains. To allow the operation of trains at speeds of around 350 km per hour, the industry has developed high technologies in sectors such as electronic information, steel and modern equipment manufacturing. The development of these domestic industries has provided the solid foundation for building high-speed railways.

The coming into operation of the Wuhan-Guangzhou high-speed railway demonstrates that China has successfully developed all the technologies needed for high-speed railway design, construction and maintenance. The domestic railway sector has surprised the world with successive innovative breakthroughs and technological development in areas such as ballastless track, railway information management and centralized traffic control systems.[23] Some key elements of the high-speed rail projects, such as ballastless track and rolling stock, are produced domestically and the incorporation of

---

[22] "The Speed of Beijing–Shanghai's High-Speed Railway Could Reach 380 km Per Hour", *BBC News*, http://news.bbc.co.uk/chinese/simp/hi/newsid_7590000/newsid_7592600/7592676.stm, 13 May 2010.

[23] "On an Innovative Track", *Beijing Review* 52 (2009).

these technologically advanced components has boosted the overall level of the railway sector. The development of relevant domestic industries has provided the solid foundation to build the high-speed railways. Liu Zhijun, Minister of Railways, suggests that more than 40,000 accessories and elements of carriages in the CRH train are manufactured by 140 related industries and firms.[24]

The technological improvement of China's high-speed railways is reflected by the electric locomotive, and signal control and dispatching systems. The CRH trains are equipped with advanced communication and information systems, which help the crews manage their trains' operations more efficiently. The on-board sensors can monitor the train engines, and help the maintenance team track the healthy operation of the trains by remote control.

The Beijing-based China South Locomotive and Rolling Stock Industry (Group) Corp. (CSR), which controls almost 50% of the Chinese market share,[25] and Jilin-based Changchun Railway Vehicle Co. Ltd. (CRC), which produced China's first high-speed train car,[26] are the two leading players in developing high-speed railway technology and manufacturing railway equipment.

However, China might need to continually spare efforts to develop advanced technologies. During his visit to the Beijing-Tianjin high-speed railway in September 2008, Wen Jiabao stressed that the future of China's railway sector lies in the use of advanced technologies. China must continue its effort in self-generated innovation and also keep up with the world's advanced technologies.[27] Currently, some components of high-speed trains are imported from other countries; for example, the signalling systems are provided by a

---

[24] The New Landmark in the History of Railway Construction", *Outlook Weekly Magazine*, http://finance.people.com.cn/GB/1045/7645080.html, 11 August 2008.

[25] "A Fast Train to the Future", *Beijing Review* 52 (2009).

[26] "Jilin Expects High-Speed Train Factory in 2009", *Xinhua News*, http://www.chinadaily.com.cn/bizchina/2009-05/06/content_7750398.htm, 6 May 2009.

[27] "Wen Jiabao Paid a Visit to Beijing–Tianjin Intercity Railway", Ministry of Railways, http://www.china-mor.gov.cn/detail.jsp?MSG_ID=14826, 11 April 2010.

Canadian firm.[28] Liu Zhijun frankly admits that around 15% of key parts for the CRH train are still manufactured in and imported from foreign nations.[29] The use of Germany's Siemens technology in the manufacture of the Beijing-Tianjin CRH is a further example of how domestic factories are producing high-speed rail vehicles using technology imported under technology transfer agreements.

The construction of the Beijing-Shanghai high-speed railway is widely expected to involve technical support from the world's leading railway equipment manufacturers, such as Japan's New Trunk Line (*Shinkansen*), France's Alstom and Germany's Siemens. It is very likely that foreign railway technology and equipment will be purchased for the building of this high-speed railway.[30]

Green Transportation

In comparison to other transportation means, high-speed railway scores highly on environmental friendliness in terms of greenhouse gas (GHG) output and energy consumption for both freight and passenger traffic. Average energy consumption for railways is significantly lower than that of road vehicles for long-distance journeys (Table 4). The average energy consumption per passenger mile for high-speed rail is around one-third that of road vehicles.[31] Moreover, the need for new highways and airports could be reduced, saving large amounts of valuable cultivable land for other purposes.

The CO_2 emission for high-speed rail is merely 85 grams per passenger-km, in contrast to the high CO_2 emissions of aircraft and road vehicles of 170 and 100 grams per passenger-km respectively (Figure 5). The CO_2 emission comparison reflects the much better

[29] The New Landmark in the History of Railway Construction", *Outlook Weekly Magazine*, http://finance.people.com.cn/GB/1045/7645080.html, 11 August 2008.
[30] "China's Railways to Spend Stimulus Funds at Home", *The Wall Street Journal*, http://online.wsj.com/article/SB123987956572324825.html, 13 May 2010.
[31] Federal Railway Administration, US, "Comparative Evaluation of Rail and Truck Fuel Efficiency on Competitive Corridors", Final Report, prepared by ICF International, 2009, 1–115.

Table 4. Fuel savings comparison of railway and road vehicles by distance

Distance Range (miles)	Energy Saving Range per Gallons
<300	80–160
300–500	10–250
500–1000	90–380
1000–2000	290–820
>2000	680–1100

Source: ICF International, 2009.

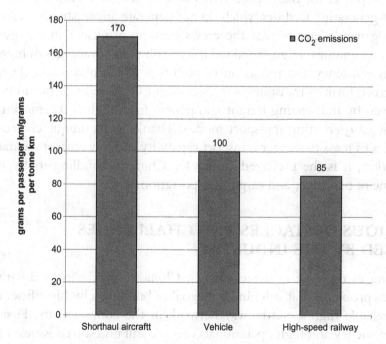

Fig. 5. CO_2 emission comparison between transportation modes.
Source: TRANSform Scotland, 2006.[32]

---

[32] David Spaven, "Are High-speed Railways Good for the Environment? A Discussion Paper" (Edinburgh: TRANSform Scotland, 2006), 1–24.

environmental performance of high-speed rail, and its huge potential in terms of energy saving.[33]

The CRH train, with its streamlined shape and aluminum alloy components, can effectively minimize running noise and air resistance. Its weight, at an average of 30% less than that of the normal train, helps to raise speed and save energy. Unlike the older single-engine trains, CRH trains are driven by multiple engines inserted within separate units. The total power output per CRH train is 8,800 kW, which is realized by multiple traction motors distributed across the underside of the entire train.[34]

The power for high-speed trains is derived from stationary electricity-generating facilities which do not generate any waste gas. Also, training would ensure that the crews become proficient in energy-saving techniques. High-speed rail has the obvious advantages of high energy efficiency and reduction of pollution which makes it a clean and green form of transportation. Significant GHG reductions can be achieved by transferring freight and people from high CO_2-emitting to low CO_2-emitting transport modes. Thanks to its unique characteristics of mass passenger transport capability and low environmental pollution, it is the preferred choice for China in handling its large volume of passenger and cargo transportation.

SERIOUS OBSTACLES AND CHALLENGES FACED BY THE INDUSTRY

Bearing in mind all its achievements, China is still confronted with serious problems that will hinder its goal of building a highly efficient and reliable high-speed railway network in the coming years. First, low efficiency and high operational costs are still unresolved issues. In terms of employee productivity comparisons, China is lagging behind most of the developed nations. North America has recorded the

---

[33] The CO_2 emissions regarding the construction and maintenance of high-speed rail are not taken into account. Also, the electric power source of the high-speed rail, which could be oil, coal and nuclear, would affect its CO_2 emissions.

[34] "On an Innovative Track", *Beijing Review* 52 (2009).

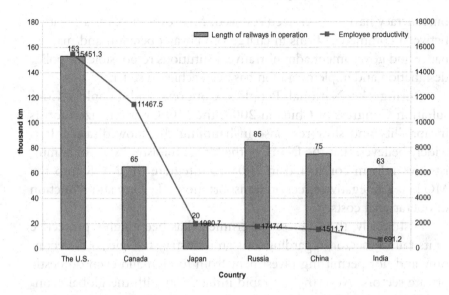

Fig. 6. World comparison of employee productivity in the railway sector, 2005.

Notes:

1. The employee productivity for the US was based on 2006 data.
2. The 2005 data of length of operational railways in the US covered all Class I Railways.
3. Employee productivity, which was taken to measure the output per employee, was measured as the ratio of (passenger-km + tonne-km)/total railway employees.

Source: Railways Databases Update 2007, The World Bank.

world's highest productivity performance. In 2006, employee productivity in the US was 15451.3 km per person, which was more than ten times higher than the 2005 figure in China of merely 1511.7 km per person (Figure 6).

The MOR has been making progress in implementing organizational reforms and taking steps to encourage competition, such as allowing around 100 branch lines to form joint ventures involving local railway administrative bureaus (RAB), provincial governments and other commercial firms; reducing high administrative costs.[35] However, the fundamental problems of monopoly control, low efficiency and

---

[35] Paul Amos and Lou Thompson, "Railways in Development: Global Round-up 1996–2005", Transport Note No. TRN-36, (Washington, DC: The World Bank, 2007).

bureaucracy have not yet been resolved. Moreover, no clear separation between commercial firms in charge of railway operation and maintenance and government administrative institutions responsible for policy designation and implementation has been achieved so far.

During the National People's Congress and People's Consultation Congress of China in 2008, the MOR was criticized for its incapability and slow response in handling the snow disaster. It is widely believed that the failure of the "large ministry" style of administrative reform conducted in 2008 to integrate the MOR into the MOT had a negative effect on transportation efficiency and reduction of operational costs.[36]

Historically, the Chinese government has been highly protective of its railway sector, regarding it as an industry strategic to the economy and not permitting investment from foreign and even domestic private sectors. Nevertheless, rapid integration with the global economy leaves the Chinese central government with no choice but to take steps to relax the tight investment control and regulation of the industry over the past few years. The dramatic increase of demand for investment in railway construction has pushed the government to lift restrictions and diversify funding sources.

In China, the majority of railways are owned and operated by the state, one of the key reasons for the general low efficiency and low employee productivity within the domestic railway sector. To reduce state investment risks and government burdens, China might need to adopt preferential policies to attract more private and foreign investment in domestic railway construction.

Currently, the MOR is both the regulator and operator of the national railway system (see Appendix 3). It is difficult for a multifunctional system of construction, operation and administrative management to accommodate a modern market economy approach. In order to increase efficiency and improve services, the government saw to the necessity of introducing a minimum set of competitive conditions for the railway sector. With this, a clear and proper defined

---

[36] "Minister of Railways: The 'Large-Department' Style Reform is Correct, It is Absolute Necessary to Reform the Railway Sector", *STNN News*, http://www.stnn.cc/china/200803/t20080307_743581.html, 13 May 2010.

relationship between the administrative institutions and commercial operating firms could be established, allowing the railway operating enterprises to transform into self-managing and self-profiting commercial entities.[37]

Guangshen Railway Co., Ltd. (Guangshen Railway) provides a sample case of reform in the domestic railway sector. It was separated from local railway administration in 1984, and in 1996 it was established as the first joint-stock railway firm in mainland China.[38] Guangshen Railway mainly engages in passenger and cargo transportation along the Shenzhen-Guangzhou-Pingshi railway, and with Hong Kong-based MTR Corporation Limited operates Hong Kong Through Train freight and passenger transport services. However, the operations of this company have been concentrated only in Guangdong over the last two decades. Their service territory may need to be extended to boost competition and increase the overall efficiency of China's railway sector.

China may want to learn from the experience of other countries when reforming its own railway system. The "British model", which increases efficiency and achieves better management in the railway industry through the introduction of competition is worthy of consideration; the British government encourages the participation of private sector in public infrastructure.[39]

---

[37] Wong W.G. *et al.*, "Evaluation of Management Strategies for the Operation of High-speed Railways in China", *Transportation Research, Part A* 36 (2002), 277–89.

[38] "Development and History", Guangshen Railway Co., Ltd., http://www.gsrc.com/en/article.php?article_id=102, 12 April. 2010.

[39] The core spirit of the UK model is to permit competition among various railway operating firms over a single, publicly owned line network. For more detailed analysis on the experience of the EU and United Kingdom, please refer to the following sources: (1) G. Driessen *et al.*, "The Impact of Competition on Productive Efficiency in European Railways", CPB Discussion Paper, 2006, 1–40. (2) E. Godward, "The Privatization of British Rail 1994–1997", *Journal of Rail and Rapid Transit* 212(1998) 191–200. (3) Louis. S. Thompson, "Privatizing British Railways: Are There Lessons for the World Bank and its Borrowers?" Transport Paper TP-2, Transport Sector Board, (Washington, DC: The World Bank, 2004).

Second, the railway sector may have to struggle to maintain market share and increase profitability. With perceived certainty, it would face fierce competition from the civil aviation and road transportation sectors. For example, in order to compete for passengers with the newly built high-speed Hefei-Wuhan and Hefei-Nanjing rail lines, the travel fares for flights and buses between Wuhan and Shanghai were reduced by up to 70% from 1 April 2009.[40]

It increasingly appears that cut-throat competition is inevitable among the various transportation providers. Railway companies would have to compete with airlines and bus firms in terms of price, service and efficiency to achieve long-term profitability targets. Considering the age and backwardness of the existing rail network, the modernization of the entire railway system is a momentous undertaking.

Safety is the last issue which needs to be addressed by the industry. In the past its safety record has not been good. For example, in April 2008, a serious high-speed train crash in Shandong Province led to more than 70 people killed and 400 injured. During the same year, a high-speed train hit a group of track-maintenance workers in Shandong, resulting in the death of 18 people.[41] China has a long way to go to replace a backward and ageing railway infrastructure built several decades ago. The chairman of Central Japan Railway, which operates Shinkansen high-speed rail between Tokyo and Osaka, echoed concerns over China's high-speed rail safety when he accused the high-speed rail system of running too close to its maximum safety level.[42]

Building an efficient and reliable national railway network is a challenging task. However, it can be handled if the industry takes action and, with state backing, the development of domestic high-speed railways is very likely to continue in the future.

---

[40] "High-Speed Rails to Slash Travel Time", *China Daily*, http://www.chinadaily.com.cn/china/2009-03/25/content_7615623.htm, 25 March 2009.
[41] "Dozens Die in China Train Crash", *BBC News*, http://news.bbc.co.uk/2/hi/asia-pacific/7370375.stm, 13 May 2010.
[42] "JR Central Attacks China Over Rail Safety", *Financial Times*, 6 April 2010, 1.

APPENDIX 1

Operational High-Speed Lines in China

Line	Length (km)
Wuhan-Guangzhou	1068
Beijing-Tianjin	120
Hefei-Wuhan	350
Shijiazhuang-Taiyuan	190
Nibo-Xiamen	860
Qinhuangdao-Shenyang	404
Qingdao-Jinan	393
Chongqing-Chengdu	368

Source: Authors' calculation based on available information.

APPENDIX 2

Medium and Long-Term Railway Network Plan

The Medium and Long-Term Railway Network Plan (referred to as the Plan) was designated and released by the State Council in 2004. This Plan was further revised in 2008. According to the revised Plan, China aims to put up to 90,000 km of rail lines into operation by 2010, of which 7,000 km will be dedicated to passenger services. The proportion of railways using electric power is expected to reach 45% by 2010. Moreover, 120,000 km of rail line is due to be in operation by 2020, 16,000 km of which is expected to be dedicated to passenger-only lines. The proportion of railways running on electric power is expected to reach 60% by 2020.

By achieving these development goals, on the one hand, it is anticipated that high-speed rail can greatly improve rail services and allow further freight transport growth on existing rail lines; on the other, all provincial capitals and important cities would become connected by it. The major equipment used on the domestic railways is intended to be of an internationally advanced standard.

Besides addressing existing challenges, the Plan has set ambitious goals for upgrading technological levels for high-speed rail, raising the percentage of domestically made parts in CRH trains and increasing R&D spending on technology.

Source: Ministry of Railway, People's Republic of China, 2009.

APPENDIX 3

Overview of the Structure of the Ministry of Railways

The Ministry of Railways			
Selected Railway Administrative Departments	Selected Local Railway Administrative Bureaus	Commercial Railway Enterprises	Selected Other Directly Supervised Institutions
Policy and Regulation Department	Beijing Railway Administrative Bureau	China Railway Parcel Express Co., Ltd.	Railway Capital Clearing Centre
Development and Planning Department	Shanghai Railway Administrative Bureau	China Railway Container Transportation Co., Ltd.	Audit Centre
Finance Department	Harbin Railway Administrative Bureau	China Railway Special Cargo Services Co., Ltd.	Supervision Bureau for Railway Project Quality and Safety
Science and Technology Department	Shenyang Railway Administrative Bureau	China Academy of Railway Sciences	Railway Project Management Centre
Human Resource Department	Taiyuan Railway Administrative Bureau	China Railway Investment Corporation	Information and Technology Centre
Construction and Management Department	Hohhot Railway Administrative Bureau		Management Centre for Foreign Investment and Imported Technology
International Cooperation Department	Zhengzhou Railway Administrative Bureau		Human Resource Service Centre
Railway Safety and Supervision Department	Wuhan Railway Administrative Bureau		Economic Planning and Research Academy
Transportation Department	Xi'an Railway Administrative Bureau		China Railway Museum
	Jinan Railway Administrative Bureau		China Railway Cultural Troupe
	Nanchang Railway Administrative Bureau		
	Guangzhou Railway Administrative Bureau		
	Nanning Railway Administrative Bureau		
	Chengdu Railway Administrative Bureau		
	Kunming Railway Administrative Bureau		
	Railway Administrative Bureau		
	Lanzhou Railway Administrative Bureau		
	Urumqi Railway Administrative Bureau		
	Qingzang Railway Company		

Source: Table compiled by authors using information from the MOR.

10

China's Airports: Reform, Development and Challenges

Xiuyun YANG and Hong YU

The air transport sector is the fastest developing sector among China's various transportation modes. China has also recorded the highest growth of air passenger traffic in the world. The impressive improvements in China's airport industry since the early 1990s have been mainly due to state investment and various reforms. China's airport deregulation reforms have taken place in four stages, with each involving different combinations of airport ownership, management and governance structures. From 2002, the state has further loosened its regulatory controls over the airport industry to speed up the commercialization of airports. Through implementing new reform measures, the government provided more investment opportunities for the non-state sector. Nevertheless, China's airport industry faces three severe challenges to full modernization, namely, uneven regional distribution, overall poor performance, and fierce competition within the domestic transport industry.

RAPID DEVELOPMENT

China's airport industry has made impressive improvements over the last decade. Back in 1992, merely 16.6 million people, 0.4 million tons of cargo and 0.5 million aircraft movements passed through 104 airports. For a vast country of 9.6 million km² and a population of 1.3 billion, the air transport capacity was obviously too low. Nevertheless, by 2008, these three business volumes had increased dramatically, reaching 192.5 million people, 4.1 million tons of cargo and 4.2 million aircraft movements, with average annual growth rates of 12.9%, 18.1% and 12.8% respectively between 1992 and 2008. Cargo traffic has grown faster than either passenger traffic volume or aircraft movement (Figures 1, 2 and 3).

Events such as the Asian financial crisis of 1997–1998, SARS (Severe Acute Respiratory Syndrome) disease in 2003 and the global financial crisis of 2008 have generated various effects on China's airport business. However, despite the negative effects brought about by these unforeseen events, China's airport industry has maintained an upward growth trend since the early 1990s (Figure 3). Moreover, passenger and

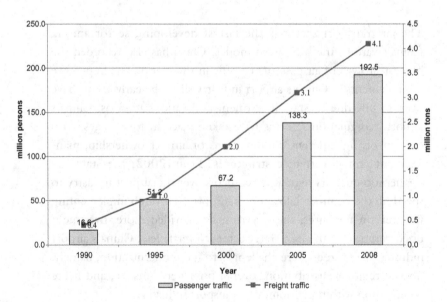

Fig. 1.   Indicators of passenger and freight traffic handled by China's civil aviation.
Source: China Statistical Yearbook 2009.

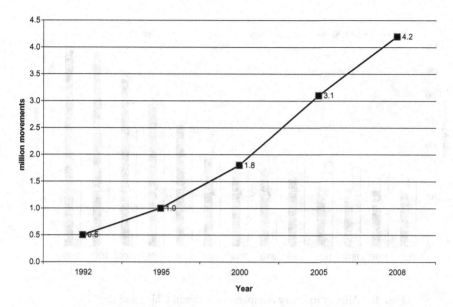

Fig. 2. Aircraft movement handled by China's airports.

Source: China Statistical Yearbook 2009.

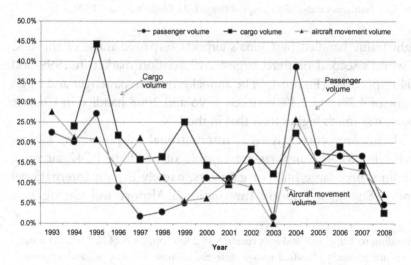

Fig. 3. Growth of business volume handled by China's airport industry.

Sources:
1. CAAC.
2. *Statistical Data on Civil Aviation of China, 2009.*

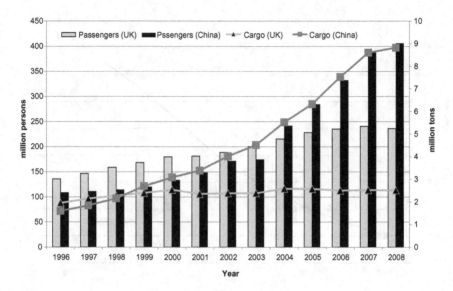

Fig. 4.   Airport industry comparison between China and the UK.

Sources:
1. CAAC.
2. *Statistical Data on Civil Aviation of China*, 2009.
3. UK Civil Aviation Authority, UK Airport Statistics: 2008 — annual; http://www.caa. co.uk/default.aspx?catid=80&pagetype=88&sglid=3&fld=2008Annual, 13 May 2010.

freight traffic handled by China's airports surpassed those of the UK, the world's second or third largest civil aviation market in 1999 and 2004 respectively (Figure 4). The annual growth in passenger and cargo volume of 4.7% and 2.1% between 1996 and 2008 handled in Chinese airports was much higher than that in the UK.

There are currently 42 international airports in China. Specifically, 31 4E[1] airports are capable of handling B747 aircrafts, including three large hubs or gateways, namely Beijing International Airport, Shanghai Pudong International Airport and Guangzhou

---

[1] According to Yang, Tok and Su's research in 2008 (pp. 243–244), "Internationally, airports are primarily classified into 4 different groups, 4E, 4D, 4C and under 3C, depending on the length of their runways, wingspan of planes taking off/landing, and space between felloes of undercarriage. Specifically, the usual classifications are 4E: a minimum 1,800 m-long runway, and capacity of allowing a plane with wingspan of

Baiyun International Airport, which have the capacity for A380 aircraft. Passenger volume of Beijing Airport reached 6.53 million in 2009 to become Asia's largest hub and the world's third largest. Forty airports can support the landing and taking off of B767, B757 and MD82 aircraft, and about 142 airports can house B737 aircraft. Total terminal area for China's airports increased to 3.99 million m² in 2007 from merely 0.23 million m² in 1991. By 2008, China had formed a relatively developed air transport network, as evident from the changing capacity structure of Chinese aviation airports between 1991 and 2008 (see Appendix 1).

The total number of air routes had dramatically increased to 1532 by 2008 from 437 in 1990 and domestic and international routes increased to 1235 and 297 in 2008 respectively (see Appendix 2). Weekly flight frequency rose from 5200 to 40000 flights while the number of civil aviation aircraft increased to 1259 in 2008 from 315 in 1992. The new airline network has coped well with the dramatic increase in air travel demand on these air routes. China's civil airlines recorded 288.3 billion passenger-km and 12 billion freight ton-km in 2008. In the same year, passenger and cargo traffic figures were 192.5 million persons and 4.07 million tons respectively.[2] China ranked No. 2 in the world for air transport traffic and passenger traffic by 2005.[3] Significantly, not only has China's air transport sector been the fastest developing among various transportation modes in China, the country has also recorded the world's highest average growth in air passenger traffic between 1991 and 2008 (Figure 5).

In recent years the domestic airport sector has begun modernizing and diversifying its products to meet the changing needs of

---

52 m–60 m and space between felloes of 9 m–4 m to takeoff/land; 4D: a runway of at least 1,800 m, wingspan of taking off/landing plane is 36 m–52 m, space between felloes is 9 m–14 m; 4C: a minimum 1800 m long runway, 24 m–36 m width wingspan and 6 m–9 m space between felloes; and under 3C: all airports with runway under 1800 m, and wingspan under 36 m and space between felloes under 9 m."

[2] *China Statistical Yearbook 2009.*

[3] Planning and Development division of CAAC, 2006; *Statistical Data on Civil Aviation of China*, 2007.

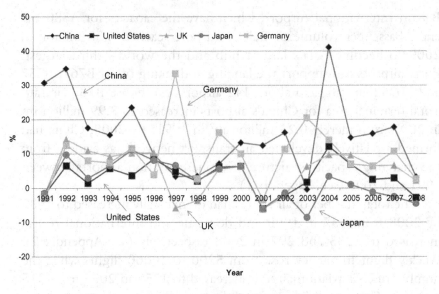

Fig. 5.   World comparison of annual growth of passenger–km for air transport.

Sources:
1. Calculated according to the data from CAAC.
2. *Statistical Data on Civil Aviation of China, 1992–2009.*

airlines and customers. Many airports have diversified into real estate, logistics and freighting, and advertising. For example, according to an estimate by Shenzhen Airport, its advertising revenue will amount to 730 million *yuan* between 2008 and 2011. In 2008 it accounted for around 50% of its total revenue.[4] With China's airports offering more commercialized services, airport services have flourished. The services provided by China's airports to passengers, airport workers, local farmers and local businessmen have expanded to cover technical support, ground services, ground transport, restaurants, banking, shopping, pharmacies, warehousing, parking, unaccompanied minor services, offices and conferencing, leisure and entertainment.

---

[4] "Advertising Revenue of Shenzhen Airport will see Rapid Growth", http://www.p5w.net/stock/news/gsxw/200807/t1748632.htm, July 2008.

STATE CAPITAL INVESTMENT IN AIRPORTS

The economic boom in China has boosted the rapid growth of air transport volume. In order to catch up with this fast development in air transport, airport reform has been a priority for the Chinese government since 1986. Reform measures could be generally grouped into three stages: separating domestic airport operations from airline operations and developing them into independent units, joint-equity reform, and localization reform.

Over the last two decades, the Chinese central government has encouraged local governments to invest in and run local airports and, with their increasing involvement in airport operation and management, local governments have now become the largest investors in regional airports. New airport construction has also become an important source of local economic growth. Compared to the semi-military style of airport management before 1980,[5] the reforms in airport functionality, service targets and scope have removed many restrictions on the operation of airports. Local airport authorities have enjoyed more autonomy and power in providing airport services and running operations; China's airports have become more commercially oriented over the last decade.

More significantly, as a consequence of state investment, airport infrastructure has improved remarkably over the last two decades. In order to cater for the rapid increase in air transport demand and number of large aircraft landing and taking off, the capacity of China's airports has been expanded, and their facilities have been updated and modernized. Between 1990 and 2005, the government had invested 120 billion *yuan* in the construction of 45 airports and rejuvenation of more than 90 airports. From 2006 to 2008, around a further 100 billion *yuan* was invested in constructing 18 new airports and renovating and upgrading another 25 airports.[6]

---

[5] Zhang Anming, "Industrial Reform and Air Transport Development in China", *Journal of Air Transport Management* 4 (1998), 155–164.

[6] "China will Increase Investment in Civil Airports", http://content.caixun.com/ NE/01/ej/NE01ejr5.shtm, 11 May 2010.

To improve safety and service capability in line with the increasing demand for air transport, the central government plans to invest 140 billion *yuan* to upgrade the three key airport hubs of Beijing, Shanghai and Guangzhou, 24 medium hubs and 28 small airports, and to build another 42 new airports during the period of the 11th Five-Year Development Plan (2006–2010). By the end of 2010, the total number of airports is expected to reach 186, and it is estimated that air transport services will cover 66% of the county-level cities, 72% of total population and 89% of the total national GDP.

Furthermore, the Civil Aviation Administration of China (CAAC) issued the Civil Airport Distribution Plan of China[7] in February 2008. As outlined in this ambitious development plan, by 2020, per capita flight is expected to increase by a proportion of 0.47, total passenger volume to reach 700 million and number of airports to increase to 244. Five airport clusters are planned in the northern, eastern, central, southwest and northwest regions of China. It is anticipated that air transport services will cover 74% of county-level cities, 78% of total population and 93% of China's total GDP by 2020.

In 2008, the global economic crisis had hit China and negatively affected its overall economic growth. The central government quickly responded and announced a 4-trillion-*yuan* stimulus package in November 2008. Most of the stimulus spending was allocated to airports and other infrastructure construction. The investment on airport construction and upgrading during that year was 30 billion *yuan*. In November 2008, the CAAC announced an airport investment plan of 450 billion *yuan* for the following two years. With a scale that is larger than that of the 11th Five-Year Development Plan, the plan is intended to speed up the implementation schedule of the Civil Airport Distribution Plan of China. With the coming to fruition of these plans, China should be able to develop an efficient airline network serving all its main population centres.

---

[7] CAAC, "全国民用机场布局规划", http://www.caac.gov.cn/I1/I2/200808/t20080819_18371.html, 19 August 2008.

DEREGULATORY AND DECENTRALIZATION REFORMS: THE KEY TO DOMESTIC AIRPORT DEVELOPMENT

In 1986, China started to deregulate its airport industry. Its main objective was to boost airport development, and to diversify airport investment, reduce the government's burden, and improve industrial efficiency. Several key factors underlie such a move. First, the operational environment for the international airport and aviation industries has changed. In line with clients' demand for high-quality connections, short transfer times, lower fares and high frequency of flights, the civil aviation market has become more unstable and greater competition has emerged among airports. Since the 1980s, it has become common for the state to deregulate airlines and push for implementation of "open sky" agreements. These moves have led to a reduction of regulatory restrictions and airline companies becoming "freer" in their decision-making processes.

The second factor was China's airline deregulation. The state began to deregulate local airline companies from 1986. By 1994, 6 state-owned airlines and 11 regional carriers had been founded. After 2002, three large airline groups were established and the government deregulated flight prices and imposed a price cap. Increasing competition in the airline industry led the airlines to devote more effort to cost-saving and demand services from airports. These airline reform measures put pressure on airports to react to the new environment by providing a more comprehensive range of customer-focused services. The third factor was the emergence of low-cost carriers in 2005 which further changed the traditional operational practices of China's airports. By 2009, 11 low-cost airlines had been established.[8] To satisfy their demand for maximum aircraft utilization, fast turnaround times and lower operational costs, domestic airports had to provide fast and efficient service at lower prices. The fourth factor was in the demand for diversification of airport services and increased

---

[8] CAAC, "Statistical Data on Civil Aviation of China", China Civil Aviation Press, 2009.

levels of investment in airport construction. This provided the impetus for airport industry deregulation. The Chinese central government had to ease its strict entry requirements in order to raise capital to fund airport construction and development.

Airport deregulation has been implemented in four main stages to attract more non-state investment from both foreign and domestic sources. Each stage was intended to provide new opportunities for foreign and private investment and was characterized by a different combination of airport ownership and management structures and hence, a different pattern of regulatory governance (see Appendix 3).

The first stage of deregulation took place from 1980 to 1986. In order to implement the "opening-up" policy and change the management structure of state-owned enterprises within the civil aviation industry, civil airports were separated from and no longer controlled by the military with the founding of the CAAC in 1980. Six regional branches and 31 provincial branches of the CAAC were established to represent the CAAC in the management of local civil aviation affairs. An airport administration system with three levels was formed. Nevertheless, domestic airports, which remained in the tight control of the CAAC and under the direct supervision of the State Council of China, were merely dependent administration units.

The second deregulation stage, from 1986 to 1992, concerned airport administration regulation. In July 1986, the Interim Measures on Management of Civil Airports[9] were issued and the first airport enterprise, Chengdu Airport, was set up. Airport administration was separated from civil aviation administration. From 1987, China's airports have been permitted to charge landing and takeoff fees and passenger service fees for airlines. By 1989, four airport enterprises, Chengdu Airport, Beijing Airport, Shanghai Airport and Xi'an Airport, were under the control of the local CAAC. A new system of contract management responsibility was applied to these airports.

The spillover effect of airport development to local economic growth became apparent; local governments were eager to invest in

---

[9] "关于机场归口管理的暂行规定", Civil Aviation Administration of China (CAAC), 1986. The provision became defunct in 2001, http://www.caac.gov.cn/B1/B6/200612/t20061220_926.html, 20 December. 2006.

airport construction and expansion and were permitted to invest in the airport industry from 1987. For example, the CAAC transferred the governance of Xiamen Airport to the Xiamen government in 1988. A total of 4.42 billion *yuan* was spent in the upgrading, expansion and construction of 46 domestic airports between 1986 and 1992.[10] However, regardless of whether investment came from the local or central government, airports were still owned by the central government. This gave rise to a kind of airport administration regulation which was more responsive to political than commercial needs. The CAAC was solely responsible for running all civilian airports in China. It concurrently acted as the owner, investor, policy maker and regulator of the management of China's civilian airports. As a consequence, the airports' mission was relatively straightforward: to provide aviation services to local regions by maximizing flight connections. Their lack of commercial responsibilities frequently resulted in relatively high operational costs.

The third deregulation stage was one of "limited relaxation" of airport administration regulation carried out between 1993 and 2001. In order to implement the Ordinance for Changing State-Owned Industrial Enterprises' Operating Mechanisms[11] in the civil aviation industry, cut costs of airline companies and improve service, the climate of airport investment was gradually loosened, and the scope of airport business operations expanded. The Implementation Measures for Changing State-owned Civil Aviation Enterprises' Operating Mechanisms[12] and Interim Measures for Civil Airport Operation Management[13] were issued by the CAAC in 1993. China's airports were then corporatized and their services marketized.

---

[10] *Yearbook of Transportation and Communication*, 1993, Year Book House of China Transportation and Communications.

[11] "全民所有制工业企业转换经营机制条例", The State Council of PR China, 1992. State Council file No. 103.

[12] "全民所有制民航企业转换经营机制实施办法", Civil Aviation Administration of China (CAAC), 1993. The provision was defunct in 2005, http://www.caac.gov.cn/B1/B6/index_8.html, 13 May 2010.

[13] "民用机场运营管理暂行办法", Civil Aviation Administration of China (CAAC), 1993. The provision became defunct in 2005, http://www.caac.gov.cn/B1/B6/index_8.html, 13 May 2010.

The third stage also witnessed the government's first efforts in attracting non-state investment in airports. The first obvious sign of deregulation of investment was marked by the publishing of the Notice on Foreign Investment Policy in the Civil Aviation Industry.[14] Xiamen Airport was listed on the domestic stock exchange in 1996, and Shanghai Airport and Shenzhen Airport were listed in 1998, when they raised 2.56 billion *yuan*. To encourage investment of air transport enterprises in airports, the Interim Measures for Domestic Air Transport Enterprises Investing in Civil Airports[15] were introduced in 1998. Hainan Airlines was the first airline to be approved for its investment in Haikou Meilan Airport. This milestone event was then superseded by the listing of Beijing Capital Airport on the Hong Kong Stock Exchange in 2000. Both private and foreign capital started to flow into the airport industry via capital markets. China's airport ownership metamorphosed into a mixed form. Nevertheless, the central and local governments still held their roles as the largest group of bankrollers and managers of airports at this stage.

Another sign of deregulation was the liberalization of ground services. Traditionally, ground services at respective airports were wholly undertaken by airport managers. Beginning from the early 1990s, however, some medium- and large-sized airports started to outsource certain ground services to external operators, including check-in, maintenance and airline catering. For example, Shanghai Hongqiao International Airport Co. Ltd. set up a professional ground handling services division in 1993 while Guangzhou Baiyun Airport detached part of its ground support functions to form independent ground service companies in the late 1990s.

The changes to airport ownership led to the emergence of a new CAAC-led regulatory structure in which the local governments were participants. The CAAC was responsible for formulating and

---

[14] "关于外商投资民用航空业有关政策的通知", Civil Aviation Administration of China (CAAC), 1994, http://fdi.gov.cn/pub/FDI/zcfg/tzxd/hyxd/P020060619621161719859.pdf, 13 May 2010.
[15] "国内航空运输企业投资民用机场的暂行规定", Civil Aviation Administration of China (CAAC), 1998, Year Book House of Transportation and Communications, 1999.

implementing airport regulation and managing 90 airports owned by the central government. However, a lack of functional separation, especially between policy formulation and regulation, greatly restricted further commercialization of airport services and resulted in relatively low operational efficiency. With low airport commercialization at this stage, the main regulatory approaches adopted were based on costs and a simple weight-based aeronautical fee to ensure some kind of real rate of return on the airports' assets.

REFORM AND PRIVATE INVESTMENT OPPORTUNITIES SINCE 2002

After 2002, China's airports entered a new era of limited and more relaxed economic regulation. The government has further loosened its regulatory controls over many aspects of the airport industry to speed up equity ownership reforms and commercialization of airports. Through the implementation of a series of policies, more opportunities for non-state investment have appeared in the airport industry.

Measures for Reform of the Civil Airport Management Administrative System[16] were implemented in 2003, and with the exception of Beijing Capital Airport and airports in Xizang (Tibet), the management of all the other 93 airports was transferred to local governments. Provincial branches of the CAAC were abolished and administration of airports was simplified from three levels to two. By implementing the Provisions for Foreign Investment in the Civil Aviation Industry[17] and the Provisions for Domestic Investment in the Civil Aviation Industry,[18] the state lowered the barrier to

---

[16] "民用机场管理体制和行政体制改革实施方案", The State Council of PR China, 2003. State Council file No. 93.

[17] "外商投资民用航空业规定", Civil Aviation Administration of China (CAAC), 2002, http://www.caac.gov.cn/B1/B6/200612/t20061220_918.html, 13 May 2010.

[18] "国内投资民用航空业规定", Civil Aviation Administration of China (CAAC), 2005, http://www.caac.gov.cn/B1/B6/index_3.html, 13 May 2010.

private investment in domestic airports. It has not only allowed private and foreign capital to take greater shareholding in airport management and enter a wider operational area, but also widened investment opportunities to include a range of airport facilities and services.

Under the framework of the Closer Economic Partnership Agreement, Hong Kong and Macau investors enjoy the benefits of reduced restriction as they are permitted to independently acquire concessionary management rights in medium-sized and small airports, provide airport management consultation services and invest in ground services. Whilst large and medium-sized airports remain under state control, domestic and private capital may now be invested in these airports, and the purchase and operation of small airports and engagement in infrastructure construction, management and operational activities are all allowed.

To further enhance the appeal of investing in China's airports, the state has also taken steps to liberalize airport charges. The Civil Airport Charges Reform Plan[19] was approved in December 2007. It aims to give more freedom to airports to price their services according to the nature of the business, and airport charges are price-cap regulated. These moves have greatly accelerated the growth of the airport industry. These airport charge reforms were expected to decrease overall costs of mainland airlines by 2–3%.[20]

To offer a more open and conducive investment climate, China has signed bilateral cooperation agreements and established coordination mechanisms on air traffic rights and services with 42 countries and regions in Asia Pacific, North America and Europe, and has experimented in regional aviation liberalization with the Association of Southeast Asian Nations (ASEAN). The Chinese government has also opened up air traffic rights by granting Fifth

---

[19] "民用机场收费改革方案", Civil Aviation Administration of China (CAAC), 2007, http://www.caac.gov.cn/dev/ghfzs/WJK/YJXX/, 13 May 2010.
[20] "The Reform of Airport Charges Enable Airlines to Reduce Costs", http://www.topcj.com/html/1/CJXW/20080226/137875.shtml, 13 May 2010.

Freedom Rights to ten domestic airports.[21] The introduction of more foreign carriers into the market and the establishment of new international flight routes are expected to strengthen the structure of China's nascent aviation network and gain the industry more international recognition.

Localized airport reform, diversification of airport ownership and deregulation of market entry have achieved the separation of roles between owners, managers and regulators; likewise, distinctions between airport management, policy formulation and industrial regulation have become clearer. A relatively independent regulatory institution has gradually emerged as a main feature during this stage. Administrative controls by the state have gradually given way to more professional regulatory practices. As deed owners, local governments are responsible for approving airport projects and securing investment funds. The airport groups, as part of their affiliation to the provincial governments, have taken on management and operational responsibilities. The CAAC no longer acts as the owner or manager of the airports; it has been transformed into an independent and professional regulator in charge of policy-making and enforcement, coordinating with other governmental bodies and serving as an information node for the industry.

To encourage airports to expand their commercial activities, pricing has deviated from the previous cost-plus principles to become increasingly incentive-based. This approach also aims to make domestic airports more attractive to capital investors by guaranteeing airports and their investors a reasonable rate of return. Airports have been given relative freedom to set prices within price caps set by the CAAC, thus promoting maximization of profits and efficiency. Under

---

[21] The fifth right means an airline of a country or region has the right to stop at an airport to carry or load passengers and goods and then fly to a third country. The ten airports are Shanghai Pudong International Airport, Wuhan International Airport, Chongqing International Airport, Tianjing International Airport, Hainan International Airport, Nanjing International Airport, Xiamen International Airport, Kunming International Airport, Sanya International Airport, and Guangzhou International Airport.

the new pricing policy, both aeronautical and "important" non-aeronautical fees[22] are now determined by negotiation between airports and their client-users; non-aeronautical fees not belonging to the first category are set according to market demand to encourage further commercialization of extended airport services.

Airports are defined as public infrastructure in the Management Ordinance of Civil Airports.[23] The function of airports is to provide the management of services. Their management mode will include production management in the flight area and asset management in the terminal area. As franchises are expected to be the main operating mode, professional airport management companies are now permitted to engage in airport operation in China. Airport deregulation has led to a gradual diversification of airport ownership in China. Liberation of the airport investment climate has also helped to develop a diversified range of capital financing methods, boosting the capitalization process and developing infrastructure.

ENTRY OF NON-STATE INVESTORS INTO CHINA'S AIRPORTS

Investment from non-state sectors is essential for the sustainable development of China's airport sector. This includes investment from domestic private and foreign sources, as well as domestic institutions. Foreign airport investors are important non-state investors. They may enter China's airport industry in three ways: buying airport equity via direct investment, buying shares through the stock market and investing in non-aeronautical business.

Hong Kong International Airport, for instance, invested 19.8 million *yuan* and obtained 55% equity to establish the Hong Kong-Zhuhai Airport Management Co. Ltd. and manage Zhuhai Airport with the

---

[22] Those considered "important" non-aeronautical charges in China include first-class and business-class lobby rent, office rent, ticket desk rent, check-in desk rent and ground service fees.
[23] "民用机场管理条例", Civil Aviation Administration of China (CAAC), 2009, http://www.caac.gov.cn/B1/B5/, 13 May 2010.

Zhuhai government in 2006.[24] Hong Kong International Airport Authority, on the other end, was in joint venture with Hangzhou Xiaoshan International Airport in December 2006, taking 35% equity of the airport. Beyond Hong Kong, the Lufthansa group signed a contract with Xi'an Airport in March 2007, committing some US$63 million to acquire 25% equity in the airport. Singapore's Changi Airport signed a contract with Nanjing Airport in January 2007 to invest 0.9 billion *yuan* for a 29% share of Nanjing Airport. In July 2007, Changi Airport established a joint venture with Shenzhen Airport, taking 49% equity to invest in and manage 50 airports in China.[25] In the early 1990s, Beijing Capital Airport set up BGS, AMECO and GAMECO joint venture ground service companies with Singapore Changi Airport Terminal Corporation. In 2004, Singapore Keppel Integrated Engineering formed a joint venture with the Ground Service Company of Guangzhou Airport, acquiring a 25% shareholding to set up a company to manage and maintain the operating system of Guangzhou Airport.[26]

Meanwhile, foreign investors have also entered the Chinese airport industry through the purchase of equity from the stock market. When Beijing Capital Airport was publicly listed on the Hong Kong Stock Exchange in 2000, Paris Airport Management Company took about 10% of equity shares; Wellington Fund and the Road Fund also bought about 2% and 5% of equity respectively. Copenhagen Airport bought a 20% share of Hainan Airport from the Hong Kong stock market in 2002, and transmitted its share to Oriental Patron Resources Investment in 2007.[27] By the end of 2008, UBS AG and

---

[24] "Hongkong Airport Invest 0.2 Billion to Take Over Zhuhai Airport", *First Finance Daily*, 3 August. 2006.

[25] "Shenzhen Airport Cooperates with Changi Airport", http://business.sohu.com/20070719/n251146462.shtml, 13 May 2010.

[26] "Singapore Keppel Integrated Engineering Invested in Guangzhou Baiyun Airport Logistics", http://news.sina.com.cn/o/2005-01-08/11484760523s.shtml, 13 May 2010.

[27] "The Largest Foreign Shareholder of Meilan Airport Has Sold Its 20% Equity", http://news.stockstar.com/info/Darticle.aspx?id=JL,20070607,00052250&columnid=2483, 13 May 2010.

Goldman, Sachs & Co. possessed 1.96% and 0.73% of equity respectively of Guangzhou Baiyun Airport. Oriental Patron Financial Group Limited and four other foreign investors accounted for 35.67% of equity of Haikou Meilan Airport. Three Taiwan companies invested in Xiamen International Airport Cargo Terminal Limited, each accounting for a 14% share.[28]

In addition to foreign institutional investors, domestic firms and individuals have started to invest in airports. For example, Wang Xuewen, commonly known as the first private investor in Chinese civil aviation, invested 60 million *yuan* in the construction of Suifenhe Airport in 1998. This airport began operations in 2003. Another private investor, Wang Junyao, invested 350 million *yuan* to buy Yichang Airport and spent a further 250 million *yuan* to rebuild the airport in 2003.[29]

Furthermore, domestic airlines and other institutional investors are equally keen to invest in airports. China Southern Airline invested 630 million *yuan* in joint ventures to construct an aviation cargo station in Baiyun Airport in 2004. It further invested in a new terminal in the city of Dongguan in 2005. China Southern Airline, holding 45% of shares, established a joint venture with Shenyang Airport and Sinotrans Air Transportation Development Co. Ltd. to set up Shenyang Airport Logistics Co. Ltd. in 2009.[30] It also invested 510 million *yuan* to expand Nanyang Airport in Henan Province.[31] Hainan Airlines is currently the majority shareholder of Haikou Meilan Airport. It has also invested in Sanya Airport (Hainan

[28] "Three Taiwan Companies Invested in Xiamen International Airport Cargo Terminal", http://www.fj.xinhuanet.com/hyzx/2003-08/14/content_815955.htm, 13 May 2010.
[29] Yang X. Y., Tok S. K., and Su F. "The Privatization and Commercialization of China's Airports", *Journal of Air Transport Management* 14 (2008), 243–251.
[30] Liu Jin and Chen Yang, "TaoXian Airport, China Southern Airlines and Sinotrans Logistics Joined Together to Build a New Model of Shenyang Airport", *Air Transport & Business* 26 (2006).
[31] "The New Terminal of Nanyang Airport, An Airport Wholly Owned by China Southern Airline Was Built", http://news.carnoc.com/list/147/147682.html, 13 May 2010.

Province), Weifang Airport (Shandong Province), Yichang Airport (Hubei Province), Yingkou Airport (Liaoning Province) and Hailaer Airport (Inner Mongolia Autonomous Region) to boost its passenger catchments.

By the end of 2007, except for airports in Tibet, all airports had undergone equity reform. Private capital has entered many airports. For example, Hunan Airport Company Limited was established in July 2007, with Hunan Investment Holdings Limited, Changsha City Trust & Investment Co. Ltd. and Hunan Trust & Investment Co. Ltd. as its main shareholders. Also, Jinan Airport Company Limited was launched by investors from ten organizations in June 2003. In December 2009, Sichuan Development Holding Co. Ltd. invested three billion *yuan* and obtained 27.23% of shares to speed up airport construction in Sichuan Province.[32]

During the process of airport deregulation reform, the central government has issued a series of policies to remove entry barriers and offered more opportunities to the non-state investor. Nevertheless, the average share of the non-state sector in total airport investment was only 10% between 2000 and 2007.[33] Boosting non-state investment in the airport industry will be an important issue both the central and local governments will have to deal with in the future.

SERIOUS CHALLENGES AHEAD

Despite of all its achievements, China's airport industry still faces three severe challenges to its full modernization program, namely, unequal airport development, overall poor performance, and fierce competition from other modes of transportation.

First, uneven development is reflected in two aspects. One is the unbalanced development among airports. There were 158 operational

---

[32] "Sichuan Airport Group was Listed after Reform and Restructure", Cheng Du Daily, http://www.cdrb.com.cn/html/2010-01/01/content_795134.htm, 13 May 2010.
[33] Calculated based on data obtained from *Year Book of Transportation and Communication*, 2001–2008.

airports by 2008. The top ten airports accounted for 55.5% of China's total passenger volumes (see Figure 6 and Table 1). The 47 airports which handled more than one million passengers in 2008 accounted for more than 95% of the total number of passengers. In contrast, the

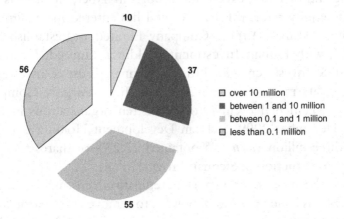

Fig. 6. China's airport distribution by passenger traffic volume.

Sources:
1. Calculated according to data from CAAC.
2. *Statistical Data on Civil Aviation of China*, 2009.

Table 1. China's top 10 airports 2009

Airport	Passenger Traffic Handled (million persons)	Cargo Traffic Handled (million tons)
Beijing (Capital)	65.4	1.5
Guangzhou (Baiyun)	37.0	1.0
Shanghai (Pudong)	31.9	2.5
Shanghai (Hongqiao)	25.1	0.4
Shenzhen (Baoan)	24.5	0.6
Chengdu (Shuangliu)	22.6	0.4
Kunming (Wujiaba)	18.9	0.3
Xi'an (Xianyang)	15.3	0.1
Hangzhou (Xiaoshan)	14.9	0.2
Chongqing (Jiangbei)	14.0	0.2
China's Airports Total	486.1	9.5
Share by the top 10 in China (%)	55.5%	75.8%

Source: CAAC, 2010.

56 airports which recorded poor figures of less than 0.1 million passengers accounted for less than 1% of national passenger volume.[34]

Air traffic has been highly concentrated in the airports located in provincial capitals, coastal or hot tourism regions. This puts enormous pressure on these heavily occupied airports' infrastructures, leading to increasingly acute slot shortage, with flight delays and congestion becoming common occurrences. In contrast, the facilities and capacities of airports located in the remote, undeveloped and rural areas have been far from fully utilized.

Uneven development among different regions is another burning problem. Compared to the corresponding figures of 29.5% and 43.8% for airports located in the eastern region, the northwest region accounted for only 4.7% and 1.9% respectively of China's total passenger and freight traffic in 2008. The northeast region and southwest region together accounted for only 20.8% and 13.4% of total volume (Figure 7).

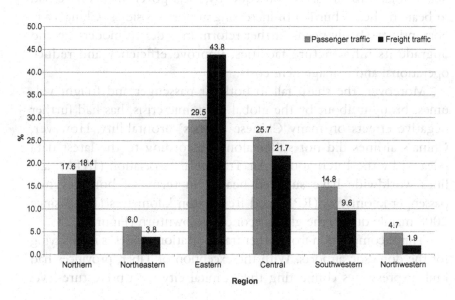

Fig. 7.   Business distribution for airports among Chinese regions.

Source: "Public Report on Airport Business in China 2009" CAAC.

---

[34] *Statistical Data on Civil Aviation of China*, 2009; CAAC, 2010.

Second, the overall performance of China's airport industry is far from satisfactory. Many of the airports with passenger traffic of less than 0.1 million remain financially unprofitable to date. For example, in 2004, there were only 43 profitable airports in China. In 2005, 85 airports, which handled less than 0.5 million passengers, faced operational difficulties. In 2006, all profitable airports were located in provincial cities or hot tourism cities. In general, 75% of Chinese airports are unprofitable.[35] China's airport sector has registered persistent financial losses in recent years, after taking into account government subsidies. In 2007, 70% of the 90 airports which handled less than 0.5 million passengers were in financial deficit. As released in the CAAC report, 114 airports which handled less than 1.2 million passengers faced operational difficulties in 2008. In fact, a total of 123 small- and medium-sized domestic airports received government subsidies in 2007.

Overall, high growth in air transportation demand failed to bring financial gain to airports. Consequently, local governments have had to bear the heavy burden of increasing airport subsidies. China's airport industry badly needs further reform in order to modernize and upgrade its infrastucture facilities, improve efficiency and reduce operational and management costs.

Moreover, the sharp fall in both air passenger and freight volumes, brought about by the global economic crisis, has had further negative effects on many Chinese airlines' profitability. However, China's airlines did not suffer alone. According to the latest data released by the International Air Transport Association (IATA), airlines worldwide have suffered heavily in terms of both revenue passenger-kilometres (RPK) and freight ton-kilometres (FTK) since 2008 mainly due to the global economic downturn (Figure 8).[36]

Third, competition from other transportation modes is intensifying for the domestic airports. With the exception of Tibet, provinces had built expressways connecting their capital city with prefecture-level

---

[35] Yang X.Y., Tok S.K and Su F., "The Privatization and Commercialization of China's Airports", *Journal of Air Transport Management* 14 (2008), 243–251.
[36] "Monthly Traffic Analysis", IATA, 2009.

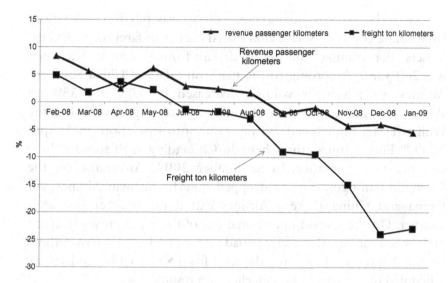

Fig. 8. Growth indicator of the RPK and FTK for the world's air transport industry. *Source*: IATA, 2009.

cities by 2009. Furthermore, starting from November 2008, the government plan of the "7918 expressway network" has been launched.[37] The plan is expected to further boost the development of the highway system.

Particularly, the rapid development of high-speed railways is anticipated to strongly challenge airport and airline development. The government's stimulus package is designed to further boost the development of high-speed rail. The Wuhan-Guangzhou[38] and Zhengzhou-Xi'an[39] passenger-dedicated high-speed railways were put into operation in December 2009 and February 2010 respectively.

---

[37] 7918 refers to the construction of 7 radically organized expressways around Beijing, 9 vertical expressways and 18 horizontal expressways by 2020.

[38] "The Top Speed of the Wuhan-Guangzhou Passenger-Dedicated Line is Up to 394 km/h", *Xinhua*, http://news.southcn.com/z/2009-12/09/content_6957117.htm, 9 December 2009.

[39] "The First High-Speed Rail for the Central and Western Regions was Put into Operation: It Only Took Two Hours from Zhengzhou to Xi'an", *Yahoo*, http://hk.news.yahoo.com/article/100206/4/ghk4.html, 9 February 2010.

Since the Wuhan-Guangzhou railway was put into operation, large airline companies have announced cuts in air fares to attract customers. For example, the lowest air fare from Wuhan to Shenzhen was 260 *yuan*. According to the marketing data of China Southern Airlines, its passenger volume decreased by 70% and 35% on Wuhan-Nanjing and Wuhan-Shanghai routes respectively after the Wuhan-Hefei high-speed railway came into operation on 1 April 2009.[40] Furthermore, the Chengdu-Chongqing high-speed railway was put into operation in September 2008. Air traffic on the Chengdu-Chongqing route dropped quickly: Sichuan Airlines, Air China and China Eastern Airlines exited this market one after another. On the second operational day of the Shijiazhuang-Taiyuan high-speed railway, the average load factor of China Eastern Airlines on the Beijing-Taiyuan route declined from 85% to 49%, and several scheduled flights had to be cancelled as a result.[41]

The experiences of high-speed railway operation in Japan, France and South Korea have shown that when the speed of a train reaches 200–250 km per hour or 300–350 km per hour, air transport passenger traffic will go down 30–60% on inter-city routes with a distance of less than 1000 km or 2000 km respectively.[42] The severe competition among different transport modes will reduce flight numbers on related airline routes or lead to cancellation of some routes. Therefore, such effects are expected to hit the Chinese airport industry in the future.

The airline sector will have to struggle to maintain its market share and increase profitability. With perceived certainty, it will face fierce competition from the high-speed railway and road

---

[40] "Competition Among a Variety of Transport Modes Has Brought Convenience and Benefits to People", http://news.xinhuanet.com/fortune/2010-01/07/content_12768535.htm, 7 January 2010.
[41] "Air Transportation will be Connected with Railway Transportation After Two Years", http://news.airtofly.com/Html/zhuguo/2009-12/19/113644091219113 64481339647_2.htm, 19 December 2009.
[42] "Civil Aviation of China Should Look Ahead to Meet the Challenges", http://www.bizteller.cn/trade/news/newsSearch/newsContent/tradenews/67925876.html, 13 May 2010.

transportation sectors. Cut-throat competition is likely to occur among the various transportation providers. Considering the backwardness of the existing domestic airports, the modernization of the entire airport industry is a momentous undertaking for the government.

APPENDIX 1

The Capacity Structure of Chinese Airports, 1991–2008

Year	Total	4E	4D	4C	Under 3C
1991	97	11	26	17	43
1992	98	11	28	18	51
1993	104	11	22	25	46
1994	109	13	27	25	44
1995	118	14	29	29	46
1996	122	14	35	37	36
1997	121	17	38	35	31
1998	121	19	35	35	32
1999	119	22	35	40	22
2000	121	23	34	43	21
2001	126	23	36	40	27
2002	125	25	34	47	19
2003	132	25	34	50	23
2004	137	25	34	52	26
2005	142	25	35	53	29
2006	147	26	38	57	26
2007	152	29	37	61	25
2008	160	31	40	71	18

Note: The military airports used by China United Airlines are not included.
Sources:
1. CAAC.
2. *Statistical Data on Civil Aviation of China*, 1992–2009.

APPENDIX 2

Number of Air Routes, Countries and Cities Flown from 1990–2008

Year	Total Air Routes	Domestic Air Routes		International Air Routes		
		Air routes	Cities	Air routes	Countries	Cities
1990	437	385	94	44	24	32
1991	452	395	96	49	29	44
1992	563	492	109	58	38	53
1993	647	563	113	71	38	53
1994	727	630	121	84	39	56
1995	797	694	133	85	31	51
1996	876	757	134	98	33	58
1997	967	851	135	109	31	57
1998	1122	983	135	131	34	64
1999	1115	987	132	128	33	60
2000	1165	1032	133	133	33	60
2001	1143	1009	130	134	33	62
2002	1176	1015	130	161	32	67
2003	1155	961	125	194	32	72
2004	1279	1035	132	244	33	75
2005	1257	1024	133	233	33	75
2006	1336	1068	140	268	42	91
2007	1506	1216	146	290	43	96
2008	1532	1235	150	297	46	104

Sources:
1. CAAC.
2. *Statistical Data on Civil Aviation of China*, 1992–2009.

APPENDIX 3

The Four Stages of China's Airport Deregulation

Stage	Ownership	Governance Structure	Pricing Method
Civil airports separated from the military (1980–1986)	Central government ownership	Airports became dependent administrative units of the CAAC	N/A
Airport administration regulation (1986–1992)	Central or local government ownership	The CAAC concurrently acted as the owner, investor, policy maker, regulator as well as management supervisor of China's civil airports	The simple weight-based aeronautical fee
"Limited relaxation" of airport administration regulation (1993–2001)	Diversification of airport ownership, with the monopoly control of central government	A new CAAC-led regulatory structure with local governments as participants	The cost-based regulation method and a simple weight-based aeronautical fee
Limited relaxation of economic regulation (since 2002)	Airport ownership diversification	Local governments are responsible for approving airport projects and securing investments. The CAAC is no longer the owner or manager of airports; it has been transformed into an independent and professional regulator	Price cap

Source: The authors' own compilation based on various sources.

Index

253